The Era of Global Transition

This page intentionally left blank

The Era of Global Transition

Crises and Opportunities in the New World

Robert W. Davies
Senior Visiting Fellow, Cass Business School, UK

© Robert Davies 2012

Softcover reprint of the hardcover 1st edition 2012 978-0-230-34876-9

All rights reserved. No reproduction, copy or transmission of this publication may be made without written permission.

No portion of this publication may be reproduced, copied or transmitted save with written permission or in accordance with the provisions of the Copyright, Designs and Patents Act 1988, or under the terms of any licence permitting limited copying issued by the Copyright Licensing Agency, Saffron House, 6–10 Kirby Street, London EC1N 8TS.

Any person who does any unauthorized act in relation to this publication may be liable to criminal prosecution and civil claims for damages.

The author has asserted his right to be identified as the author of this work in accordance with the Copyright, Designs and Patents Act 1988.

First published 2012 by
PALGRAVE MACMILLAN

Palgrave Macmillan in the UK is an imprint of Macmillan Publishers Limited, registered in England, company number 785998, of Houndmills, Basingstoke, Hampshire RG21 6XS.

Palgrave Macmillan in the US is a division of St Martin's Press LLC, 175 Fifth Avenue, New York, NY 10010.

Palgrave Macmillan is the global academic imprint of the above companies and has companies and representatives throughout the world.

Palgrave® and Macmillan® are registered trademarks in the United States, the United Kingdom, Europe and other countries.

ISBN 978-1-349-34575-5   ISBN 978-1-137-28348-1 (eBook)
DOI 10.1057/9781137283481

This book is printed on paper suitable for recycling and made from fully managed and sustained forest sources. Logging, pulping and manufacturing processes are expected to conform to the environmental regulations of the country of origin.

A catalogue record for this book is available from the British Library.

A catalog record for this book is available from the Library of Congress.

10 9 8 7 6 5 4 3 2 1
21 20 19 18 17 16 15 14 13 12

In memory of my father, Trevor Davies (1920–2011)

This page intentionally left blank

Contents

List of Figures and Tables	x
Acknowledgements	xii

Introduction		1
1	**From Blue Skies to Ambiguity**	3
	Hope and fear	3
	A word about transition and globalisation	6
	Using this book	7
2	**Exploration**	11
	Ambiguity and uncertainty – A time for retrenchment or innovation?	11
	Too darned dangerous	12
	Starting out	19
	Conclusion	24
	Reflection points	25
	Additional reading	25
3	**Power, States and a World in Transition**	26
	Five critical questions	26
	Trenches and bayonets	27
	Power and actors in the 21st century	34
	Smart and soft?	40
	Questions, answers and new states	43
	Conclusion	45
	Reflection points	46
	Additional reading	47
4	**A 21st-century medievalism?**	48
	Is the future in the past?	48
	A 21st-century medievalism?	51
	Conclusion	69
	Reflection points	70
	Additional reading	71
5	**Pathways**	72
	Reflections on a conundrum	72
	What do we mean by transition?	73

	Lessons from the past: Peace or conflict?	82
	Questions, answers and a framework for the future	91
	Conclusion	95
	Reflection points	95
	Additional reading	96

6 Solitary, Poor, Nasty, Brutish and Short? — 97
Tearing apart the accepted — 97
All for one or all for many? — 98
Secularism and a clash of globalisations — 102
So everyone wants democracy? — 110
Despots waiting in the wings? — 115
Conclusion — 117
Reflection points — 117
Additional reading — 118

7 Another Way — 119
TINA – There is no alternative? — 119
A religious capitalism? — 121
China: Autocratic capitalism? — 128
Conclusion — 137
Reflection points — 138
Additional reading — 138

8 An Engine of Growth? — 140
The excitement — 140
And a challenge — 141
The hopeful economies: A brief overview — 142
Challenges everywhere — 145
Historic rivalries and a problem of borders? — 145
The South China Sea — 148
A problem with the basic staple of life? — 150
Rare earths and persuasion — 151
Management and resolution — 152
Reflection points — 153
Additional reading — 153

9 The Long Test — 154
Into practice — 154
Step 1: Deep assumptions or deep pitfalls? — 156
Step 2: Looking forward — 165
Step 3: Rethinking globalisation — 180
Step 4: Revisiting strategy — 182
This complex world — 186

Reflection points	186
Resources	187
Reflections	**188**
Bibliography	198
Index	217

Figures and Tables

Figures

2.1	Stability–change: Managing capabilities in transitioning worlds	20
2.2	Stability–change: A view of the future	23
3.1	Hard power: 1980	29
3.2	Hard power: 1990	30
3.3	Hard power: 2000	30
3.4	Hard power: 2010	31
3.5	Hard power: 2020	32
3.6	Hard power: 2030	33
4.1	A 21st-century quadrilemma	61
4.2	Familiar worlds	64
4.3	The collapse of the market elites	65
4.4	The rise of the post-state elites	66
4.5	Post-state elites and social movements	66
4.6	A world without states	67
5.1	The 21st-century quadrilemma	73
5.2	The liberal order – Start and evolution	78
5.3	Pathways of transition	93
6.1	The 21st-century quadrilemma	98
6.2	Do you believe that universal global values exist?	100
6.3	The architects of personal values	101
6.4	After the Soviet Union: Approval of change from a planned to a market economy	105
6.5	After the Soviet Union: Deterioration in values and behaviour	107
6.6	From chaos to order, from the void to representative democracy	112
7.1	Three opposing perspectives	121
7.2	From chaos to order and democracy's crisis: The potential smoothing effect of the 'China Model'	136
9.1	Developing a future view: The process	155
9.2	Future choices: Which world or worlds?	158
9.3	Passing the long test: Power maps (2010–2030)	166

9.4	The dissonance matrix	169
9.5	Dissonance and smart power 2020 – Passing the long test	172
9.6	The year 2020 – A change in influence	175
9.7	The challenging road – Failing the long test	176
9.8	Dissonance and smart power 2020 – The challenging road	178
9.9	A shift of influence – Failing the long test	180
9.10	Stability–change: A view of the future	182
9.11	Memo to the leadership team	184
9.12	Stability–change: A second look	185

Tables

2.1	Success during uncertainty: An action framework	19
4.1	Critical actors – Some examples	60
5.1	Pathways	80
9.1	Deep assumptions – The verdict	164

Acknowledgements

There are very many people who have helped me on this journey.

I should start with all my friends and colleagues at Cass Business School, UK, and City University, UK. I would like to mention in particular Dr Julie Verity, Dr Anastasia Nesvetailova, Dr Sara Silvestri, Prof. Scott Moeller, Dr Joanna Zaleska and Dr Wes Harry who have provided support, advice and guidance in very different ways. Their input, ranging from the challenges of book writing, getting to grips with the international relations literature to comments on content and introductions to contributors, has been invaluable. A special mention must also be made of Prof. Axel Johne for the encouragement, over the years, to progress to do 'something better'.

I would also like to thank Prof. Ronen Palan for his reflection on my early thoughts that formed a foundation for this book and Jeremy Kourdi for his guidance on entering the world of book authorship. The contributors to the chapter 'Reflections' must not be forgotten as their thoughts have added a further dimension to this book.

Then we have the 'review panel' who spent so many hours going through and commenting upon chapter drafts. Very many thanks to Rita Jeffery, Stuart MacAdam, Sally Sanderson, Duncan Simpson and Jo-Anne Watermeyer.

I must also record my appreciation of the input of Henry Davies, who provided so much help with background research, chapter reviews and, in particular, the preparation of chapter material for Chapter 8, titled 'An Engine of Growth'.

As usual, my daughter Phoebe has been resolute in her support, for which I will be always grateful.

My wife Grace has played a special role. This book, in many ways, was her idea. After hearing me talk for hours over the dinner table about the problems of 'transition', she has spurred me on to start writing. For her, this book has been a considerable investment. Firstly, she once again saw me locked away for days (weeks) in my study. Secondly, she spent much of her spare time reviewing chapter drafts in their many versions. I am deeply grateful for that investment.

My cluttered memory will have omitted the names of many who have provided help; my apologies for omitting you all, but please do accept my appreciation.

Dr Robert Davies
Cass Business School, London, UK
March 2012

This page intentionally left blank

Introduction

In 2006, I wrote a set of long-term global business scenarios. In the process of doing this, I researched the assumptions that businesses and their leaders were making about the future. These views, that I will call 'deep assumptions', worried me. They seemed to represent only the very best of futures, the bluest of blue horizons. The talk was of unending globalisation, the spread of wealth, consumerism and, above all, 'Westernisation'.

There appeared to be no other alternative view or scenario. Everything was going to be great.

I spent a long time considering these deep, underlying assumptions and the longer that I thought about them, the more worried I became. There was little, if any, talk about power transition, the unknown pitfalls that would await the world as it took the little known journey from unipolarity to multipolarity. I asked myself the question: 'what do we know about the process of moving away from a world dominated by one power, the United States?' The answer was 'very little'.

All these worries came to fruition with the banking crisis of 2008 and the idea for this book was born.

The world changed at that point, but we still seem to cling to the same deep assumptions, in the hope that the bluest of blue horizons will return. They might. But there are many other outcomes. There are new forces and actors at play. The time has now come for everyone involved in strategy making in any organisation to test, challenge and debate their views about the way the world works. That is what this book is all about, testing deep assumptions and building pictures or views of the future. This involves discovering and understanding who will be the real architects, who will reshape our world. The importance of going through this process cannot be overstated. The type of transition that we face, as we say goodbye to a unipolar world, is totally unique. We will not see another like it during the lifetimes of the readers of this book, and possibly, of their offspring.

Challenging deep assumptions will surprise you. And it will fundamentally change the way that you think about the world, the purpose of business and, of course, strategy.

1
From Blue Skies to Ambiguity

Hope and fear

> Economic hope but political fear.

This very short statement (James, 2011, p. 530) sums up for many the new world that the Great Recession ushered into our lives. For the United States the Great Recession officially spanned the period December 2007–June 2009. Lasting for around 18 months, this was one of the longest periods of economic upheaval to hit the United States, and earned it the accolade 'Great'. Interestingly it wasn't really a global recession. Some countries suffered just a slowdown. But the less fortunate are still faced with stagnation, uncertainty and lengthening queues of the real casualties, the unemployed.

It was far more than a mere economic recession. It was like reaching the end of a book. A book that had spanned the living years of every reader and described the world we knew. For many of us the book had provided a feeling of comfort, a feeling of stability and security as well as a great foundation for businesses and organisations of all sizes to think about plans that stretched out into a blue horizon of seemingly limitless opportunities.

But the Great Recession acted as a catalyst to pour doubt onto most, if not all, of the written and unwritten assumptions that had, until its arrival, underpinned the blue horizon, especially for businesses headquartered in the West.

Just a few years ago, the future seemed to be so much brighter.

The fall of the Berlin Wall in 1989 had opened a new chapter, both for mankind and for business. It promised to mark more than the end of the Cold War, the decades-long confrontation between military superpowers that had threatened mutually assured destruction and the wiping out of civilisation. It was the start of a new dawn, a new era and a very West-influenced era. It appeared that economic co-operation, free market capitalism and the spread of democracy would replace the spectre of state-versus-state conflict. This message of hope and brightness was embodied in a paper written by Francis Fukuyama in the same year, which was entitled *The End of History?* (Fukuyama, 1989). Fukuyama pointed to the prospect of a world characterised by democracy and Western capitalism. As democracy spread, so war would be consigned to the history books. We had entered the age when no democratic state would turn and fight another democratic state. The world had finally matured. Both politically and economically the 20th century and beyond would see the universal adoption of 'the Western way', or the heady mix of democracy and capitalism that would bring wealth and peace to all. The world would become truly globalised both economically and culturally. This new place was summed up by President Bill Clinton in 1992 when he said 'in a world where freedom, not tyranny, is on the march, the cynical calculus of pure power politics simply does not compute. It is ill-suited to a new era' (Clinton, 1992).

Further fuel was added to this fire of globalisation by Goldman Sachs with the publication of the now seminal paper entitled *Building Better Global Economic BRICs* (O'Neill, 2001) that introduced a picture of massive growth opportunities for Western businesses in four key new emerging economies – Brazil, Russia, India and China – opportunities that Western companies would rush to take advantage of (Bremmer, 2010). All this spawned a range of optimistic books trumpeting the opportunities that a world united under the banners of democracy and capitalism could offer. In the words of one text, '[t]he simple fact is that globalization makes us richer – or enough of us richer to make the whole process worthwhile' (Micklethwait and Wooldridge, 2001, p. 335). The 'golden arches' theory appeared (Friedman, 2006), which forecast that multinational corporations could become more powerful than states. Increasing economic interlinkages across national borders would do away with the need for military forces (Ohmae, 1990). The sky couldn't get bluer.

But possibly it was the theme at the World Economic Forum's 2005 Davos meeting that encapsulated the flavour, assumptions and hope in those pre-recessionary years, when the atmosphere of this meeting was summarised in these words:

> The global economic mood music just would not stop.
> (Weber, 2005)

Well, the 'global economic mood music' has stopped.

Instead of blue skies we are surrounded by the fog of ambiguity. Whilst some are still acclaiming the virtues of both capitalism and globalisation, louder voices are appearing that question the capability of capitalism to both create and spread wealth in a fair and just manner. Surprisingly these voices can be heard from both inside (Lambert, 2011; Packer, 2011; Roubini, 2011) and outside (Callinicos, 2010; Harvey, 2010) capitalism's camp.

The fog of doubt is thickened by the realisation that the power and influence of the architect of the post-Second World War order, the United States, is now perceived to be in decline (Wike, 2011), and its influence may be slipping away faster than the dead empires of the past.

We have all lived, been educated, worked and made critical business decisions in a world crafted, largely single-handedly, by the United States. Certainly since the fall of the Berlin Wall and the Soviet Union, the United States has been the only superpower. We have been living in a unipolar world. But now we have entered the period when the world is moving from a unipolar environment dominated by the United States to a multipolar landscape. There are others who are surging forward with new ideas and different perspectives. There may be old scores to settle too.

The hard reality is that we know all too little about the opportunities and challenges that the transition, the pathway, from a unipolar to a multipolar world will hold. Neither the strategy textbooks nor the textbooks of the political scientists hold the answer. We are in uncharted territory.

It could well be that the liberal world order of democracy and free-market capitalism that came to grow and flourish as the Berlin Wall fell will rise again and continue into the distant horizon. But there is also the possibility that the forces of globalisation that we have unleashed could produce exactly the opposite of what was intended – either a deeply fractured world with capitalism and democracy broken into many different shards (Gray, 2009) or even a world where historic cultural divides and wounds will reopen (Huntington, 2002).

No one knows what the coming decades have in store, but this book aims to help you chart a course for your business into the future that is coming our way and is designed to help readers answer these and other questions:

How will a world in transition affect my business?
Where does globalisation go from here?
Who might influence the shape of our future markets?
Will the transition from the old unipolar world to the new multipolar world be a peaceful one?
How will capitalism change in a multipolar world and what does this mean for the way we do business?

A word about transition and globalisation

The issues of transition (that is the process of moving from a unipolar world dominated by one superpower to a mutlipolar world with many powers) and globalisation are closely intertwined and almost inseparable in our current environment. In fact the transition that we face is a direct product of the globalisation process that we have witnessed in recent decades. The problem is, however, that the word 'globalisation' is so widely used today and appears so frequently in conversations that we could assume that it has a universal meaning, understood by all. As we progress through this book it will become apparent that the meaning of 'globalisation' is far from clear and that this problem of meanings is one of the major obstacles that the world faces. However we will start with the following description of the 'phenomenon' of globalisation:

> Fundamentally it is the closer integration of the countries and peoples of the world which has been brought about by the enormous reduction of costs of transportation and communication, and the breaking down of artificial barriers to the flows of goods, services, capital, knowledge, and (to a lesser extent) people across borders.
>
> (Stiglitz, 2002, p. 9)

This description of globalisation, as put forward by the economist Joseph Stiglitz, is a good start, as it both alludes to the popular evidence of globalisation that is all around us in the form of cheaper consumer goods, the industrialisation of developing countries, the drive to continuously slash the costs of doing business, the integrating force of the Internet and of course the assumption that a newfound wealth and freedom will unite us all.

The 'breaking down of artificial barriers' that Stiglitz refers to has helped to stimulate economies in the developing world and, in turn, has presented us with the challenge of transition. When we refer to 'globalisation' in the early chapters, we will have this description in mind.

Using this book

Returning to the question 'how will a world in transition affect my business?', this book is designed to help leaders at many levels in organisations to produce a route map that will help them to move forward and explore the uncertain and unknown era of transition. It is not designed just for CEOs. This book has been created as an easily accessible guide that can be used by leaders across an organisation.

Why?

Because in businesses that work successfully in difficult and uncertain times, strategy-making is a shared process where many contribute. Strategy and planning, especially during periods of ambiguity, do not solely remain within the domain of the top-level leader or of some distant head-office department. It is essential that a broad range of staff are involved, particularly those whose work means that they interact with the outside world.

Research from the fields of strategy, the management of change in organisations and international relations has been used to create this book. At first sight these may seem to be unlikely bedfellows, but they embrace the knowledge and awareness that leaders will require to look into a totally unknown world. Large parts of this book draw upon research in the field of international relations, particularly power transition theory and new emerging thinking regarding the future role of the state, subjects that are not found in traditional strategy textbooks but are essential if we are trying to understand the process of change and transition that lies ahead.

In these years, the subjects of strategy and international relations will become closely intertwined.

As you progress through each chapter new ideas and frameworks will be introduced. Using these frameworks and ideas will help you to develop your own view of the future and what this future holds, in terms of opportunities and challenges, for your business. Every chapter includes suggested issues to explore with your colleagues. You can use this approach to build your own picture or scenario of a world in transition.

This book can be thought of as a journey in three parts. Chapters 2–5 form the first part of the journey and aim to provide the reader with tools and techniques specifically designed to explore a world in transition. The second part, Chapters 6–8, presents concepts for debate. These chapters are designed to challenge established assumptions regarding the way the world works. Issues such as the end of growth, the return of communism and the rejection of democracy are all introduced for discussion. Chapter 9 brings us towards the conclusion of the journey and introduces approaches that can help translate our findings into thought, debate and practical actions. At the end of the book the section *Reflections* includes thought pieces from a range of writers and thinkers drawn both from the academic and business environments. These pieces are aimed at adding depth to the discussions that this book is designed to stimulate.

In Chapter 2, **Exploration**, we introduce the characteristics of successful leadership during times of great uncertainty and ambiguity. Drawing primarily upon change management and strategy literature, a framework of key 'conditioning tasks' or critical actions is presented for leaders wishing to outperform their competitors in these unpredictable times. Chapter 2, in common with each subsequent chapter, concludes with suggested reflection points and additional reading. Before leaving this chapter readers are encouraged to map the deep assumptions that underpin their organisations' current strategies. These assumptions can then be challenged, developed and redefined as readers progress through later chapters. To help this process we introduce a fictional insurance organisation as an example and examine both its strategy and the deep assumptions that underpin it.

Chapter 3, **Power, States and a World in Transition**, sets out to explore if we are faced with anything more than a simple transition in economic power from the old economies of the West to the new emerging economies. We start by taking a traditional view, drawing upon established thinking in the international relations arena, and ask if the popular projections of the 'advanced' and 'emerging' economies paint a complete picture of the future. Or is viewing the world as a collection of states, economies and armies something that may have been relevant in the 20th century but is something that could be totally misleading in the 21st century?

Chapter 4, **A 21st-Century Medievalism**, proposes that we have to look beyond economic projections and just seeing the world as a fabric of states. The forces of globalisation may have produced unfortunate and unplanned side effects. The side effects are introducing new players, or, as they are called in the field of international relations, 'actors', who must be considered. Surprisingly the real clues as to what is really going on can be found back in the 17th century, and it is proposed that the final shape of our world will be determined by a new confrontation between four major interest groups.

Chapter 5, **Pathways**, looks closely at the potential transition pathways or routes that the process of transition could take in the coming decades. We tackle the critical question of whether or not the world faces conflict and, more hopefully, the peaceful transition that we expected before the Great Recession. If we do face conflict, which form will such conflict take and who could be the protagonists? Are the great military power wars of the 20th century a thing of the past and, if they are, how will tomorrow's conflicts be fought? Understanding the characteristics of the pathways of transition is of essential importance in planning for the future, even more important, surprisingly, than attempting to forecast what the world will look like as the era of transition draws to a close. Focusing only on developing an end point, a future picture of the world, is a hollow exercise without also considering the more important issue of how we will get to that end point. This chapter therefore focuses on providing a framework to help leaders and their teams debate potential pathways.

Chapter 6, **Solitary, Poor, Nasty, Brutish and Short?**, looks carefully at two of the deep assumptions that have driven globalisation. Firstly that globalisation will produce a world where we all share the same values. We look at the values underlying different definitions of 'globalisation' and debate whether or not we are now facing a clash of two different globalisations. Secondly the permanence and durability of democracy are also brought into the debate, and we question whether or not it is seen as a universal panacea that is suitable for all contexts.

Chapter 7, **Another Way**, holds that the Great Recession may have fatally wounded free-market capitalism, sometimes called the 'Washington Consensus', and two alternative models are examined, the 'China Model' or the 'Beijing Consensus' and, following the Arab Spring of 2011, we look at the potential paths that democracy and capitalism could take in the Middle East.

Chapter 8, **An Engine of Growth?**, examines the challenges of continued growth, but from the perspective of the emerged and emerging economies in Asia. We place particular emphasis on looking at a selection of the hurdles that must be overcome if growth is to continue.

Chapter 9, **The Long Test**, helps readers to assemble conclusions from the previous chapters and, using our fictional insurance organisation as an example, we construct a route map that will enable their organisations to take the first tentative steps towards the future.

Reflections presents key thought pieces expressing a range of different perspectives that both challenge and develop themes introduced throughout this book.

2
Exploration

Ambiguity and uncertainty – A time for retrenchment or innovation?

For any organisation it can be tempting, when once rock solid assumptions fall away, to cut costs and retrench; to defend the portfolio of clients, products and services that have been built up over the years; and to wait for times to get better. In other words, sit it out and hope that a familiar past will return. Common sense and caution tell us that we should stand still and wait for things to become clearer before we make decisions. But research, coupled with experience from past recessions, particularly the economic depression of the 1930s and the downturn of the early 1990s, can tell us a very different story.

In times of crisis, proactive change, exploration and innovation are surprisingly not options; they are mandatory actions for business leaders (Applegate & Harreld, 2009). In other words, the last thing that we should do is hide away and reappear when the dust settles. So, looking back into the past, economic crises are not times for inward thinking; they are, possibly surprisingly, times for exploration, experimentation and outward thinking.

The depression of the 1930s provides us with excellent examples. During the period 1930–1931, the luxury magazine *Fortune* was launched, *Motorola* introduced the first car radio and the cosmetics brand *Revlon* was born. These, and other organisations, broke established industry rules to carve out new markets whilst others just waited (Chakravorti, 2009). So, the danger is that if your organisation does not look for new opportunities in a changing landscape, others will. Just waiting and hoping for a clear picture of the future to appear will mean that your organisation could face the prospect of massive change to play catch up and it is worth remembering that large-scale organisational change projects have, in turn, massive failure rates of up to 70% (Beer & Nohria, 2000). It is just too risky to stand still.

So all this leads us to consider what leaders should do. If cost cutting, retrenchment or just waiting can produce the prospect of a disastrous failure, is a more far-sighted approach, using tried and tested approaches, to long-term business planning the answer? Should you sit down now and take time out with the leadership team and create a new, well thought out long-term plan and use that to drive change?

Too darned dangerous

The cold reality is that conventional business planning, with its foundation of one view of a future world and one strategy to face it, with a set of predefined implementation steps and performance scorecards, just cannot deal with an ambiguous future. Some say that such an approach is 'too darned dangerous'.

If we analyse how businesses have successfully met the challenges of ambiguity and uncertainty, we can see that a subtly altered picture that requires a different approach to leadership and strategy making emerges, to the ones that we may use in more stable times. Specifically, if we go back to lessons from the recession of the early 1990s there are seven learning points to consider.

Learning point 1: Don't just think about planned strategy

Over 20 years ago Henry Mintzberg and James Waters thought that there were two broad ways that leaders can craft strategy in their organisations (Mintzberg & Waters, 1985). The two ways of building strategy that Mintzberg and Waters talked about are *planned* and *emergent* approaches. Planned strategy is the type that we are used to and probably most comfortable with. As its name suggests, planned strategy is about a structured, step-by-step process to analyse the organisation's marketplace and project its future, identify customers, analyse competitors, decide which products and services are to be provided and what action steps and performance measures are necessary to implement the strategy. All these activities are usually controlled by the most senior people in the organisation.

This is a very structured process and the strategy is implemented as planned, hence the label *planned strategy*.

As Henry Mintzberg went on to add, there are two basic assumptions that underpin this approach (Mintzberg, 1990).

The first of these assumptions is that strategy formulation should be a controlled, conscious process of thought. Action only takes place once the strategy has been constructed, usually following a step-by-step process, and then formally agreed, both tasks frequently being undertaken by the top-level management team. The total process is therefore usually controlled and directed by top-level management, with the CEO, the master strategist, at the helm.

The second major assumption is that there will be no major upsets and that the future will unfold as planned, events being as predicted. If anything does happen that is not predicted, then these events will be benign in nature or totally under the control of the organisation.

But clearly we are not in this position. Neither of these assumptions hold true. The environment is not predictable and it may not be friendly or benign.

So, relying on this approach to guide the organisation, planned strategy making, presents us with three very great dangers.

The first very great danger is that decisions are made without exploring and learning from a new, changing external landscape. Decisions are made based upon a picture of a past world, not a future world.

The second very great danger is that the way we think the world works is not challenged. Researchers have a name for this 'thought picture'. They call the thought picture 'interpretive schemes'. Interpretive schemes represent the values and interests of staff, particularly those of the top-level leadership team, and, critically, these interpretive schemes strongly influence the way that both the external world and the organisation itself are seen (Ranson, Hinings & Greenwood, 1980).

The 'thought picture' or 'interpretive schemes' act like a massive filter or lens that can distort or cut off views of what really is happening. What this means in practice is that information about the outside world is heavily filtered, narrowed and even unknowingly remanufactured by members of the organisation (Weick, 1995). Interpretive schemes are therefore powerful and influence both what we see or look for in a changing world and in turn define 'what will work and what won't work'. Interpretive schemes therefore shape and guide actions too. In short, the big issue is that we can fall into the trap that we only see what we want to see and we only do what worked for us in the past. So, the very great danger is that we can work within an 'artificial bubble' that does not reflect what is really going on outside the organisation. It may seem a rather strange concept, but every organisation possesses, to one degree or another, its own artificial bubble.

The third and final very great danger in just relying on top-down planned strategy is that no attempt will have been made to develop new skills and knowledge. The organisation will step out boldly into a new world armed only with the capabilities gathered from a past time.

All this leads us to conclude that a process to challenge established views of 'what will and won't work' must be instigated as soon as possible, otherwise critical decisions about the organisation's future will be formed in that comfortable, but dangerous, artificial bubble.

So, taking time out to formulate a new all-embracing long-term plan is arguably the last thing that an organisation should do when faced with uncertainty. Rather, the initial effort should be to create an environment for learning and experimentation, which is the focus of the remaining points.

Learning point 2: Think about emergent strategy too

All this leads us to consider the other type of strategy, emergent strategy, which Henry Mintzberg and James Waters introduced. Rather than being planned, emergent strategy appears as the organisation interacts with a changing environment, experiments and learns. It can be thought of as learning, based upon a dynamic interaction with a new and unfolding environment, an interaction that leaders in the organisation actively participate in and encourage.

Any organisation looking to succeed in a world that is changing needs, as early as possible, to set up a framework for exploration and learning. Strategy research is full of this idea of setting up a framework to learn and then to take the learning and use it to form longer-term planned strategies. We can think of this emergent strategy as 'strategy through doing, experimenting and learning'.

The challenge in turbulent times is not to totally tie down the organisation in a planned strategy framework. The temptation may be to go for total control, but this could well just result in rigidity and life within that artificial bubble.

Learning point 3: Develop two organisational focal points

Rather than creating an environment of total, centralised control, there is a need to encourage a balanced approach that supports control whilst allowing for probing, debate, experimentation and learning. This can be thought of as almost creating two parallel organisations or focal points, one with a leaning towards planned strategy, the other having the principal role of exploration and experimentation. Some members of the top-level management team focus on stability, whereas others focus on experimentation. The organisation with a leaning towards planned strategy develops and defends the existing portfolio of customers and offerings and we can call it the 'stable' organisation, whilst the second organisation, or the 'exploring' organisation, looks for opportunities in a changing world and is charged with the duty of crafting emergent strategy. The exploring organisation is responsible for probing the new unfolding world and its marketplaces, then sharing the learning with the organisation as a whole. Without such a strong emergent focal point, the entire organisation will become isolated from the new world and, ultimately, fail.

But the stable organisation has another critical role to play. The cold, hard fact is that in uncertain times organisations will experience periodic large-scale threats that will endanger their future existence (Sull, 2005). The stable organisation must excel in responding rapidly to these unforeseen threats when they spring up and quickly contain any ensuing crises (Augustine, 1995). The purpose of the stable organisation is to protect the heart of the organisation's business against such threats, so ensuring a steady stream of profit, whilst the exploring organisation experiments and gathers the learning and experience that, in turn, will grow into the strategies and profit streams of the future.

Learning point 4: Value experimentation, value failure

An apparently strange title. We have made it clear that a central part of success is the encouragement of the exploration of the new world. This typically forms a series, or a raft of simple small-scale experiments. These experiments are important for a number of reasons, including the following:

- They confirm or deny views inside the organisation as to how the outside world is changing. In short, they help to, if necessary, break the artificial bubble.
- The development of new capabilities, new knowledge and new experiences.
- The contribution to a better, planned strategy. Organisations will always have planned strategies and defined future visions. The learning generated through experimentation helps the organisation eventually to create planned strategies that really reflect the opportunities in a changing landscape.

But going back again to the recession of the 1990s, there are some ground rules for experimentation. These are as follows:

1. Create a lot of small-scale experiments. Do not throw all the effort and available resources into one or two major projects or experiments.
2. Initially, base these experiments around changes that you think are occurring in the outside world.
3. Control the downside. By definition, many of the experiments will fail. Ensure that the downside, both financially, and culturally, is carefully ring fenced. In times of recession and ambiguity, most organisations' balance sheets are pressurised. Ensure that any financial downside can be strictly limited. You will also need to ensure that failure can be celebrated.
4. Celebrate failures. What? The fact is that failed experiments are very, very valuable and can lead to important insights into what will work in the new world. It is critically important therefore not to discard failed experiments, but to analyse the reasons for failure and try again. The process of analysing failures and initiating new experiments can produce the knowledge and experience that will form the foundation for new winning long-term strategies.

Learning point 5: Top team alignment

As the title suggests, we are concerned with building a top-level team whose members are committed to the need for exploration, innovation and change. The members of this team are prepared to demonstrate, individually and collectively, both their commitment to change and the rejection of the view that the organisation can survive by relying on 'what worked before'.

Leaders, from the outset, need to give careful thought with regard to both the construction of their leadership teams and the artificial bubbles, or ways of seeing the world, that are embedded within these teams. It must be made quite clear that failure to create a team that is aligned around the need to explore a shifting external environment and to champion exploration, experimentation and learning will result, at some point in the future, in confusion, followed by failure.

The process of ensuring top-level team alignment is within the sole domain of the CEO. The central part of the task is to ensure that team members are committed to the need for change and are prepared to abandon obsolete 'interpretive schemes'. Some (Aitken & Keller, 2007) talk of leaders producing a matrix to assess team members with say 'business performance' on one axis and 'commitment to change' on the other. This is not just something that can be done by a new incoming CEO, the task can be just as effectively conducted by incumbent CEOs too (Pettigrew & Whipp, 1991).

Learning point 6: Team diversity

But there is more to be done than just creating a change-focused team. Studies consistently show that diverse leadership teams work more effectively during times of environmental uncertainty (Cannella et al., 2008).

We have to consider two types of diversity in leadership teams. The first is called *intrapersonal functional diversity*. This refers to individual members of the leadership team who have had experience in working *across* a range of different functional areas in the organisation. Many organisations are designed around rigid functional structures, which give stability and order when times are certain. But when times are uncertain, flexibility is required, and critically decisions have to be made rapidly that span these internal boundaries (Arrata et al., 2007; Ibarra, 1992). Leaders with a background of working in a wide variety of functional backgrounds are, when quick decision-making is required, less likely to take a parochial perspective and more likely to know where to locate the knowledge and experience in the organisation that is key to rapid holistic decision making (Bunderson, 2003).

The second type of diversity that has to be considered is referred to as *functional diversity*, in other words the range of functions represented by the team *as a whole*. The broader the range of functional experience represented within the leadership team, the less likely it is that the team will be exposed to a condition known as 'groupthink' (Janis, 1972). When dealing with uncertain and complex environments a more diverse and challenging atmosphere is needed. So, as Mauboussin (2011) notes, what is really needed is a 'team of rivals', people who can come up with different points of view and, constructively, challenge an established consensus. The greater the capacity within the team for constructive rivalry and debate, the more likely it is that the team will generate really creative solutions when problems appear.

Learning point 7: Getting the story together

The 'story' sets out why the organisation needs to invest effort in exploring and learning from a changing environment.

Research (e.g. Sull, 2005) tells us that successful leaders in periods of turbulence invest time in communicating. Indeed, during turbulence, leaders spend considerably more time in face-to-face communication, or developing and telling the story. As Aitken and Keller (2007) observe, it is important to make the case for exploration and change. If staff deeply understand the need to explore, innovate and change and how the effort can deliver success in uncertain times, then a tremendous amount of constructive energy can be realised. But without such a deep understanding, confusion will rule. The development of a story, reasons why the organisation cannot stand still and the need to go out and learn, is very much within the personal domain of the CEO. Whilst the story must be unequivocally echoed by the entire leadership team, it is the role of the CEO in difficult times to personally engage with staff across the organisation, taking the story to them.

Critically, during times of turbulence, successful CEOs invest their time in different ways from the lesser-successful CEOs (Johne & Davies, 1999). The successful CEOs spend more time interacting with both customers and staff at all levels than their lesser-performing counterparts who focus largely upon interacting with their fellow managers.

Together, these seven points create a framework for action, as shown in Table 2.1. This book can be used to help put such a framework into action.

Table 2.1 Success during uncertainty: An action framework

Success in times of ambiguity and uncertainty: Key pointers	
POINTER 1	Do not rely on a rigid long-term strategy.
POINTER 2	Think about how you can create an emergent strategy, one based on experimentation, exploration and learning.
POINTER 3	Create two focal points in your organisation, one to defend current business and the other to explore.
POINTER 4	Value experimentation and learn from failure.
POINTER 5	Ensure that the top-level leadership team will not shun change.
POINTER 6	Create a diverse top-level leadership team that can cut across functions and think laterally in a crisis.
POINTER 7	Invest time in personal communication.

Starting out

Rather than merely providing a description of a future world, this book aims to help readers to produce their own views and to define the implications for their businesses. It does this by using a stability–change model, as shown in Figure 2.1.

The model has been constructed to reflect the reality of life in a transitioning world. Uniquely, we will have to deal simultaneously with two worlds: a familiar, expiring old world and the emerging, new world. These are represented by the two circles at the centre of the model. The left-hand circle represents the old, familiar world. The right-hand circle represents the unknown new world, which is only just starting to form. The new world will share some, but by no means all, of the characteristics of the old world, which is why the two circles overlap.

Living in both worlds will be a fact of life for one or more decades. The forms of both the old and new worlds that we hold in our minds are driven by 'deep assumptions'. Together, these deep assumptions form the 'thought picture', 'interpretive schemes' or 'artificial bubble' that we introduced earlier. For any leadership team, it is essential that the deep assumptions are rigorously debated and tested. The deep assumptions are shown by the

20 *The Era of Global Transition*

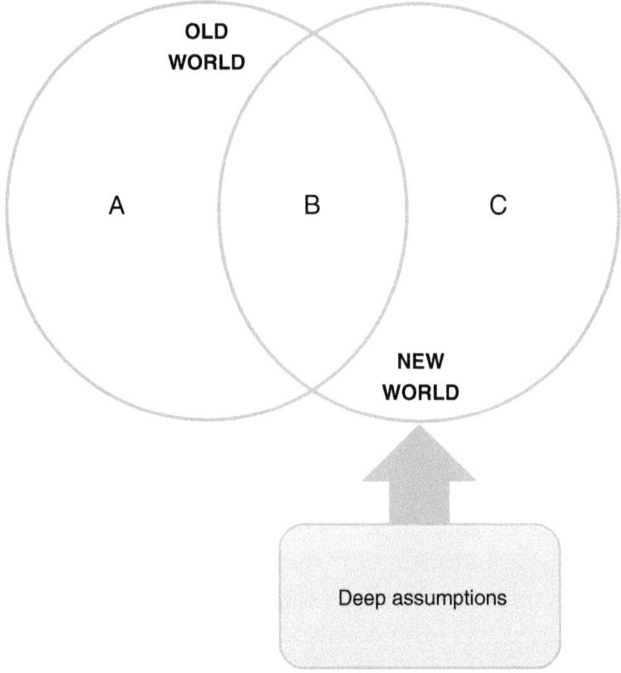

Figure 2.1 Stability–change: Managing capabilities in transitioning worlds

upward-pointing arrow. The assumptions shape, in our minds, the rise of the new world and the decline of the old.

But there is more to be done than just the production and testing of assumptions. The capabilities that the organisation needs to survive and flourish must also be considered. One of the central messages in this book is that any organisation must nurture and develop a careful mix of capabilities that will enable it to succeed in both worlds: the old and the emerging new. These capabilities are a combination of skills, experience and know-how carefully nurtured within the organisation. In turbulent times, such a carefully selected set of capabilities can do more to aid long-term success than a mere portfolio of products and services. Products and services have a life cycle and therefore grow and die. A portfolio of carefully selected capabilities does more and can spawn a flow of offerings to see a business through the toughest of times.

The stability–change model can be used to define not just the deep assumptions underpinning an organisation's view of a world in transition. It can be used to identify and map the capabilities that an organisation needs in the old world, the transitioning world and the new world. These three worlds are shown as areas 'A', 'B' and 'C' in the model. Area 'A' embraces the capabilities that are needed only in the old world. These have little use in either the transitioning world or the new world. As time progresses, these capabilities will become less and less relevant. Area 'B' represents the transitioning world, a period where we have to live in both a declining old world and the emerging new. The capabilities that appear here help us to succeed in both worlds. These must be nurtured and defended at all costs. Finally, 'C' is the area for totally new capabilities that are required for success, but only in the new world. It is important to consider these capabilities now, as they will provide the foundation for the initial exploring and experimental work that was discussed earlier.

An example will help to demonstrate the process.

We will take a fictional insurance business with global aspirations. Its strategy, before progressing through this book, is shown in the stability–change model in Figure 2.2. The illustration shows the capabilities that our fictional business thinks it will need to succeed in the coming years. After careful reflection and debate, the leadership team has defined the deep assumptions that drive its pictures of the old and new worlds. These are as follows:

Deep Assumption 1: The world will always consist of a network of states or countries. Looking at the world in this manner and judging the importance of each state by the size of its economy and economic growth rate are the best ways of seeing the future world.

Deep Assumption 2: Globalisation is an unstoppable force, driven increasingly by technology.

Deep Assumption 3: Globalisation will bring wealth, and a reasonably fair distribution of that wealth, for all.
Deep Assumption 4: Everyone wants to live in a democracy.
Deep Assumption 5: As wealth rises, so will secularism. We will forget old cultures and beliefs and adopt the same universal, largely Western values. The importance of religion will fade away as globalisation marches on.
Deep Assumption 6: Everyone wants to be a consumer.
Deep Assumption 7: We have reached the end of an era of conflict. There will be no more major state versus state conflicts. Prosperity and democracy will bring peace.
Deep Assumption 8: In the medium term, Asia will drive the next round of consumer-fuelled growth. This growth in turn will fuel a sustained global recovery.
Deep Assumption 9: Growth. We will innovate and find solutions to resource, energy and environmental concerns.

It can be seen that our leadership team has invested an unusual amount of effort setting out some fundamental assumptions, many of which are not usually discussed in a typical strategy and business planning workshop.

These assumptions have driven the definition and positioning of capabilities based on the following conclusions.

Traditional face-to-face distribution and marketing routes will rapidly become relics of the past, driven out particularly by mobile telephone technology. Asia, not Europe, offers the big growth prospects, so existing branch and retail store locations across Europe will become increasingly irrelevant. If we look at the stability–change model in Figure 2.2, 'Face-to-face distribution', 'Retail stores (Europe)' and 'Community agents', the relics of the past are shown at the periphery of the old world as they now have rapidly declining relevance.

The leadership team has also concluded that ongoing relentless cost reduction will be the key to survival in both old and new worlds. Mobile telephone technology will drive a new wave of expense-based competition. Driving cost reduction by 'virtualising' traditional processes, cutting out costly human involvement and using mobile telephone devices as distribution tools are all needed to maximise profitability in both the old and new worlds.

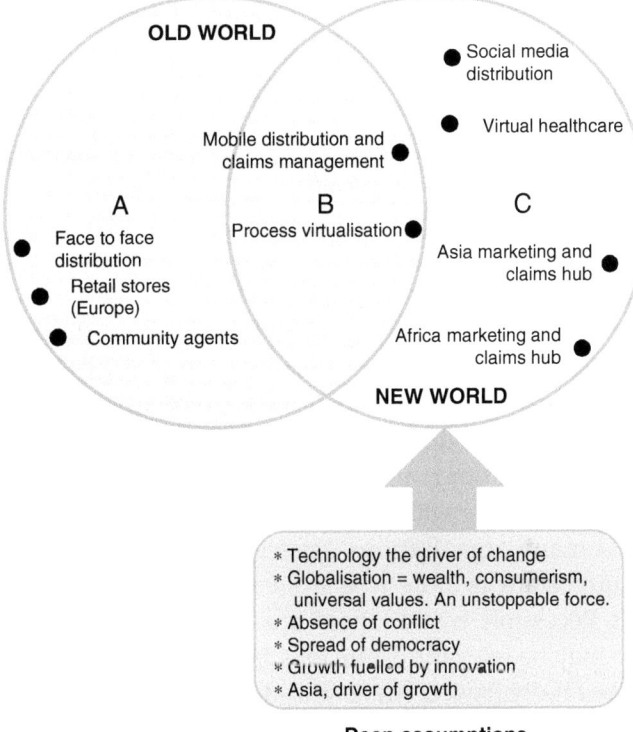

Figure 2.2 Stability–change: A view of the future

These capabilities are shown as 'Mobile distribution and claims management' and 'Process virtualisation' in the overlapping areas of the two worlds, area 'B', as they are the key to survival in both worlds and must be both nurtured and defended.

Outstanding growth opportunities, on a scale not yet witnessed, will appear in Asia and Africa as both continents industrialise and foster a burgeoning middle class, hungry for luxury goods and, of course, the insurance to protect them. These are the economies that will, in turn, dominate, shape and control the future, which is why these opportunities are shown solely in the area of the new world's circle.

Finally, disruptive, ground-breaking innovation in both healthcare and the application of social media will revolutionise insurance, taking it from a mere product to a complete healthcare diagnostic and treatment solution. These are disruptive shocks for the insurance industry that affect only the new world.

Conclusion

Developing a framework for exploration and experimentation is an essential element when preparing an organisation to face ambiguity. But exploration and experimentation require a foundation, a view of both the future world and the transition pathway that we are about to follow.

It may be helpful now, before going any further, to define the deep assumptions underpinning your organisation's current strategy and its view of the future. We introduced nine 'deep assumptions' that underpinned both globalisation and the process of transition in our fictional organisation. These were, and in many cases still are, the widely held assumptions that in turn underpin a great many organisations' strategies and views of the future. But it is important to note that from where we stand now, in a post-Great Recession world, these are entirely untested assumptions. Some may be relevant. Some may belong to the last century. Others may be fatally flawed, mere wish-dreams. Now is the time to set out and debate your organisation's deep assumptions.

If we are to understand a world in transition, we have to challenge and debate such deep assumptions. After all, they may have hidden frailties. The process of debate will in turn help us to paint a more accurate picture of the future.

This process is important; after all, before 2008 many believed that derivatives and other sophisticated financial instruments would prevent a stock market meltdown and that the world would never face another recession.

So, our next task, in the following chapter, is to tackle the first of these nine assumptions – that we should see the world primarily as a network of territorially defined states.

Reflection points

1. What are the deep assumptions that underpin your strategy?
2. Do these assumptions still hold after the Great Recession?
3. How reliant are they upon the dominant influence of the United States?
4. Is your organisation reliant purely upon planned strategy?
5. Do you have a framework to explore the post-Great Recession world?

Additional reading

For many leaders, facing ambiguity means managing change. Both these publications provide guidance:

Baden-Fuller, C. and Stopford, J., 1992. *Rejuvenating the Mature Business: The Competitive Challenge*, London: Routledge.
Balogan, J. and Hope Hailey, V., 2008. *Exploring Strategic Change*, Harlow: Financial Times Prentice Hall.

For an overview of the challenge of leadership and innovation, including a practical workshop exercise try:

Davies, R. et al., 2010. Innovation: mapping the role of the corporate leader, London: Cass Business School/The Chartered Insurance Institute. Available at: http://www.cassknowledge.com/sites/default/files/article-attachments/475~~robert_davies_cii-cass_innovation_aug2010_fullreport.pdf.

3
Power, States and a World in Transition

Five critical questions

It has been said that 'What money is to economics, power is to international relations' (Mearsheimer, 2003, p. 12). Understanding power, who holds it and how it can be used is at the heart of understanding a world in transition. One of the major approaches used by researchers to help understand a changing global landscape is even called 'Power Transition Theory'. So getting to grips with the term 'power' is an essential first step in envisioning the possible paths of transition that lie ahead of us. But the problem is that power, just like globalisation, is such a widely used word that one could assume that it has a universally agreed meaning. The truth is that there is no agreed meaning. Power, especially in the international arena, has many facets and, like a living organism, is growing and changing, spurred on, at least in part, by technological progress.

To grasp the concept of power and its application in the changing global landscape, we have to answer five critical questions:

1. Are there different types of power?
2. How is power defined?
3. How is power measured?
4. Who can own or wield power?
5. Will power continue to evolve and change?

The answers to these questions will form a foundation from which to consider the transition paths that potentially lie ahead of us. This chapter focuses upon answering these five questions and drawing critical conclusions. Chapter 4 then builds on these findings to present a framework through which we can construct possible future worlds. Chapter 5 will specifically look at the potential transition paths that lie between the present and the worlds that await us. But first we have to understand power and how it is used to form and shape the future world.

Trenches and bayonets

Power, from a classically realist perspective, is 'the capacity to produce an intended effect' (Waltz, 1959, p. 205). From this position, Waltz, one of the most influential figures in the field of post-Second World War international relations, goes on to assert that power, and he has in mind physical force, is held only by the state. It is one of the primary tools that states can use in pursuing their goals. This theme, that power is held solely by states and primarily takes the form of physical force, echoes resoundingly in the thinking of many other international relations writers and researchers. Gilpin (1981), for example, sees power functioning to ensure that weaker states will obey the commands of more powerful dominant states.

We see further evidence of this perspective when we look at the work of researchers who have attempted to measure power. Lemke (1997) uses an economic perspective, in terms of Gross Domestic Product (GDP), to illustrate the relative power possessed by emerging and declining states, as does the more recent work of Subramanian (2011). Some researchers include other factors, most notably military expenditure. Lebow and Valentino (2009) go even further and consider both GDP and the size of a state's population in an attempt to capture latent military prowess 'since population is a key determinant of a state's ability to mobilize military forces' (Lebow & Valentino, 2009, p. 396). The Composite Index of National Capabilities (CINC), used for research in this field, takes these perspectives too, looking at population, industrial capabilities (including iron and steel production) and military capabilities (Kim, 2010).

So power is classically seen as the primary tool that states can use to pursue their goals and, in the final analysis, it takes the form of military power. Military power is, in turn, a function of the size of a state's economy and the population it can draw upon.

These apparently confrontational approaches to viewing power can have their uses.

We can apply these seemingly hard-edged dimensions of power to chart the distribution of power over the post-Second World War decades. This will give us a perspective on how the global landscape is changing. In the illustrations below, starting with Figure 3.1, three measures are applied to chart the global distribution of this hard-edged power:

(1) Economic growth trajectory. Here we take economic growth rates over a ten-year period. This provides us with a view of a state's 'economic trajectory', how quickly it is growing or contracting. It also provides us with an indication of the potential levels of growth, or contraction, in coming years too. This is a more dynamic approach than just looking at a one-year snapshot. We can see this measure on the vertical axis.
(2) Military prowess. Military spending as a percentage of GDP in the year of analysis is shown along the horizontal axis of the illustrations.
(3) Economic size (GDP). The relative size of a state's economy is shown by the bubble area in each illustration.

This is a convenient approach too, as it will allow us to view the popular economic growth projections of the emerging economies from a totally different perspective, not merely looking at the relative size of economies, but the capacity of states to develop and wield hard-edged power. Using this methodology, six illustrations or 'power maps' are presented, and in each the world's top eight economies by size of GDP are shown.

The first, Figure 3.1, shows the distribution of hard-edged power in 1980, during the Cold War years, nearly ten years before the Berlin Wall was to fall. This illustration clearly shows a balancing of power between the Soviet Union on the one hand and the United States and its allies on the other.

The Soviet Union is alone, its economy smaller than that of the United States, but this disparity is made up for in terms of its military spending, a massive and, history would prove, unsustainable near 16% of its GDP. But the Soviet Union is countered by the United States, with its allies tightly clustered behind it. This was an era of power balancing, nuclear-backed 'mutually assured

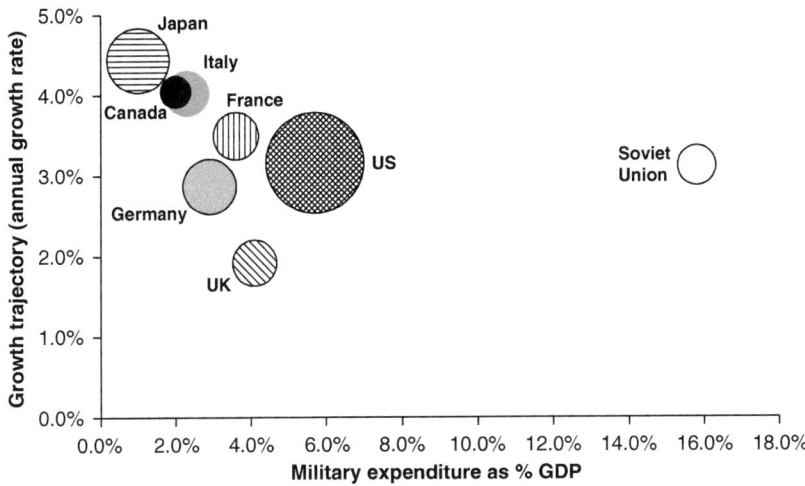

Figure 3.1 Hard power: 1980

Note: Real GDP is calculated at 2005 US$ values. The Soviet Union's military expenditure is shown at 1988 levels.

Source: Historic GDP – the United Nations. Historic military spending information from the Stockholm International Peace Research Institute (SIPRI) http://www.sipri.org/databases/milex. Some sources estimate the Soviet Union's GDP at approximately 50% of that of the United States. For a discussion of the Soviet Union's GDP, see Dikhano (1999) and Maddison (1998).

destruction', a clash of superpowers bringing the prospect of total global annihilation.

We move on ten years in the second power map, Figure 3.2. The Berlin Wall has fallen and the Soviet Union is now in obvious decline, set to finally disintegrate in 1991, weighed down by declining growth rates and the now impossible burden of military spending. The United States and potentially Japan appear destined to be the dominant powers in the coming decades. So the long-term dominance of the United States appears to be assured and it still enjoys the support of a cluster of old friends.

By 2000, a US-dominated unipolar world is at its peak, as shown in Figure 3.3. The Soviet Union's successor, Russia, has fallen, albeit temporarily, out of the world's top eight economies, lying now behind a nascent India. China makes a quiet and almost unseen entry into the world's eight largest economies.

Interestingly, it was in these post-Berlin Wall decades that triumph was declared for democracy and capitalism. Fukuyama published his essay 'The End of History?' (Fukuyama, 1989) promising a

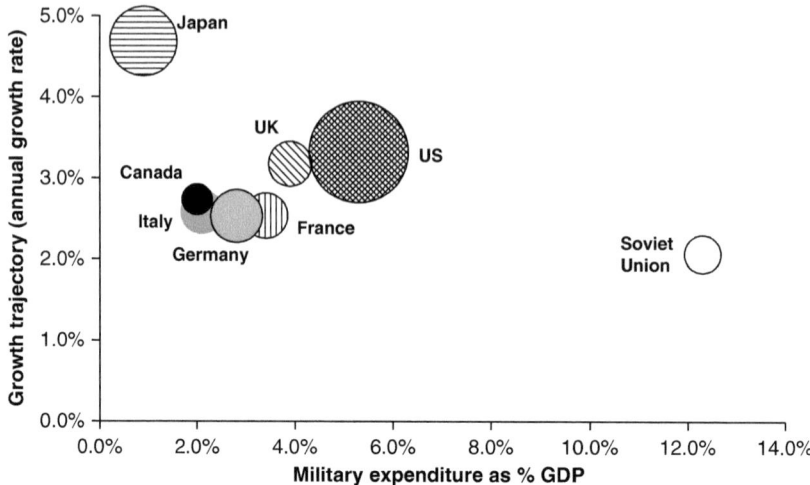

Figure 3.2 Hard power: 1990
Note: Real GDP calculated at 2005 US$ values.
Source: Historic GDP – the United Nations. Historic military spending information from the Stockholm International Peace Research Institute (SIPRI) http://www.sipri.org/databases/milex. Some sources estimate the Soviet Union's GDP at approximately 50% of that of the United States. For a discussion of the Soviet Union's GDP, see Dikhano (1999) and Maddison (1998).

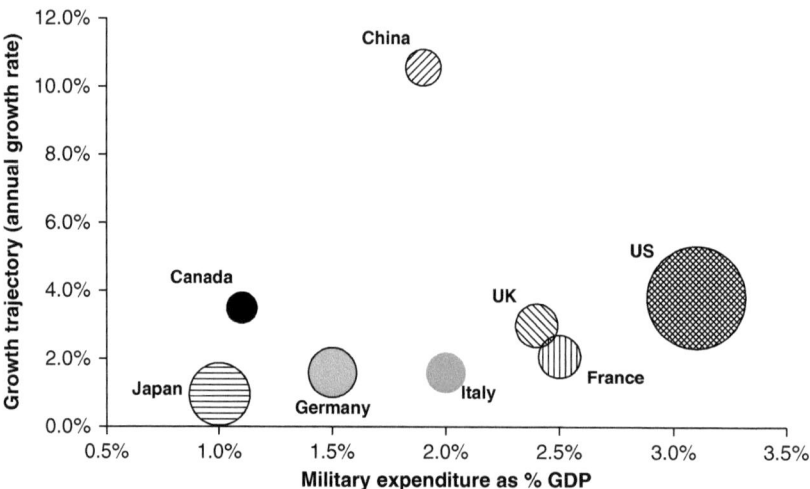

Figure 3.3 Hard power: 2000
Note: Real GDP calculated at 2005 US$ values.
Source: Historic GDP – the United Nations. Historic military spending information from the Stockholm International Peace Research Institute (SIPRI) http://www.sipri.org/databases/milex.

mature world where conflict between democratic states was a thing of the past. President Clinton too declared:

> We are at a turning point in human history. Immense and promising changes seem to wash over us every day. The Cold War is over. The world is no longer divided into two armed and angry camps. Dozens of new democracies have been born. It is a moment of miracles.
>
> (Clinton, 1993)

Whilst most voices were hailing a triumph for democracy and capitalism, there were emerging signs of trouble ahead. The growth rates of the United States' historical allies were starting to fall, raising questions of their relevance in the decades to come. Was the United States also moving in the Soviet Union's footsteps, shouldering the burden of a defence budget that would be unaffordable in future years?

But the United States still dominated the global power map in 2010 (Figure 3.4). It stood alone in terms of its level of military spending, rather as the Soviet Union did some 30 years earlier.

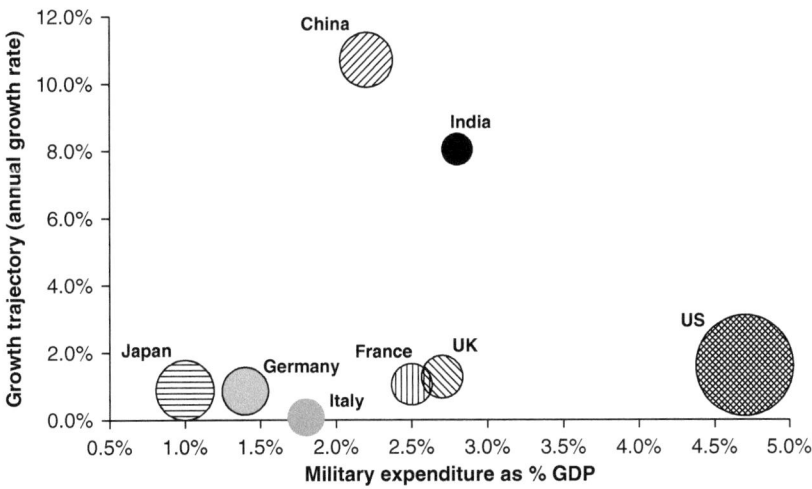

Figure 3.4 Hard power: 2010

Note: Real GDP calculated at 2005 US$ values.

Source: Historic GDP – the United Nations. Historic military spending information from the Stockholm International Peace Research Institute (SIPRI) http://www.sipri.org/databases/milex.

An old friend, Canada, has departed the ranks of the top eight economies, to be replaced by India. Russia and Brazil are just outside the ranks of the top eight economies.

All these illustrations span our formative years, years when our preconceptions of the way that at least the business world operates were formed. Assumptions, such as the permanence of consumer-fuelled growth, the spread of democracy and the end of superpower wars, have been accepted, without rigorous testing, as fact. All these preconceptions were of course formed during an era of US dominance and influence. The obvious question is: will this dominance and influence continue? To try to answer this question, we will move ahead to the year 2020.

So, it is when we look forward to 2020 (Figure 3.5) that we see the most significant changes, if that is, the new economies continue their rise. Clearly, the Great Recession has had a long-term impact upon both the United States and its friends. It is almost as if there are two worlds. The old economies seem stuck in a low-growth trap. The new economies, notably China and India, together race

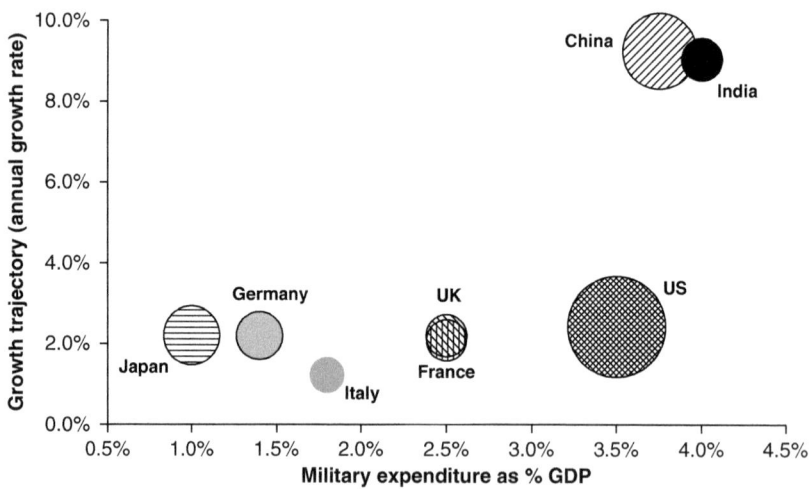

Figure 3.5 Hard power: 2020
Note: Real GDP calculated at 2005 US$ values. With the exception of China and India, military spending is assumed to decline due to sovereign debt pressure.
Source: Historic GDP – the United Nations. Historic military spending information from the Stockholm International Peace Research Institute (SIPRI) http://www.sipri.org/databases/milex. Other projections – the Author.

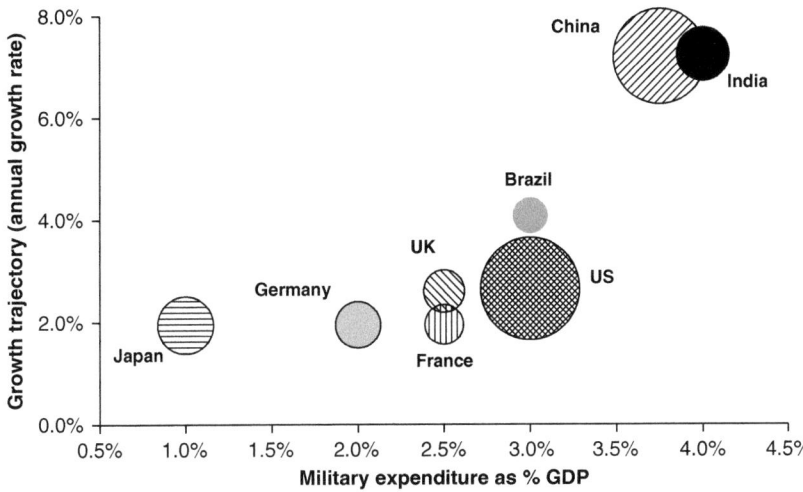

Figure 3.6 Hard power: 2030
Note: Real GDP calculated at 2005 US$ values. With the exception of China and India, military spending is assumed to decline due to sovereign debt pressure.
Source: Historic GDP – the United Nations. Historic military spending information from the Stockholm International Peace Research Institute (SIPRI) http://www.sipri.org/databases/milex. Other projections – the Author.

ahead. It is almost as if the United States is leading a different, low-growth world.

A further ten years on and it appears as if the United States is starting a journey to the bottom left of the power map in Figure 3.6, to join other old empires. China, India and a new entrant, Brazil, with Russia just outside the 'G8', are the states with buoyant economies set to exert influence as we approach the middle of this century.

These maps of hard-edged power help us to see a landscape that provides a perspective that differs from conventional economic projections. They seem to clearly indicate that an era of US dominance is coming to an end. The all-too-clear potential outcome is that the batten will pass to China, that is if China wishes to accept it.

Although these maps of power are useful and provide us with a new picture of the future, we are left with a feeling that this is very much an early 20th century way of viewing power and the workings of the world. Images of troops lined up in trenches along national borders, bayonets glinting in the sun, supplied by factories belching smoke and munitions, appear in the mind.

Power and actors in the 21st century

So, are these perspectives still valid as we look ahead through the second and into the third decades of the 21st century? Are we missing new elements in the emerging landscape? Are there new sources of power? Do we have to consider new actors or players that can hold and wield power? These are all questions that spring to mind.

Susan Strange (Strange, 1988) opens the door more broadly in three key areas. Her first message is that we need to look beyond states when we consider the holders of power. Strange refers to a number of non-state holders of power (that we will call 'actors') that we must reflect upon, especially when we think about activities that span the traditional borders of states. She says, 'Corporations, banks, religious leaders, universities and scientific communities are all participants in certain important kinds of transnational relations' (Strange, 1988, p. 21).

Strange's second major contribution is to broaden our viewpoint, when we consider the forms that power can take, introducing the position that there are two main forms or types of power. She refers to these as relational power and structural power. Relational power is the hard-edged power that we have discussed above, which Strange calls 'the power of A to get to B to do something they would not otherwise do' (p. 24). This is hard, arm-twisting power, and the stuff of traditional state versus state military conflict.

But structural power is different and may be potentially of far more interest to us. Strange puts forward this definition of structural power: 'the power to shape and determine the structures of the global political economy within which other states, their political institutions, their economic enterprises and (not least) their scientists and other professional people have to operate' (Strange, 1988, p. 25).

This second type or form of power is a major advance. It refers to the power to be the architect of the global economic and business environment. A clear example of the use of structural power can be found in the closing years of the Second World War. In July 1944, the United States used its newly reinforced structural power to act as, arguably, the prime architect and designer of the post-war economic environment. It used structural power to establish the rules and institutions, including the International Monetary Fund and World Bank, which in turn would govern the global international monetary systems for decades to come.

This leads us to the question that if structural power is so important, then what are its sources? What drives its creation? This is Strange's third major contribution and she points to four critical and interrelated sources of structural power:

1. Security. This is the capacity to provide security, notably the ability to protect people from violence.
2. Production. Control over, in terms of goods and services, what is produced and how it is produced.
3. Finance. Who controls the supply of credit. Critically, Strange has in mind the issue of gaining confidence: 'whoever can so gain the confidence of others in their ability to create credit will control a capitalist – or indeed socialist – economy' (Strange, 1988, p. 30).
4. Knowledge. The power to create and control knowledge that is valued by others.

These sources of structural power seem to be increasingly relevant now, especially when we reflect upon the near collapse of the world's banking system in 2008, the indebted position of many of the advanced economies and the leaps, in terms of knowledge, that will be required to overcome impending energy, water and food supply crises.

But, as we have seen, the most important facet of structural power is its capacity to confer upon the holder the ability to be the architect of the liberal order, or its successor, just as the United States did in 1944, when it drove the creation of the rules and institutions that would govern the post-war international monetary system. At its simplest, we can regard structural power as the power to make the rules that will decide how things are done in a future world.

Susan Strange has taken us forward in terms of both the types of power that we need to consider and the actors that hold or wield power. Whilst the concept of non-state actors has been introduced by Strange, we are still left with the strong view that we should only see the world as a collection of states. We still have the trenches and the bayonets, but the horizon is now cluttered with images of glass tower blocks that are the bankers' offices, joining the chimneys of the factories belching out smoke, armaments and munitions.

But is this right? Is the state still the dominant actor? Or is something else, something bigger going on?

Philip Bobbitt can help us to expand our view when he talks of the death of the state (Bobbitt, 2003, 2008).

At the centre of Bobbitt's argument is the proposition that states have had their day. This has its roots in Strange's view that many holders of power, or actors, have appeared that can transcend the traditional physical borders of states. In other words, the existence of traditional borders does not really get in the way of their operations.

The concept of states, land masses with physical borders, was first recognised in the Treaty of Westphalia in 1648 and this concept has become an established way of thinking over the following decades. The primary reason why states exist, according to Bobbitt (2003), is to maximise the welfare of the state itself and its citizens.

But Bobbitt argues that, after some 350 or so years, the state has reached the end of its useful purpose. In a globalised, technology-driven world, states find that they are both losing control over the ability to maximise welfare and are unable to respond to the challenge of maximising opportunities for their citizens.

The argument is that new entities may be needed to replace states in the emerging world order – entities that can, in particular, respond to the challenges of a globalised, technology-driven world.

Bobbitt is not alone in calling the end of time for the state. There are many others. From totally different perspectives, Ohmae (1990, 1995), Strange (1996), Clark (2000) and Cooper (2004) all carry similar messages.

Cooper refers to the state's successor as the 'post-modern state'; Bobbitt uses the term 'market state'. For the time being we will use Bobbitt's label, before developing his concept further towards the end of this chapter.

The idea of the evolution of states into market states, it is proposed, is driven by both the intended and unintended by-products of globalisation and technology. Perversely, the forces that drove the emergence of globalisation will, it is proposed, lead to the death of the state in the decades to come.

Some see this as a positive development, allowing economic rationality to prevail over arguably less rational political interference (Ohmae, 1995), but others have a different perspective. The danger, as Cooper sees it, is that these unintended by-products of globalisation bring 'new, more foreign enemies whose motives we barely understand' (Cooper, 2004, p. xi).

In short, drawing upon Bobbitt (2003; 2008) the demise of the state will be driven by a series of 'globalisation's challenges', these being:

1. Human rights. The increasing importance attached to human rights. The concept that basic norms and standards of behaviour must be adhered to, irrespective of national boundaries.
2. Weapons of mass destruction (WMDs). The proliferation of WMDs and the availability of WMDs to non-state actors, including terrorist groups, and even individuals.
3. Transnational threats. An increased exposure to disease, pandemics and natural disasters.
4. Economic management. Free flow of capital across borders which reduces the ability of a state to fully control its own economic destiny or even to protect the jobs of its own citizens.
5. Information. The creation of the Internet that allows information and opinions to flow across national boundaries as if they were figments of imagination. The product is a challenge to national languages, customs, routines and culture. Access to information has played a key role in empowering individuals and small groups, even enabling them to topple state leaders. We will return to this important topic again in the following pages.
6. Legislation. The inability of the state to protect its citizens, and leaders, from prosecution in other territories.

Monk (2009) sees the Great Recession as evidence that states and their post-war institutions are now unable to keep up with the pressures and demands of ongoing globalisation. What is required is a new form of organising that will provide some better defence or resilience to globalisation's challenges and pressures.

From a different perspective, Fry (2000) sees problems for both the state and the future course of globalisation. Fry's view is that commonly accepted views of globalisation overestimate the homogeneity of interests on the world stage. He sees not overarching globalisation, but a move to states grouping on a regional basis around cultural values:

> The increasing links between peoples within a region and the promotion of a cultural identity and community by states is creating further demands for wider participation in the regional contest over values and practices. It is no longer simply a project of states.
>
> (Fry, 2000, p. 131)

There is some evidence too that Fry's views are coming to fruition. Crandell (2011), for example, notes that new allegiances and groupings are appearing in Latin America following the United States' dwindling influence, and not all such alliances may unequivocally support either democracy or free-market capitalism.

So the decline of the state and the emergence of its scions could potentially be the next 'epochal' upheaval in the evolution of world order.

Simply put, there are growing views that the concept of the state is approaching its sell-by date. The economic growth and decline of states is only one dimension to reflect upon when looking forward towards a future world. Just seeing the world as a map where states, their economies and armies are the major architects of change could be missing a point. The potentially fitful rise of nascent market states, or other forms, such as globally interlinked cities as new actors, replacing or living alongside states, will be another and far more important dimension to consider when we think of the future.

The real problem is that we have only really a vague notion of what any replacement for the state could look like. The most popular conception is probably Bobbit's 'market state'. It can be held that the European Union is a very early market state prototype, designed in the pre-technology era. Others see another embryonic market state in China as it spreads its influence across the globe.

More advanced prototypes of market state could be thought of as 'virtualised' in form, bound together by shared perspectives on, for example, human rights and capitalism, rather than mere physical proximity.

In our scenario planning sessions with MBA students at Cass Business School, the future of the state, and the possible form of any successor, is a common theme. Several of our future scenarios envisage economies and societies that are not defined by geographic boundaries at all, but by common attitudes to the role of the individual in society and the legitimacy of capitalism. This type of thinking reveals new structures that could replace the state including, for example, global networks of aligned cities.

But for now, we will follow Bobbitt (2008) and consider just two successors to the state: the *market state* and, another emerging entity that Bobbitt foresees, the *state of terror*. It is the state of terror to which we will now turn.

As technology and globalisation act as catalysts to drive the emergence of the market state, so technology and globalisation will spawn the market state's nemesis, the state of terror. Technology and globalisation will in turn empower states of terror, in other words all who rail against the values that market states seek to protect. Al Qaeda is put forward by Bobbitt as an 'early prototype' of a state of terror. But we should not let the word 'state' cloud our view of the size or even form of a 'state of terror'. Theoretically, a state of terror could be as small as one person. But however small such states are, states of terror will be bound, like market states, by common values, potentially in both physical and transnational 'virtualised' forms.

Size, particularly in economic terms, will not therefore be an indicator of power. States of terror are enabled by the dark side of technological progress. Joseph Nye's observations are salient at this point when he observes that technology has empowered terrorism, noting that events on 11 September 2001 showed us how a small group of individuals could kill in one day more US citizens than could a state (Japan) on 7 December 1941, when the surprise attack on Pearl Harbor took place (Nye, 2011b). The purported capability of hackers to bring down the Internet in a matter of hours is another chilling example of the power of individuals empowered by technology.

So power, particularly hard-edged relational power, is no longer within the sole domain of the state. Flash mobs and individuals can be holders of relational power too. And the relational power that they can wield may equal or exceed that of many states (or indeed nascent market states).

The best recent example that we have of the role of newly empowered non-state actors is the 'Arab Spring' of 2010–2011. The self-immolation of Mohamed Bouazizi, in a small town in Tunisia after his fruit stall was closed by officials, is largely credited as being the catalytic event that instigated popular uprisings across the Middle East, which in turn toppled many established heads of state (Bone, 2011).

We can now see how dangerous it is to view the current world and a possible future landscape in the form of a series of economic projections based just around states. We have more actors to consider than just states and more structural forms to think about too. But just as we have looked for the emergence of new actors beyond the state, so we must see if new forms of power are emerging, beyond those highlighted by Susan Strange.

Smart and soft?

'Soft' power is a term that has fallen into frequent usage. Nye (2011a) defines soft power as 'the ability to obtain preferred outcomes without coercion or payment'. It can be considered as the opposite of the hard-edged relational power introduced at the beginning of this chapter. Soft power has the same end in mind as hard-edged power, in Nye's words, 'affecting others to get the outcomes that one wants' (Nye, 2011a), but it does so through persuasion, not blunt, arm-twisting force.

Just as Strange (1988) pointed to four sources of structural power, so Nye (2011b), from the perspective of the state, points to three sources of soft power, being:

1. Culture, expressed in social behaviour and values,
2. Political policies and
3. Foreign policies.

We can immediately observe that these sources of power are framed from the concept or perspective of the state. But just as hard relational power can now be wielded by non-state actors, so can soft power. States of terror can use soft power as can corporations. This is what Friedman (2006) had in mind when he suggested his 'Golden Arches Theory', a theory that posits that multinational corporations could wield more power than states and bring peace by not investing in countries with war-like intentions. Whilst Nye's three sources of soft power may be relevant for states and market states, they may not be for other actors. For others, culture, or the attractiveness of the values and ideals that a corporation or collection of individuals stands for, may be the sole source of soft power.

It is important to note that all these sources of soft power are very much like the concept of beauty – the perception of the strength of these sources of power lies not with the holder, but with the beholder. If culture, political values and foreign policy are seen as attractive, then soft power can be a powerful seducer. Wolf (2005) points to soft power as historically being one of the key assets of the first prototype market state, the European Union, soft power acting as a magnet to attract aspiring members. In this context, some see such soft power as having the capacity to lead to a 'reconciliation of civilisations'.

Naturally, if the mix of culture, political policy and foreign policy (or indeed any one component) is not attractive to the beholder, then soft power becomes irrelevant. Of these three, culture may be the most important and, as Kissinger observes, the West may place too much emphasis on the efficacy of persuasion, underestimating the resilience of culture (Kissinger, 2011).

This is the rub that soft power faces in a world in transition.

But soft power, as a relatively new and untested concept, faces another rub.

And that is its permanence. A large army is a relatively permanent source of power, so long as its soldiers are fit, well fed and supplied with up-to-date tools of their trade. The question with soft power, from the perspective of whoever holds it, is its durability. We have already seen that the European Union has been held out as an important holder of soft power (Wolf, 2005). However, the 'Euro Crisis' of 2011, centring around the creditworthiness of many of the European Union's most established member states, is seen as removing, in a few short months, the European Union's soft power capabilities (Popescu, 2011).

We are not merely concerned with states as actors and holders of power. We are concerned with the prospect of emerging market states and other newly empowered actors, each being a separate holder. This of course leaves us with an unanswered question: is it possible for states, either states or emerging market states, to possess forms of soft power that can appeal to the broad range of actors that have appeared on the global stage?

Whilst in most minds, soft power must be the preferred tool to achieve 'the outcomes one wants', we must question its efficacy during the transition decades. Is it a new form of power that represents a world that wishes to avoid the hubris that the deployment of hard-edged relational power brings in its wake, or will it fail the test of time?

There is finally a third rub. It may not be possible for states, either states or market states, to have soft power as the only tool in their armouries. Some (Cohen & DeLong, 2010) hold that a state's capacity to deploy soft power is contingent upon the size and health of its economy, which is clearly illustrated in the example of the 'Euro Crisis' above. Building on this position, we can see that for any *state* actor, soft power stands with its feet on two platforms, a relational power platform and a structural power platform. Indeed, it is the use of a mix or confluence of relational power, structural power and soft power that some call the use of 'smart power'.

Smart power was originally conceived as a tool that would become the mainstay of US foreign policy, one that would spread liberal internationalism on the assumption that 'a global system of stable liberal democracies would be less prone to war' (Nossel, 2004). We can see that smart power, like soft power, stands on the platforms of relational power and structural power when Nossel illustrates the application of smart power through 'wars against terrorists and rogues, the rehabilitation of failed states, and the liberalization of repressive societies' (Nossel, 2004, p. 137).

Wilson (2008) helps by providing us with a succinct view of smart power when he defines it as 'the capacity of an actor to combine elements of hard power and soft power in ways that are mutually reinforcing, such that the actor's purposes are advanced effectively and efficiently' (Wilson, 2008, p. 110).

But Wilson makes the point even clearer when he demonstrates that smart power is not limited to the domain of the West, its states, corporations and other associated actors. China has proved itself to be a skilful user of smart power, leaving the United States in its wake.

The message to take from Wilson's work and others is that although soft power is attractive, it may not be viable on its own. At the very least, from the perspective of a state actor, it requires the support of a strong economy, in addition to a culture, combined with political and foreign policies that are attractive to the beholders.

Questions, answers and new states

We opened this chapter by posing five key questions. We will now draw the chapter to a close by setting out responses to these questions for debate.

Question 1: Are there different types of power? We have identified a hierarchy of power. The two foundation stones are Strange's (1988) relational power and structural power. Relational power is a traditional perspective, focusing on economic and military might, the capacity to inflict physical damage. Structural power is a more recent development and is the power to act as the architect of 'how things are done'. Probably of the two, structural power is the most relevant. Understanding who, or which group of actors, holds the balance of structural power can help us to predict the workings of the world. Soft power sits on the relational and structural foundation stones, surmounted by smart power, which is the ability to apply a mixture of soft, structural and hard-edged relational power. A major uncertainty in our minds must be the use of power in the era of transition. Will soft power, smart power, structural power or even hard-edged relational power dominate?

Question 2: How is power defined? All the common definitions of power retain the arm-twisting theme that Waltz (1959) and Gilpin (1981) introduce. In an attempt to reflect the more subtle approaches of soft and smart power, Nye's definition, being 'the ability to alter others' behaviour to produce preferred outcomes' (Nye, 2011c, p. 10), is the preferred one.

Question 3: How is power measured? Trying to measure power can be really misleading and runs the risk of reification, or building an artificial construct and then believing that it is real. Arguably, even the established measures of hard relational power are mere indicators and they provide us with no assessment of an actor's ability or, importantly, motivation to use power. We can conclude here that there are no reliable measures of structural power, soft power or smart power.

Importantly, relying on any of the established measures gives us a distorted view of a world in transition and ignores any of the new actors who may be pivotal in designing the emerging global landscape.

Question 4: Who can own or wield power? Or who are the actors that own power? Just one or two decades ago, the answer would have been states. Many of the economic projections dealing with the emergence of new economies still paint pictures of the world as consisting purely of states. The forces of globalisation and technology have materially changed the scene. A whole raft of new actors has been empowered, from multinational corporations, through religious groups to individuals and 'flash mobs'. The 'Arab Spring' of 2010–2011 is an excellent example of the power that now rests outside the state. Individuals, pressure and belief groups can access relational power, soft power and therefore elements of smart power, arguably at levels that can equal or exceed the capacities of some states.

In this new environment, it would be erroneous to think that states are the most powerful of all, having sole access to the constituents of smart power. They may be the weakest. Non-state actors may prove to be more nimble than traditional state actors in their use of power in its various forms.

As we have seen, the concept of the state is one that is showing its age. After more than 350 years the state is creaking, its borders offering little defence against the unintended poison found in the chalices of technology and globalisation. As states struggle against the by-products of these forces, we hold that their successors could well emerge during the *Era of Transition*. Bobbitt (2008) refers to just 'market states' and 'states of terror'. Although this is a good starting point, Bobbitt has in mind a strict delineation between market states that are organised along democratic and capitalistic principles and states of terror whose primary objective is the destruction of their nemesis, market states. In other words, it is held that capitalism and democracy together form the major organisational driving force or magnet behind the emergence of the successor to the state.

After the Great Recession it has become clear that we cannot merely assume that capitalism and democracy are the only viable frameworks or driving forces. In addition, it should not be forgotten that the Westphalian concept of the state reflects very much a Western perspective and may blinker us from the perspectives of others (Falk, 2000) and that there is a need to move away from historic Western images (Fry & O'Hagan, 2000).

We must remember too that after the Great Recession, capitalism, for some, is in crisis (Callinicos, 2010; Hadar, 2010) and indeed the universal appeal of democracy too may be in question. It is therefore too early to dismiss the emergence of structures typified by centralised control that eschew democracy and free-market capitalism. To do so would severely restrict our field of view.

But we need to consider another force too. We need to reflect upon the concept of culture or values as a primary driving force. As we have seen, Fry (2000) warns us not to underestimate the issue of cultural identity, and in general, the issues of culture and identity have been, until recently, badly neglected when studying world politics (O'Hagan, 2000).

On this point, we can draw upon the observations and suggestions of Samuel Huntington, writing in *The Clash of Civilisations* (Huntington, 2002). Broadly, Huntington sees the world dividing into cultural groupings or layers. The collapse of the Soviet Union is seen as a catalyst in this respect with political ideology being replaced by culture as the new 'magnet of attraction and repulsion'. In Huntington's words, 'in the emerging global politics, the core states of the major civilizations are supplanting the two Cold War super powers as the principal poles of attraction and repulsion' (Huntington, 2002, p. 155). States organised around cultural norms owe little, if any allegiance, to concepts of capitalism, democracy or communism. Instead, they look to shared cultural beliefs and identities as the primary dimensions of organising.

Assuming that states, in their current form, are the major architects of change may therefore be a big mistake when we look out to see a future world.

Question 5: Will power continue to evolve and change? This cannot be discounted, but we now have a broad enough view of power to start to consider how it could be used and the issue of transition. Of more importance is the question: who will use power, what type of power will they use and what will act as a catalyst for its use?

Conclusion

The first *deep assumption* that we looked at in Chapter 2 was that the world will always consist of a network of states. The conclusion of this chapter is that looking just at states and economic projections can provide us with a dangerously misleading view of the future global landscape and omits some unintended by-products of the process of globalisation.

Two major shortcomings in looking at the world merely from the perspective of states have been observed.

Firstly, the assumption of the continued dominance of the state. In other words, states are the most powerful actors or architects when we consider a world in transition. This is not now the case. We are now in the position where groups of individuals or even a single person can possess as much power as a state, a position that is well illustrated both by the attack on the Twin Towers, New York, in September 2001 and the 'Arab Spring' of 2010–2011. Secondly, the inference that power, defined as 'the ability to alter others' behaviour to produce preferred outcomes', can be measured in purely economic or military terms. The 21st century has brought with it new forms of power, most notably 'soft' power and 'smart' power. Soft and smart power could be major tools to be used during the years of transition, but there are doubts as to their robustness and durability.

Just looking at the world from a traditional perspective presents us with the risk that we will ignore the central issue that we need to consider when thinking about a world in transition; that it is a potential assault on the state from newly empowered groups, or 'non-state actors'. Many feel that states will react to these challenges by 'clubbing together' and forming market states, very much like the European Union, but there are other outcomes that may await us. Interestingly, this is not the first time in history that this type of challenge has appeared. By looking back to the Middle Ages in Europe, we may find some clues to second guess future events. In the next chapter, we will focus upon that journey back in time to search for answers.

Reflection points

1. Who will be the most influential actors in deciding the form of the post-Great Recession world?
2. What forms of power will these actors use?
3. Will soft power become the hallmark of the 21st century? Will this mark a new level of maturity in international relations?
4. Will we witness a 'clubbing together' of states to protect themselves from the pressures of globalisation?

Additional reading

For those interested in learning more about international relations try:

Sutch, P. and Elias, J., 2007. *International Relations: the basics*, London: Routledge.

For a realist perspective on the world that challenges the popular view that the process of globalisation will proceed peacefully try:

Mearsheimer, J., 2001. *The Tragedy of Great Power Politics*, New York: W. W. Norton.

To explore the issue of power, try:

Nye, J., 2011. *The Future of Power*, New York: Public Affairs.

4
A 21st-century medievalism?

Is the future in the past?

The great twist of globalisation is that it may take us back into the past. The type of future that we may face could be the same that parts of the world, notably Europe, experienced some 600 years ago.

As we have seen, there are some unintended consequences, or poison, in the chalice of globalisation. The confluence of technology and the push for global economic integration has produced the empowerment of a range of actors, who are, in turn, challenging the historic authority of states. Many of these actors' interests have nothing to do with the state. They have nothing to do with business or capitalism either. For many of the newly empowered, allegiance to the interests of any single state or economic growth is at best of secondary importance. These 'out of state' or transnational interests can embrace a diverse range of issues from the rapid accumulation of personal wealth through to saving the environment, eliminating land mines, promoting human rights and, of course, religion.

For these actors, it is the cause that is important for them.

Some (e.g. Rapley, 2006) call this, quite aptly, a process of 'gnawing at the edges' of states. Perversely, the traditionally stronger states, including the 'superpowers' of the 20th century, may well prove to be the most vulnerable to these 'gnawing away' attempts. An example of this eating away process came during the Euro Crisis of 2011. Pressure from money markets contributed both to the exit of democratically elected prime ministers (George Papandreou of Greece and Silvio Berlusconi of Italy) and, additionally, to the establishment of a cabinet constructed, in Italy's case, of unelected 'technocrats'. All this leads to a raft of questions being asked, such as 'Must democracy be sacrificed to save Europe?' (Reinhardt, 2011) and:

> If democratically elected leaders do not satisfy the markets, the IMF and the European Commission, they are now, in effect, summarily dismissed, without any reference to the wishes of the people.
>
> (Skelton, 2011)

But there is another perspective to consider. Others see this process of gnawing away from a different view, observing that the empowerment of the money markets is a positive element of globalisation. The argument here is that money markets can be more effective and efficient decision makers than governments, especially in times of crisis (Altman, 2011).

But there are earlier examples of the vulnerability of states.

Terrorism, or more particularly, the attack on the Twin Towers in New York, is a recent example of an assault upon a state by a non-state actor.

However, an earlier victim was the Soviet Union. Cerny (2005) argues that the collapse of the Soviet Union was not solely due to its decline as a military superpower, but that its downfall really was the result of two other underlying, deeper struggles. The first was the ineffectiveness of military force, or relational power, to gain victory in conflicts, both in Afghanistan and Angola. The second struggle was the inability of the Soviet Union to defeat an emerging hunger for consumerism amongst its citizens. One lesson to be taken from the fall of the Soviet Union is that military prowess, or relational power, may be helpful in ensuring that weaker states will obey the commands of more powerful dominant states, but it is of little use against other actors, particularly the newly empowered (Judah, 2011).

All this of course means that the long-established sources of traditional power available to the state become increasingly questionable, as we progress further into the 21st century, a conclusion that we reached in Chapter 3.

The problem becomes obvious.

Traditional military-based or relational power's only relevance will be when states come to confront each other. This type of power becomes increasingly less effective when states venture out of their traditional comfort zones and enter the rather amorphous area where they confront newly empowered actors. One could say, drawing upon our discussion in the last chapter, that states can draw upon soft or smart power in these situations. However, these are as yet untested tools. The more likely conclusion is that the limitations of military force will both hasten the decline of the old 20th-century powers and herald a period for these states that Cerny (2010) refers to as the 'New Security Dilemma'. The dilemma, or paradox, that these states face is that the more they invest in conventional weaponry, the more they will attract those that wish to 'gnaw away' at their boundaries.

It is almost as if the forces of globalisation are 'unravelling' the sovereignty of the state.

But the real product of this 'unravelling' or 'gnawing away' process is that the ability of the state to perform its primary activities is being eroded. These primary, historic, activities are providing for the moral and material prosperity of the state's citizens, together with, of course, their health. This leaves us with the rather obvious question of what could or will replace the state. This is a tough question to answer as we all accept the concept of the state as the primary building block of world order and we even struggle to find the vocabulary to use to describe what alternative systems of rule could look like after all this gnawing away has finished (Ruggie, 1993).

If we look back in time, the system of states is only one of a number of possible 'systems of rule' that the world could adopt.

So at this point, we should be clear about what we mean by a 'state'. We will use this definition:

> The starting point of international relations is the existence of states, or independent political communities each of which possesses a government and asserts sovereignty in relation to a particular portion of the earth's surface and a particular segment of the human population.
>
> (Bull, 1977, p. 8)

Bull then goes on to provide us with an established view of the authority of states:

> [S]tates assert, in relation to this territory and population, what may be called internal sovereignty, which means supremacy over

all other authorities within that territory and population. On the other hand, they assert what may be called external sovereignty, by which is meant not supremacy but independence of *outside authorities*.

(Bull, 1977, p. 8, emphasis added)

So using Bull's terminology, we are seeing a gnawing away of the state's internal and external sovereignty.

This now brings us to one of the hottest and most contested areas within the international relations literature, the future of the state. We are faced with these questions:

'Are we at the dawn of the emergence of a new global order?'

Is the system of states dying after a lifespan of well over 350 years?

Whilst we have been born and bred to conceive of the world as a system of states, we should remember that 'states are simply groupings of men, and men may be grouped in such a way that they do not form states at all' (Bull, 1977, p. 20).

Our position in this chapter is that the state is undergoing its most fundamental attack since it evolved out of a rather looser and less territorially bound system, medievalism, and it is indeed this medieval system of rule that operated over 600 years ago that will help us to answer the question 'what will happen to the state?'

A 21st-century medievalism?

This erosion of the state and the emergence of a world of different actors take us to a position similar to that which came into play in the medieval period, the Middle Ages, when a system of states did not exist. A different, more fluid and territorially ambiguous system of rule then operated and, for surprising periods of time, offered relative stability.

The concept of such a backward movement into the past is not new and was first introduced by Wolfers (1962) and later developed by Bull (1977).

But first a brief historical note.

In the system of rule that existed in the Middle Ages, no one ruler was in the position of being a supreme authority over a territory and its population. We had a world of power sharing. Using the terminology introduced above, no single ruler or actor had complete internal or external sovereignty. Such sovereignties had to be shared with others. As Bull notes, in Western Christendom, each ruler, a member of the local aristocracy, had to share authority with a range of other actors, from vassals subservient to that ruler to, ultimately, the Church, which held a supreme position within this system. In practice, two major holders of power pulled this system together. One was a secular power, in the form of the Holy Roman Empire and its noblemen, the other a religious power, the Church. It is important to remember that at this time territorial borders were not strictly defined and even where borders existed they were porous and 'grey' in nature.

This description of the medieval order starts to sound surprisingly similar to a new emerging order that we may well face.

With the emergence of a new range of power-sharing actors, we could well be faced with, as Bull (1977) put it, a *New Medievalism*. Bull thought of this as a system of overlapping authorities and shared loyalties. At its simplest, this can be thought of, in a modern sense, as a matrix structure, where a state shares and cedes power amongst other actors, each actor having access to different types of power from hard-edged relational power through to soft power. In addition to sharing power, the state has to contend with its citizens holding multiple loyalties too, and amongst these loyalties allegiance to the state may be far from the most important.

The concept of a new medievalism can provide us with interesting perspectives when thinking about the context that we find ourselves in now as it removes the 'blinkers' that many established state-centric approaches present (Friedrichs, 2001). In short, Friedrichs holds that research in the international relations field focuses, at any one time, only upon one of the following areas:

1. The view of the world as a collection of states.
2. The impact of globalisation.
3. The impact of cultural, religious and values-based influences.

The message here is that traditional analytical approaches look only at one perspective. We need an approach that simultaneously embraces all three. But even more importantly, there is a need, as Bull (1977) states, to escape the intellectual and imaginative

A 21st-century medievalism? 53

imprisonment of the states system, and new medievalism may be such a route out of the prison that will enable us to envision new systems and, in turn, what possible forms the future world could take. This means that we have to stop thinking about a world shaped primarily around territorially defined states. While it is hard to conceive, there may be other ways of organising our world.

But before we explore what the offspring of the current system could look like, we must ask the question:

Can we be *certain* that we are entering a period of new medievalism – is the era of the state *really* coming to an end?

There certainly appears to be *prima facie* evidence that this may be the case, when, as we have seen, financial markets can force the resignation of a G8 state leader (Bowley et al., 2011).

We need, however, a more objective test or set of tests to answer this question.

Bull (1977) sets out five tests or traits, which together may point to the fact that we are already within a period of transformation and entering the era of a new medievalism. These tests are, using Bull's descriptions:

(1) *The regionalisation of states*. This is the tendency of states to seek to form themselves into larger units as a basic defence against the gnawing process we introduced earlier. As we have seen, some (e.g. Bobbitt, 2008) see this as a natural step. States cluster together to protect themselves against the intended and unintended effects of globalisation, taking a 'divided we fall, united we stand' approach. The earliest post-war example of grouping together or regionalisation is the European Union. But we can see this trend elsewhere, for example, Prime Minister Putin's attempts to create the Eurasian Zone (Buckley, 2011), and, potentially, an East Asian free trade area (Bergsten, 2009).
(2) *The fragmentation of states*. This is a situation, in which, in parallel with states trying to integrate or join forces with other states, we have the appearance of those actors that wish to disaggregate states or smash them into pieces. Currently, we can see many examples of this, including demands for fragmentation in the United Kingdom, Belgium, Spain and post-conflict

Iraq. It is not important that these actors eventually succeed in their quests; it is the mere fact that such actors exist, proliferate and are willing to challenge the authority of a state.

(3) *The restoration of private international violence.* This means who has the right to use force and wage war. In the Middle Ages, many groups could lay claim to the right to exercise force. In our world now the established view is that only states may legitimately exercise force. Bull (1977) is concerned here with the re-emergence of the use of widespread force, on a global basis, by actors other than the state. To use the definition of power developed in Chapter 3, we are concerned with those actors who can exercise hard-edged relational power; but of course relational power is not limited to the use of guns and explosives, it also relates to other tools that can damage the infrastructure of a state and many argue that cyber warfare will be the violent tool of choice in the 21st century (Evans & Whittell, 2010; Rubin, 2010). The most notable example would be Bobbitt's (2008) 'states of terror' where organised groups, other than states, use force as a means of coercion and claim their legitimacy or right to use such force. We have of course at least one example in Al-Qaeda, which translated means 'the base', with its ability to operate without a formal headquarters (Bajoria & Bruno, 2011). Interestingly, following Cerny (2005), Al-Qaeda may be one of the most prominent and important examples that we have of organising in our new medieval world, that is, an actor that does not rely on territorial boundaries to define itself and whose operations span such traditional borders.

(4) *Growth of transnational organisations.* In short, we are concerned with actors that challenge a state's monopoly of power and its ability to determine its own destiny. Examples range from the United Nations, the World Bank and the International Monetary Fund through to the multinational corporations, investment banks, rating agencies and non-governmental organisations (or 'NGOs', examples of which are Greenpeace and Amnesty International).

(5) *The technological unification of the world.* Here we are concerned with the Internet and the creation of the so-called 'global village'. Rather than unifying the world and encouraging the development and proliferation of one culture, Bull

(1977) holds that such 'technological unification' encourages increased differences, fragmentation and hence tension. In today's language, we are talking about the Internet and mobile communication. Gray (2009) takes up this point:

> By enabling practitioners of different cultures who are geographically scattered to interact through new communications media, globalization acts to express and to deepen cultural differences.
>
> (Gray, 2009, p. 60)

Gray builds on this position to say that technology will 'break up common cultures and replace them with traces and fragments' (Gray, 2009, p. 60). The message here is that technology, with its power to cross borders, will not result in the development of one shared culture, a popular assumption, but will act as a catalyst to heighten cultural differences.

But if the tests of new medievalism have been passed, what does our new medievalist world look like? Intriguingly, little effort has been invested, until recently, in exploring the concept of new medievalism (Payne, 2003). Writers who have ventured to peer into this dimly lit area present several potential characteristics that we will now explore.

Of all these exploratory ventures, the ideas of Friedrichs (2001) lay the foundation stones. Friedrichs holds that in this new neo-medieval place there will be three 'realms' or sources of legitimacy that will act as the architectural powers of the future. These architects or groups of actors are as follows:

(1) The state. Historically, at an international level, only the state can make decisions and claim to represent the citizens of its territory. The state is still, now, the centre-piece of the system, therefore it must play some part at least in the transition to a new world.
(2) The transnational (global) market economy, or, in short, capitalism. The market economy's claim to legitimacy is its economic efficiency in the distribution of both resources and wealth. Proponents of this camp hold that capitalism is the most efficient way of allocating scarce resources, generating wealth and distributing it.

(3) Social actors, either groups or individuals who claim their legitimacy from the values that they espouse, which can range from sustainable development through to human rights and of course religion. Within this group of architects, social actors, there will be many whose motivators are directly opposed to capitalism and the central control of the state.

We can think of these three architects as forming a three-way pull or 'trilemma'.

A trilemma is a situation in which a choice has to be made between three options, but it is only feasible to choose, at most, two of the options. A satisfactory compromise between all three is impossible. A compromise between two can be made, with negotiation, to work together, but getting a lasting compromise between all three is impossible. A simple and humorous example of a trilemma would be Zizek's Trilemma (Zizek, 2007), where Zizek reflects that, in the communist system, it was impossible to be simultaneously honest, to genuinely support communism and, at the same time, to be intelligent. 'If one was honest and supportive, one was not very bright; if one was bright and supportive, one was not honest; if one was honest and bright, one was not supportive' (Zizek, 2007).

So we could be faced with a trilemma, or a competition between three groups of architectural actors, each with different interests, motivators and sources of legitimacy. We have the traditionally dominant state, the market economy and social actors. At best, the needs of only two will be satisfied at any one point in time.

This view of a trilemma of three competing legitimacies or architects is similar to the work of others who have attempted to explore the future pathways of globalisation. Rodrik (2011), taking an economic viewpoint, constructs a trilemma from the following alternative options:

(1) 'Hyperglobalization' is total global economic integration with the complete elimination of trade barriers. This equates to Friedrich's transnational market economy. This is absolute free-market capitalism.
(2) The 'Nation state', where authority rests within the state.
(3) 'Democratic Politics'.

A similar approach too is seen in the construction of scenarios by Shell, where the following options (conceived as a choice between forces, not actors) were incorporated into a trilemma (Shell International, 2005):

(1) Market incentives, again with parallels with Rodrik's 'hyperglobalization' and Friedrich's 'transnational market economy'.
(2) The force of the community or aspirations to social cohesion and justice, where we again have some parallels with Rodrik's democracy and Friedrich's social actors.
(3) Coercion, regulation where we find similarities with control being centralised within the state in both Friedrich's and Rodrik's proposed trilemmas.

Harvey (2010) too uses a similar approach in describing who will influence the post-Great Recession world. He describes a battle for the control of land, resources and even intellectual property rights that will be fought between three main actors or architects who he sees as being states, corporations and wealthy individuals.

Using these observations, and notably those of Friedrichs (2001), we can isolate the actors, or players, who will have a key role in defining the future shape of the world and its 'systems of rule'. Our primary focus here is upon individuals in groups or coalitions, not forces, choices or entities such as 'states'. We are interested in people and how they will behave. Our attention is upon the coalitions of people that could be the architects of a new order. There are of course other actors, but we need to isolate those who we think will be the key architects. Focusing on groups or coalitions of individuals and their behaviours will help us to understand the pathways of transition that lie ahead of us. The focus on groups of people and their behaviours is important. As Gilpin (1981) notes:

> Strictly speaking, states, as such, have no interests, or what economists call 'utility functions', nor do bureaucracies, interest groups, or so-called transnational actors, for that matter. Only individuals and individuals joined together into various types of coalitions can be said to have interests.
> (Gilpin, 1981, p. 18)

However, we need to stop at this point and consider our earlier observation that a successor to the territorially bound state may appear. As we have seen, Bull (1977) has noted that states are only one way for individuals to organise and there may be many others. So, in all there are four groups of individuals, each with different needs and perspectives, which we need to consider and to focus our attention on. These are individuals that form four groups or coalitions that we will call 'state elites', 'market elites', 'social movements' and 'post-state elites':

1. State elites. Members of the state elites have access to the controls and coercive influence of the state. These actors can decide to what extent authority is centred in and exercised by the state, in other words who is rewarded and who is punished. An extreme example of centralised control would be the planned economy of the Soviet Union. North Korea and the People's Republic of China also spring to mind as examples, in differing degrees, of the use of centralised decision making and control. Autocracies, oligarchies and fascist single-party systems all represent highly centralised systems of rule.

2. Market elites. Here we are concerned with key players in the market economy and their interests. These include multinational corporations, rating agencies, investment banks and the wealthy individuals that Harvey (2010) sees as being major holders of influence. These actors, or players, at an extreme point would want the total removal of all trade barriers and the minimisation of the role of the state. This is free-market capitalism, where the market economy is allowed a free hand to allocate resources and, in extreme forms, could even assume responsibility for the welfare of the individual.

3. Social movements. Here we are concerned with groups, even individuals in society whose values are of utmost importance to them. Adherence to these values or cultural norms is more important than allegiance to a state or the accumulation of financial wealth. From Thomas's (2005) definition, we can describe a social movement as:

> A segment of the population, holding a set of beliefs and opinions, that seeks to bring about in a conscious, collective and organised manner, some material change.
> (Thomas, 2005, p. 112)

For social movements, choices are made based largely upon beliefs, culture and values, as opposed, for example, to more tangible, rational, economically based decision making that we would expect to find being taken by market elites. Examples of social movements range from environmentalists to potentially the most influential of all, religious groups.

Including social movements takes us towards a perspective of society that Shankar (2010) has in mind, which is based upon the pillars of economic institutions, political institutions, the social sector and faith-based organisations.

It must be stressed for many members of social movements that legitimacy emanates from beliefs, culture and values. For many in the world, values, historic cultures and beliefs assume far more importance than the geographic boundaries of the state or the wealth generated by economic markets (Guzansky & Berti, 2011). Surprisingly, for some, these interests may not even include democracy. Democracy, as we shall debate in Chapter 6, may be more fragile than we imagine.

Importantly, social movements have been largely ignored in the international relations field (Thomas, 2000), but they may well prove to be the most influential in the formation of the new, post-Great Recession world order. As Kirill (2010) and Khatami (2010) hold, we have not just been confronted by an economic crisis or recession; we are faced with, in their eyes, a recession in terms of spiritual values and human behaviour. The relative influence of social movements could also rise if we consider that the reputation of market elites may be tarnished in the aftermath of the Great Recession.

4. Post-state elites. An important but potentially difficult point to conceive is that we must not limit our thinking to a world of territorially defined states (although it is easiest to think this way as the world stands at the moment). The concept of the world as a system of states is a relatively new one and, in medieval times, there was less emphasis on territorial boundaries. Decisions were made by a dispersed group of appointed 'princes' (kings, dukes, counts, bishops and abbots), together with the nobility of the Holy Roman Empire and authority was delegated across this broad network. As we have seen, territorially bound states are under pressure. We cannot discount the possibility that the states system could dissolve and that new forms of organising, such as networks of cities or 'super states', could appear. Any model needs to include such new actors. Table 4.1 provides examples of the actors in all four groups.

Table 4.1 Critical actors – Some examples

Actors	Examples
State elites	Parliament (UK), Congress (US)
	House of Lords (UK)
	(Unelected institution with some powers)
	The Supreme Leader of Iran
	Dictators
	Absolute monarchy
Market elites	Investment banks
	Multinational corporations
	Rating agencies
Social movements	Amnesty International
	Greenpeace
	Campaign for Nuclear Disarmament
	Faith-based groups
	Al-Qaeda
Post-state elites	Geographically aligned 'super states' or 'super economies'.
	The European Union may be an early prototype
	Virtually linked networks of cities

We can position each of these four groups of actors in a '21st-century trade-off' or 'quadrilemma' as shown in Figure 4.1. Following Gilpin (1981), in all cases we are concerned with groups or coalitions of individuals, not the 'umbrella body', which of course does not possess feelings or interests!

The essential point is that each group of actors or architects have completely different desires and motivators. State elites, at the extreme, want control of what happens within their borders or environs and they want to at least preserve, if not enlarge, these boundaries. Market elites have different motivators. Again, at an extreme, market elites are not interested in borders, they see borders as obstacles in the way of free trade as, in their view, it is only a freely operating global economic market that can efficiently allocate scarce resources and generate wealth for all. Members of social movements may not be primarily interested in material wealth. As we will observe in Chapter 6, for social movements, globalisation has absolutely nothing to do with wealth generation in material

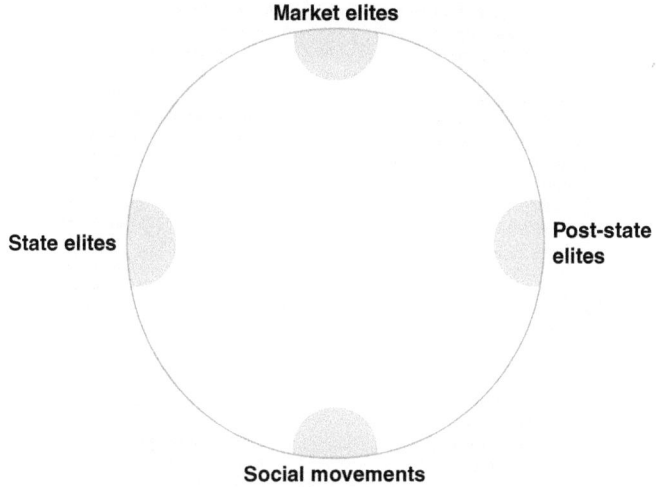

Figure 4.1 A 21st-century quadrilemma

terms. They are more concerned with wealth generation in terms of the values and behaviours that in turn are their 'central life interest'. Finally, we have post-state elites. Looking to the future, post-state elites are concerned with control and influence that may not be limited or defined by territorial boundaries.

Some may say 'where are the international institutions such as the United Nations in this model?' and 'Why have they been left out?'. The position that we are adopting is similar to that of Walt (2012) when he observes that such international institutions can have their limitations and that in practice they are influenced by the balance of power in the world (the more powerful state elites). In the final analysis, such institutions cannot force the most powerful state elites (or their successors) to act against their interests.

Each actor could of course try to organise a system on its own, without the involvement of any of the other three actors. This would present us with four extreme, or pure, forms of organising. At the left of the quadrilemma we have a situation, where power and decision-making is tightly controlled by the state. In extreme positions, this would entail the wholesale rejection of free-market capitalism and the re-emergence of the centrally controlled economies of the Soviet era. Moving clockwise to the top we have the free-market economy, where actors such as investment banks, multi-national corporations and rating agencies are amongst the most influential decision-makers. Progressing again clockwise, we have on the right the post-state elites who are interested in control and influence in their new domains, which might be the market states that Bobbitt (2008) describes.

Finally, moving to the bottom of our quadrilemma, we find social movements where culture, religion and values are the primary motivators.

These extreme positions, where only one group holds real influence, are, at best, only medium-term positions, as it will be impossible to repel the attacks from the other groups of actors for a long period of time. The situation immediately before the Great Recession may be a good example. In a move towards neo-liberalism, market elites became increasingly influential and we were headed towards a world dominated by free-market ideals. In the words of one financial trader: 'The governments don't rule the world. [The investment bank] Goldman Sachs rules the world' (BBC News Business, 2011).

This is a position that cannot be maintained indefinitely. At some point, other actors will erode this dominant position of influence. These points, where one group of actors can dominate for the short or, at best, medium term, are shown by the light grey areas in each of the four poles of the quadrilemma in Figure 4.1.

At the other extreme, we will hold that anything more than a very short-term compromise between the needs of three or more groups is impossible. It might be possible to reach a brief compromise, but this would quickly disintegrate as diverging views and opinions clashed.

Importantly, following experiences in the Middle Ages, Friedrichs (2001) holds that for a system to work and to provide relative stability in the long-term, no one group of actors must dominate, and that for stability to prevail (as it did for substantial periods in the Middle Ages), a balance or 'constructive tension' must exist between two actors. In practice, however, we will hold that there is always one group that is more influential than the other.

We can summarise all this in a set of rules, which are to be applied when using the quadrilemma to think about future worlds and who will be their architects, as follows:

> Rule 1: Compromise between all four groups of actors is impossible in anything more than the very short term. Conflicting

views will rapidly unravel any agreement. We can regard this as the 'Higgs Bosun Consensus' of the quadrilemma.[1]

Rule 2: One group of actors can dominate and impose their system of rule, but this will only exist in the short- to medium-term. It is impossible to resist the 'gnawing away' forces of the other three groups of actors in the longer term.

Rule 3: A position of long-term stability can only be achieved between two groups of actors.

Rule 4: In a long-term compromise between two groups, there is a dominant group and an influential group that has a voice, but gives way voluntarily to the dominant group. It is impossible to reach a perfect power-sharing agreement between two groups. There will always be one dominant group. This is a situation of 'constructive tension' or 'cooperative antagonism', to use Friedrichs' (2001, p. 493) vocabulary. This means that there are two potential long-term 'settling points' or areas of agreement that can be reached between two groups. We show examples of these settling points in Figure 4.2 as 'The liberal order' and 'State capitalism'. Settling points are positions that could form the basis for new world orders.

Rule 5: There will always be a dominant group and an influential group in a relationship between architects. The dominant and, to a lesser degree, the influential groups are the real architects. The voices of the other groups are heard and they may continue to exist, but their influence is limited and only passing attention is paid to them. When thinking therefore about a world in transition, we should not think about states, but we should think of which combination of two groups of actors will emerge to forge a new world order.

In Figure 4.2 we can start to see the range of possible futures that await us. Figure 4.2 looks at a world that is familiar to us, forged by the relationship between state elites and market elites.

But Figure 4.2 looks at the world as we now know it. It only shows, at best, a quarter of the possible futures that await us. The elements of 'State capitalism', 'The liberal order', 'Free market capitalism' and 'Autocracy' are familiar to us, but there are other alternatives that could be tried. Of the four positions shown in Figure 4.2 'State capitalism' and 'The liberal order' represent points of longer-term stability. 'The liberal order', which we will explore in more detail in the next chapter, represented an attempt

64 *The Era of Global Transition*

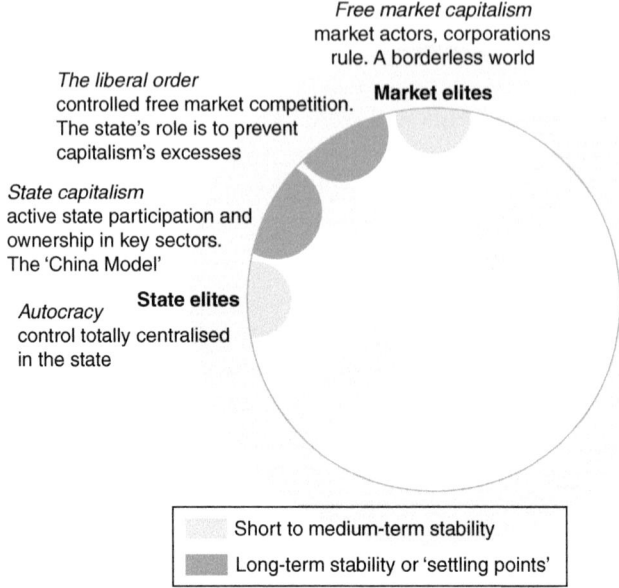

Figure 4.2 Familiar worlds

by the United States at the end of the Second World War to learn the lessons both from conflict and from the Great Depression of the 1930s. It was an order that was designed to limit capitalism's excesses. It is of interest that efforts, from the end of the 1970s, to reduce the role of the state, have ceded more power to market elites and we reached a position, before the Great Recession, where we approached a zone of only short-term stability right at the top of our quadrilemma.

But there is more to our journey and there are other worlds and combinations of actors to explore. If the influence of market elites collapsed and social movements emerged as an increasingly influential architect, then different 'rules of the game' appear as shown in our next illustration, Figure 4.3.

This is a difficult world for market elites, which is why they do not appear as an influential actor in Figure 4.3. It is a place where they must get used to being the third, and rarely heard voice. This is a place very different to the consumer-driven environment that we are used to. Values, ideals and religion replace the thirst for material goods. These are worlds where states still exist but security, control and values are cherished. Examples are shown in Figure 4.3.

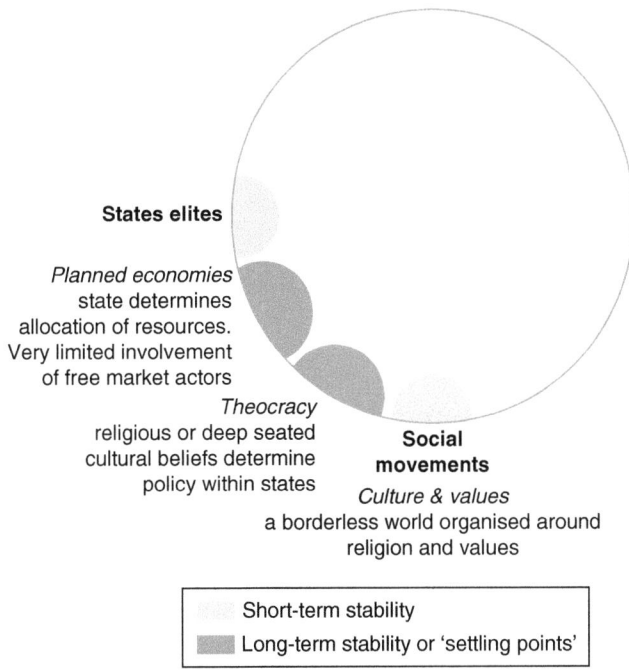

Figure 4.3 The collapse of the market elites

Another totally new configuration of course awaits if states lose legitimacy, fade away and their successors, the post-state elites, emerge. This leads us to explore the right-hand side of the quadrilemma. We can see an outline of one possible world in Figure 4.4, which shows us the relationships forged between post-state elites and market elites. This is a world of large-scale economic blocs. We can think of these relationships as 'empires'. As shown in Figure 4.4, one is an empire of free markets or market states, and another is an empire of state capitalism. The most likely form that post-state elites will take are alliances of states to produce 'super states', so we could think of these empires as massive geographical blocs.

It is quite plausible that the influence of market elites will diminish in a post-state world and a subtly different picture of a world of ideological, cultural or religious layers emerges.

This configuration is shown in Figure 4.5. Here too we have 'empires'. One, 'cultural empires', could be geographic blocs separated by culture or values where post-state elites have the upper

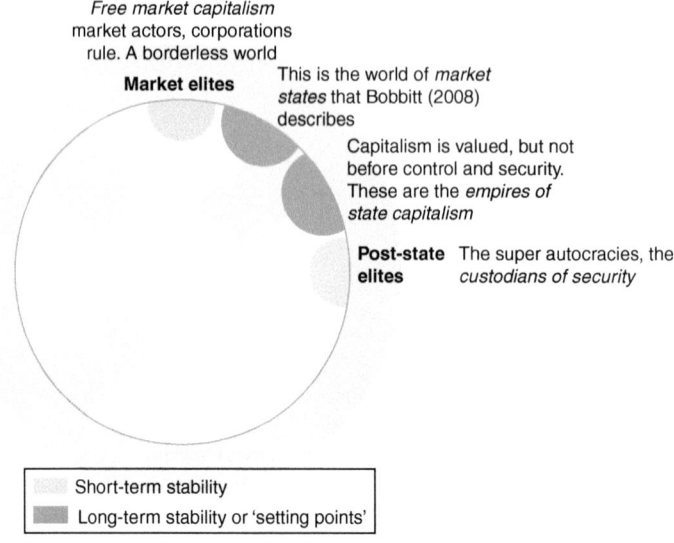

Figure 4.4 The rise of the post-state elites

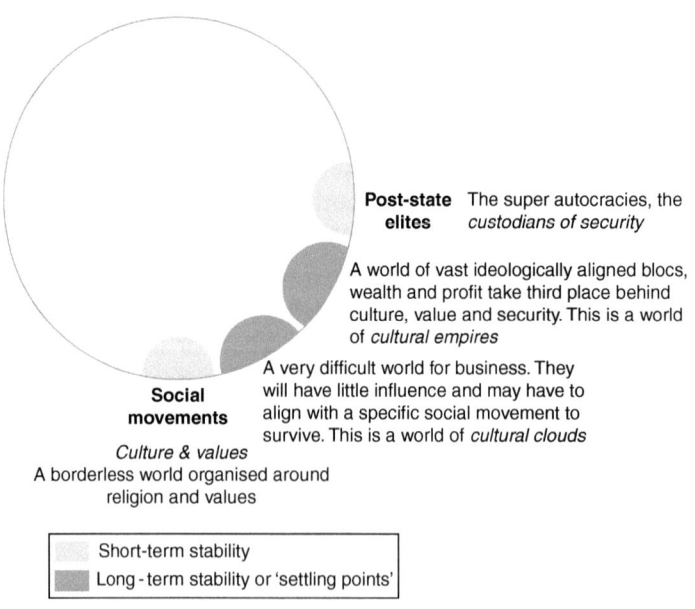

Figure 4.5 Post-state elites and social movements

hand. The other, 'cultural clouds', puts social movements firmly in the driving seat.

But we have a final plausible future that could await us. This is a future where the legitimacy and influence of states fade away and their successors fail to fill the void. The remaining architects with real influence are social movements and the market elites. Figure 4.6 shows how this vacuum could be filled. We could think of these as 'virtual worlds'.

If the credibility of market elites has been dented during the Great Recession, and the legitimacy of states elites has been eroded as globalisation has progressed, the question must be 'who will exert the greatest pull and where will new allegiances be formed?' Which pair of architects will design the next world order?

So where will all this take us?

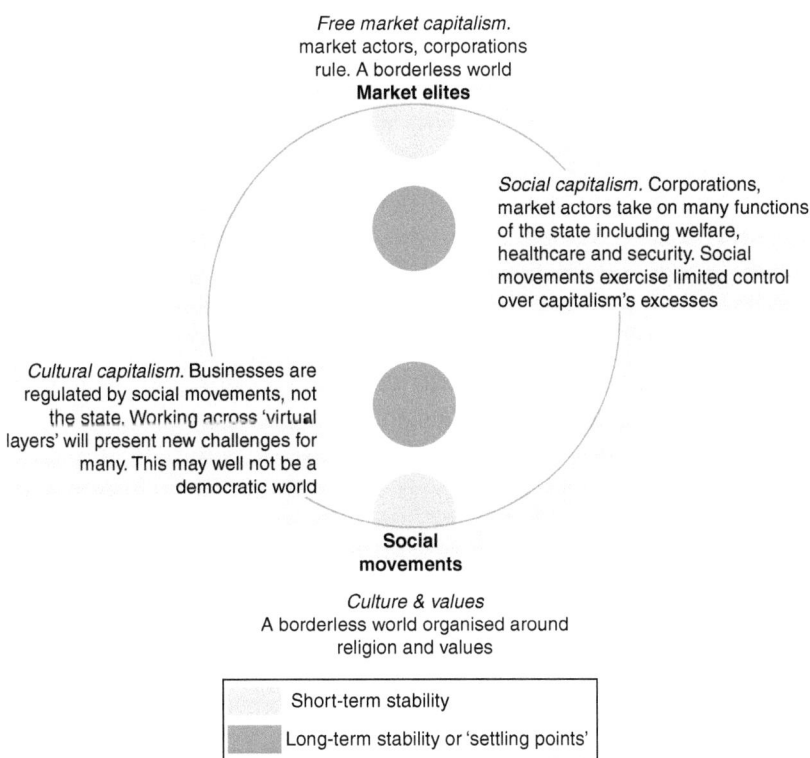

Figure 4.6 A world without states

Some writers paint a depressing view of what could follow in our new 21st-century medieval world. As an example, Kaplan (1994) foresees increasing fragmentation of identities, leading to a period of instability and conflict. But even within Kaplan's writing we can see the opposite picture emerging, one of areas or zones of stability, where two groups of architects join together in a constructive tension. The task must now be to consider the following:

(a) Have the positions of both the state and the market elites been permanently damaged by the Great Recession and its aftermath?
(b) Which groups of actors will assume the greatest influence?
(c) How will these groups combine to create new relationships?
(d) How will the two groups in a partnership of constructive tension defend themselves against more antagonistic attacks from the groups that are 'frozen out'?
(e) Will the world go through multiple zones on its journey to find one 'best way of organising'?

Going again back in time to the first period of medievalism, the stabilising force was the Church, and Kaplan (1994) sees the same force, religion, emerging in our new 21st-century medieval world. Cerny (2005) holds a similar view. He sees that 'non-territorially based groups, especially widespread ethnic and religious groups, may organize in order to control territories of their own' (Cerny, 2005, p 27). Huntington (2002) too would point to the bottom of our quadrilemma, but it is equally possible of course that the market elites could rise again. Or, then again, the state may rule supreme.

We are presented with a complex array of potential new partnerships, but this complexity is an unintended by-product of globalisation.

Drawing on the past, it is highly unlikely that one dominant marriage or 'constructive tension' will apply across the globe. The more likely picture is a proliferation of experiments as actors, free from the influence of the United States and the post-war institutions, and empowered by technology and globalisation, exercise their own views and muscle.

Apart from setting out a range of options or futures, a major value in the quadrilemma is to expand our field of view. When we read the business sections of our newspapers, or listen to economic commentaries, we tend only to be told about a world that exists in the top left quadrant of the quadrilemma, where there is a marriage of state elites and market elites.

We can too easily ignore and be blind to the remaining quadrants, where culture, religion, values and new forms of organising drive behaviour.

To answer those who say that there are no alternatives to capitalism, there are, it just depends which viewpoint one takes. Again, like beauty, it is all in the eye of the beholder.

Conclusion

We ended Chapter 3 wondering if seeing the world as a patchwork quilt of states and economies was the right approach to the challenge of transition. We asked if there were other actors and interests, to consider.

In this chapter, we have identified the four groups of actors that we need to consider and how they might interact.

We have also concluded that we must not be blind to a world without states.

It may sound absurd to think of the decline of the state as a system of rule, but there are some salient lessons from history that Ruggie (1993) draws our attention to. The most important of these lessons is that if change does occur, then it will occur quickly and suddenly. Historically, change in the systems of rule is characterised by the 'punctuated equilibrium' model. In other words, systems of rule, of which the state-centric Westphalian system is but one, tend to exist for long periods of time with little, if any, change. Then, rather than prolonged periods of small-scale evolutionary change, dramatic change occurs quickly and sometimes without any warning.

So, we must start to think about the different forms of organising that are possible and critically who the architects or powerful actors might be. The quadrilemma that we have introduced in this chapter can help us do this and to see the world in a different way. Using the quadrilemma can open a new door to looking at both the current status and the potential future structure of the world.

The message is that there are four groups of actors who will reshape the world. The coming struggle will determine which actor has the dominant voice.

The 'China Model' or the 'Beijing Consensus' is emerging as a major challenger to the US-led liberal order, and there may be more. It is by no means clear that the liberal order will win through (Soros 2011), and the 'China Model' or 'competitive authoritarianism' (Bernhard 2011) may well prove to be the foundation stone for tomorrow's super states. But as Cerny (2006) holds, whatever happens:

> It will be the product of old-fashioned more structurally open and politically more fluid, processes of conflict, competition and coalition-building carried on by a range of relevant actors seeking to create and capture the benefits of globalization for some combination of self interest on the one hand and public good on the other....
>
> (Cerny, 2006, p. 694)

Which leaves us with a major issue to explore in the next chapter, being 'what will the pathway of transition to the future look like?' Conflict, cooperation or coalition building?

Reflection points

1. Has the Great Recession permanently damaged the influence of the money markets, the market elites?
2. Will the world adopt one model or many models?
3. Will social movements mount a significant challenge, and if they do, what impact will they have on how we think about competitive strategy?
4. In ten years' time, which two actors will be the most powerful in your organisation's core markets? How could they combine to form new world orders?

Note

1. The Higgs Boson is a theoretical energy field that gives matter its mass. Scientists searching for it realise that if it does exist it only exists for a very short period of time.

Additional reading

For a greater insight into the worlds of market states and states of terror try:

Bobbitt, P., 2008. *Terror and Consent: The wars for the twenty-first century*, London: Penguin.

5
Pathways

Reflections on a conundrum

The previous chapter revealed the true nature of the transition that we face. Rather than a simple shift in power between one or two major states, as we witnessed during the 1980s and the 1990s, we have a conundrum. The future shape of the global business environment and, arguably more importantly, the characteristics of the transition pathways that are ahead of us will not be determined just by the coalitions that control states. Business interests (in the form of market elites) and social movements will have a big say too, making this transition unlike any other within living memory.

To deal with the conundrum, we have introduced the *21st-century quadrilemma*, shown again in Figure 5.1.

This quadrilemma sets out the key actors and it provides a foundation for us to see the various ways in which the world could be organised. Our attention in this chapter shifts to understanding the potential transition paths that lie ahead, for a world populated by both old and new actors, all eager to promote their interests and goals. In short, we need to consider the types of future transition paths that lie in front of us and if these are characterised by conflict, cooperation or coalition building. To do this, we will look at two questions:

1. *What do we mean by transition?* We are concerned with change in the international or world order or the 'way things are done' as a result of a transition from a unipolar to a multipolar world. But before proceeding any further, we need a clear view of both the *types* of transition or change that we could encounter and

the *routes* or pathways that such change may take. We will look both inside and outside the international relations literature to find our answers.
2. *Peace or conflict?* Again, we start by looking at the contribution of the international relations literature and then move on to look for other approaches that can help us explain human behaviour. We then look at the issue of conflict and question whether or not this will be limited merely to traditional state versus state military confrontation.

This chapter concludes by drawing together the answers to these questions and our conclusions from Chapter 4 to present a complete framework for viewing the future that we will apply throughout the rest of this book.

What do we mean by transition?

There are a number of issues that we must look at before we can answer the question 'What do we mean by transition?'

The first is 'Are there different types of change that we should consider?' To start to find an answer, we will look at research in another area within the social sciences field, that is the study of change in organisations. There are certain parallels that are of

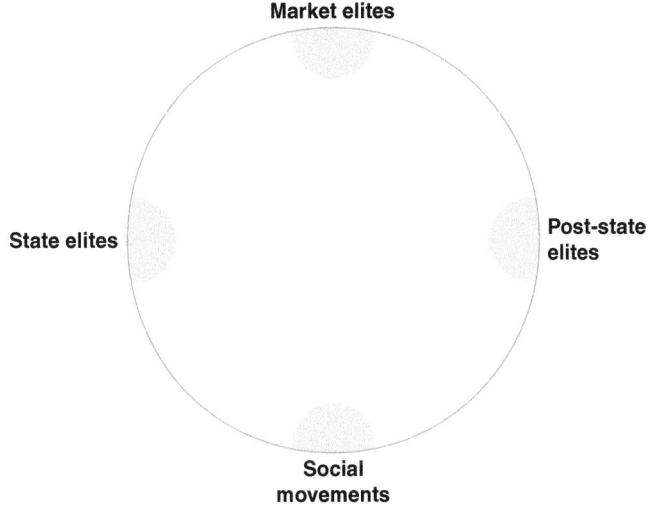

Figure 5.1 The 21st-century quadrilemma

interest. Organisations, whether for profit or not-for-profit, can be complex structures. The different dimensions that together constitute an organisation are difficult to identify. Some, such as the organisation's size, can be measured objectively in financial terms, but others, such as the guiding cultural norms, routines and beliefs, defy accurate measurement. There are multiple actors at play too, just as there are in the international arena, each having access to different types of power and driven by different interests and motivators.

One broad lesson that we can take from the study of change in organisations is that we must be careful to identify different *types* of change. Looking at change in organisations, Levy (1986) offers us definitions of first- and second-order change. First-order change consists of minor adjustments and improvements that 'do not change the system's core, and that occur as the system naturally grows and develops' (Levy, 1986, p. 10). These can be regarded as small changes and adjustments that we can take, most of the time, in our stride. Second-order change is different. Second-order change involves change across all dimensions and parts of the organisation including, importantly, culture and 'the way things are done'. So first-order change represents minor adjustments, whereas second-order change turns the whole system on its head and can upset culture and, of course, people in the process.

There are immediate parallels in the field of international relations when we look at researchers who examine power shifts between states. For example, Clark (2011) notes that when considering power shifts between states, one needs to bear in mind the issue of legitimacy. This can be described as the 'broad acceptance of a dominant state's preferred international order' (Clark, 2011, p. 14), or more simply as support for 'the United States' way of doing things'. Legitimacy in these terms can be more important than the consideration of economic growth or even the development of hard-edged relational power. Lemke (1997) came to similar conclusions when he examined the prospects for peace following the fall of the Berlin Wall, observing that the collapse of the Soviet Union represented 'the evaporation' of any challenge to the status quo and that therefore a period of peace beckoned for the world. The only clouds on the horizon that Lemke saw at that time were threats emanating from emerging states, which could become dissatisfied with the international order, as championed by the then sole dominant state, the United States.

The point that all these authors make is that the characteristics of transitions, or shifts of power from one state to another, depend largely upon the acceptance, or rejection, of the international order as crafted by the historically dominant power. When we talk about the term 'international order' (or 'world order'), Buzan's definition is useful when he refers to it as 'the deep rules of the game that states share with each other sufficiently to form a kind of social order' (Buzan, 2010, p. 6).

So we can see that we are again concerned with two broad types or categories of change in the arena of international relations, just as we are when looking at change in organisations. On the one hand, we have first-order transitions, where there is no material challenge to the international order (or 'deep rules of the game' to use Buzan's words), crafted by the historically dominant state; and, on the other, we have second-order transitions where the new rising actors are dissatisfied with the current deep rules of the game and seek to craft one or more replacements. We will explore this issue later when we discuss the issue of conflict, but it is useful at this point to define the 'current deep rules of the game' as crafted by the United States, the dominant state or, to use international relations terminology, hegemon, for the best part of the 20th century and the first decade of the 21st century.

Ikenberry (2011, pp. 169–193) sets out the characteristics of what he refers to as the 'American-led liberal hegemonic order'. This order was crafted out of the lessons emanating from both the Second World War and the preceding Great Depression. Ikenberry identifies the following characteristics, or as we shall call them, pillars, of the 'liberal order':

1. *Open markets.* A totally open world economy is seen as an essential foundation stone for enduring peace. Protectionism and the emergence of 'hostile regional spheres' are held as the precursors of both instability and conflict. The years immediately before the Second World War saw the emergence of a number of separate insular trading blocs, a situation that the United States wanted to avoid experiencing again. This approach obviously had direct advantages too for the United States, as it would give the United

States and its allies access to all growing and flourishing markets across the globe.
2. *The social bargain.* This represented the recognition that national security was directly linked to, and dependent upon, the security of individual citizens. It would be necessary in the future to ensure that citizens were protected from capitalism's booms and depressions. This would require both international cooperation and the construction of a safety net to provide protection against the ravages of unemployment, old age, sickness and disability.
3. *Multilateral institutions.* The delivery of the above goals, embracing a capitalistic world free of protectionism and a safety net to protect the most vulnerable from capitalism's extremes, would require unprecedented levels of global cooperation. Indeed, there was a belief in the 1940s (that seems to have been forgotten as the 20th century drew to a close) that if markets were left to run themselves without any form of regulatory intervention, then chaos would ensue. The result was the formation of the Bretton Woods institutions that would, effectively, police capitalism.
4. *Shared security.* Ikenberry calls this 'security binding', a good term as the objectives are two-fold. Firstly, to encourage states to group together to provide both economic and military security, therefore sharing the burden of policing the world. But the second objective was to bind states together and therefore to constrain each state's options, therefore inhibiting the emergence of strategic rivalry and power balancing. NATO and the post-war US–Japan alliance are examples of such security binding arrangements.
5. *Democratic solidarity.* Here we have the view that democracy, and primarily Western definitions of democracy, must underpin the spread and evolution of the new global liberal order. Only the West could drive the creation of the post-war liberal world order and the institutions that would craft this order must be situated within, and controlled by, the West.
6. *Human rights.* Arguably it was the US President Franklin D. Roosevelt who was the primary architect or driving force behind social advancement. His vision is encapsulated in a speech given to Congress in January 1941, 11 months before the attack on Pearl Harbor. In this speech, Roosevelt referred to four key human rights:

> The first is the freedom of speech and expression – everywhere in the world.
>
> The second is the freedom of every person to worship God in his own way – everywhere in the world.
>
> The third is freedom from want – which, translated into world terms, means economic understandings, which will secure to every nation a healthy peacetime life for its inhabitants – everywhere in the world.
>
> The fourth is freedom from fear – which, translated into world terms, means a world-wide reduction of armaments to such a point and in such a thorough fashion that no nation will be in a position to commit an act of physical aggression against any neighbor – anywhere in the world.
>
> (Roosevelt, 1941)

> These sentiments were later to be encapsulated within the Universal Declaration of Human Rights adopted by the UN General Assembly in December 1948.

7. *US global leadership*. This is the final pillar of the liberal order the assumption that the United States will be the leading architect and manager of the world order. An obvious position at the close of the Second World War, as only the United States had both the relational and structural power to drive this new order forward.

So here we have the seven pillars of the liberal order, the deep rules of the game, crafted and developed under the influence of one dominant state. Each of these pillars will be tested during the era of transition that lies ahead. If these pillars are subjected merely to cosmetic adjustment or tinkering, then we will be faced with a period of slow evolutionary adjustment, or first-order change. If the new holders of power seek to demolish, question or substantially re-craft these pillars, then we could be faced with more violent, wide-ranging and unpredictable second-order change.

The US-designed liberal order can be located in our 21st-century quadrilemma, as shown in Figure 5.2.

The liberal order considered the needs of states and markets and tried not to forget individuals. But this was a position crafted in the 1940s and it was to evolve in later decades as possibly the lessons, particularly of the Great Depression of the 1930s, were forgotten.

78 *The Era of Global Transition*

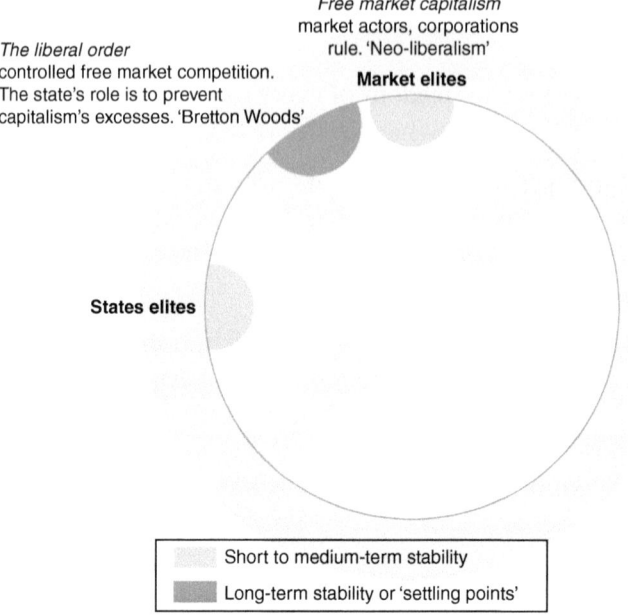

Figure 5.2 The liberal order – Start and evolution

From the end of the 1970s a new, modified order was to emerge, known to many as neo-liberalism, which as Nesvetailova and Palan (2010) note:

> [Neo-liberalism] is premised on the belief in markets as the most efficient mechanisms of resource allocation. Thus, for instance, if financial markets are left to operate freely, with little or no external interference, market distortions or imbalances ['booms and busts'] should be rare and minimal.
> (Nesvetailova & Palan, 2010, p. 798)

This movement pushed the liberal order to, and some would argue, beyond its limits. Indeed, Nesvetailova and Palan go on to hold that the Great Recession demonstrated that 'all the post-Bretton Woods systems of privatised financial regulation have failed miserably' (Nesvetailova & Palan, 2010, p. 799).

All this demonstrates that we should regard the deep rules of the game as a living organism that is continuously changing and evolving.

But understanding the process of change is equally as important as understanding the end result, that is, what the new rules of the game could be. If we are to face conflict in any form then one can argue that understanding the process of transition is even more important than getting to grips with the end result.

Looking at many economic projections, one may form the opinion that change will follow a linear path with a beginning point, a period of transition during which change takes place and the attainment of an end point, whereupon change stops. One gets this picture of linear, steady, uneventful change with a fixed end point, when looking at projections of the old economies and the 'emerging', new economies. This approach, with a defined starting point, a nice clearly defined period of change and then an end point, paints a benign picture.

In our context, this represents the very best of worlds. This is first-order change.

To understand the possible pathways of change, the routes that a world in transition could take, we need to refer to a comprehensive catalogue and not just one benign pathway. Unfortunately, much of the international relations literature focuses its attention largely upon addressing the question will or won't there be war, or two pathways.

So again, we have to look outside the international relations literature and return to research in the field of organisational change. Arguably, the most comprehensive framework for thinking about the pathways of change was put forward by two researchers in the 1980s. These researchers (Greenwood & Hinings, 1988) looked at change in organisations' 'core norms and values', the interpretive schemes that we introduced in Chapter 2, and proposed a catalogue of potential change pathways. We can use this 'catalogue' as an initial foundation to set out a range of possible pathways or routes that changes to the deep rules of the game in the international arena could take, as power transitions occur. We need however to make changes to suit our work in the international arena. The pathways, with alterations for our purposes, are summarised in Table 5.1.

This approach broadens our vision and helps us to think about a range of change scenarios or change pathways.

Although it is not meant to be a definitive model, we are provided with a far more comprehensive set of potential pathways than a simple linear or 'war or no war' model.

Table 5.1 Pathways

Change path	Characteristics
1. Stasis – no change	No change in the current order. No actors challenge the current rules of the game.
2. Incremental change	Only small, evolutionary adjustments are made to the current rules of the game by current and emerging actors. There is broad agreement in the current rules, or some may wish to hide their opposition until they are powerful enough to mount a challenge. Adjustments are negotiated without resort to conflict.
3. Transformation	A new set of rules is introduced and change follows a linear path. The transformation will probably be peaceful, especially if the dominant actor acquiesces.
4. Splintering	Attempts are made to design and implement a range of different orders, but actors give up and return to the old order. This can be seen as a situation where many newly empowered and rising actors want to experiment with 'their ways' in their 'backyard', many of which may fail and by default, the liberal order reappears as the dominant order. Localised confrontation and conflict may occur in the process.
5. Conflict	Consistent attempts are made to move to a new order. Attempts are interrupted and hampered, but single-minded determination, probably on the part of one rising actor, or a group of such actors, ensures that the new order is eventually accepted. This is a world of confrontation and conflict where the historically dominant actor resists.
6. Unsuccessful assaults	Actors have major grievances with the world order, its principles and the recognition they receive. Actors may well overestimate their power and mount direct assaults on the dominant actor, which fail.

Source: Adapted from Greenwood and Hinings (1988).

Change paths one and two, *Stasis* and *Incremental change*, are arguably the most favourable, particularly in terms of conflict avoidance. *Stasis* entails broad acceptance of the current order, or rules of the game, by all dominant actors (whether state elites, post-state elites, market elites or social movements). The seven pillars of the liberal world order hold with one exception. The new dominant actors join the United States. The seventh pillar is now one of joint consensus-focused leadership instead of the United States' single-handed captaincy. But the United States remains active as a joint decision maker and arguably is seen as a 'wise old sage'. Acceptance of, and allegiance to, the remaining six pillars is surprisingly strong. A period of stasis appears.

The *Incremental change* path too is relatively benign; we are concerned with first-order change only. Minor evolutionary adjustments to the liberal order take place. The United States remains as a consulted and respected decision maker, adviser and 'wise old sage'. Consensus is shared among dominant actors, old and new.

If paths one and two, *Stasis* and *Incremental change*, are the most favourable, then the remaining four are the most difficult, as we are concerned with at least limited attempts to achieve second-order change and with it a challenge to potentially all of the pillars of the liberal order that could well 'bring the roof down' at least once, if not several times.

The best possible of the second-order transition paths is *Transformation*. A new order appears, but it is adopted without intervention and the transition proceeds smoothly; the United States assumes a mood of acquiescence, resigning itself to a reduced position in terms of influence. Changes to the international order are material, but are accepted without resistance by the dominant holder of power, the United States. *Transformation* does, however, bring with it the prospect of conflict if the United States does not acquiesce.

But from this point the situation deteriorates.

In a world of *Splintering*, different orders are tried, but fail. Although the world eventually returns to the liberal order, this is after much disagreement. We can think of this as a world where newly empowered actors want to try and experiment with alternatives to the liberal order in their own 'backyards'. This could well be a world where a proliferation of 'Iron Curtains' appear. Eventually, the experiments fail and the liberal order returns.

Conflict takes us down a similar pathway but this time, after resistance and disagreement, a new generally accepted order appears, championed by a powerful and intransigent actor or group of actors. This new order is fundamentally different from the seven pillars of liberal order and reflects the interests and values of the new dominant actors that have championed its cause. Conflict is in most cases inevitable, unless an 'Iron Curtain' divides the major holders of power.

Unsuccessful assaults is a world where many actors are violently opposed to the liberal order, but lack the power to do anything about it. They however attempt direct assaults on the dominant actor and fail.

So a world in transition, where we move from a unipolar to a multipolar environment, can follow many pathways.

Lessons from the past: Peace or conflict?

Before we can complete a framework for viewing the process of transition, we need to consider the issue of conflict, especially if we think that second-order change could occur in the form of a substantial challenge to the US-defined liberal order.

It is an unfortunate fact that conflict raises its head in most of the change pathways or scenarios that we have introduced in this chapter. But to move further, there are three broad questions that we need to address:

(a) Which is the more stable of worlds – unipolar, bipolar or multipolar? A relevant question as we are moving away from unipolarity towards multipolarity.
(b) Has the world moved beyond conflict?
(c) If conflict does break out, what form will it take?

If we were hoping for a direct answer, at least for the first of these questions, from the international relations literature, then we will be disappointed. We find that we are faced with two camps: the realists on the one side and the idealists, or democratic peace theorists, on the other. But even amongst the realists there is disagreement.

Waltz (1959) holds that bipolar systems are the most stable as each shares an interest in maintaining the status quo. But Waltz is also of the opinion that multipolar systems are the least stable as there is the danger of miscalculation, an issue that he holds led to the First World War. Gilpin (1981), on the other hand, feels that multipolar systems are the more adaptable and can make adjustments as new powers emerge. In others words, Gilpin sees that a world with many actors that hold significant levels of power is more malleable.

But Mearsheimer (2003) would disagree, noting that war is more likely in multipolar systems for three reasons. Firstly, there are more opportunities for dyadic or 'one-on-one' conflicts; secondly, there are more opportunities for power imbalances that introduce the temptation of conflict; and, finally, Mearsheimer sees the possibility of miscalculation, where some states think that they have the power to overthrow another when in fact they do not - the opposite of Gilpin's position.

Although there is disagreement amongst the realists, Gilpin's ideas and proposals do have some relevance for us and, of all of the realist theories, Gilpin's theories have proven the most accurate in their predictive powers (Wohlforth, 2011). These ideas and proposals include (Gilpin, 1981, pp. 10–11, 13, 18–19, 156) the following:

1. States do not have interests and objectives; it is, to use Gilpin's language, the individuals who are joined together to form the dominant coalition within a state that have interests and objectives. This is in line with the group of actors called state elites, that we introduced in the last chapter.
2. Unlike Waltz, Gilpin is not disposed to the view that states are 'conditioned for war'.
3. Stability will prevail if no state believes that it is profitable to pursue change, but if a state believes that it is profitable, then the state (or more correctly the dominant elite that controls the state) will pursue change until the marginal costs exceed the marginal benefits.
4. Interestingly, the costs of maintaining stability can rise faster than the capacity of a dominant state to support these costs, which is the position that the United States finds itself in now. The dominant state faces a cost disadvantage.
5. Instability can arise when a state loses control over economic, political and social developments. Gilpin points to the dangers of social upheavals that arise when the old 'rules of the game' decay.

This is an important point. There are two dimensions to consider when we think about the 'rules of the game'. The first are the rules that guide 'how things are done' or Buzan's (2010) social order. The second is the realisation that these rules allow access to resources too. As Davidson (2002) notes, 'revisionist' states (those that seek to change the rules of the game) will have as an objective a change in the distribution of goods. When Davidson talks about the distribution of goods, he means access to territory, and when we talk of territory, we should focus on access to resources in an increasingly constrained world. So we need to be concerned if the dominant elite of a state feels that it is losing control over (a) the state's economic, political and social destiny and (b) access to critical resources.
6. This reinforces the last point. A precondition for 'hegemonic' war is where 'the contending parties have been at odds with one another on all fronts and have few interests in common to moderate the antagonism' (Gilpin, 1981, p. 238). Gilpin goes on to note that all the great wars in history have been simultaneously political, economic and ideological struggles. In other words, they have embraced both 'the way things are done' and the 'distribution of goods'.
7. Chillingly, Gilpin concludes:

> [M]ost importantly of all, hegemonic wars are preceded by an important psychological change in the temporal outlook of peoples. The outbreaks of hegemonic struggles have most frequently been triggered by the fear of ultimate decline and the perceived erosion of power. The desire to preserve what one has while the advantage is still on one's side has caused insecure and declining powers to precipitate great wars.
>
> (Gilpin, 1981, p. 239)

Rising nationalism could then be seen as a precursor to conflict.

The important points to take out of this in terms of trying to answer the question 'Which is the more stable of worlds – unipolar, bipolar or multipolar?' are firstly that it is not the configuration (unipolar, bipolar or multipolar) that may be important. Of more importance are the interests and objectives of the 'states elites'. If the states elites feel that their power of self-determination is being eroded, or that the dominant rules of the game are obsolete or are against them, then conflict could ensue. The prospect of conflict also rises if the state elites feel that it is profitable to pursue conflict. We should be careful, following our observations in Chapter 4, to note that for some 'profitable' might be calculated in ideological and not economic terms.

But of course, the idealists would throw all these arguments out, which takes us to the second question 'has the world moved beyond conflict?'

Supporters of the 'democratic peace theory' would argue that war is now unthinkable amongst the 'leading members of the international system' (Jervis, 2002, p. 1). This is in some ways a similar position to that taken by Fukuyama (1989) and the democratic peace theorists in general, which is that established democracies will not fight each other. This is indeed a powerful and influential school of thought that first emerged in the early 1970s. It has been held that the absence of war between democracies comes as close as anything we have to 'an empirical law in international relations' (Levy, 1988, p. 662). Indeed it seems as if it has seeped into the textbooks of corporate and business strategy, where there is little if any reference to conflict. A world of peace seems to have become an impermeable law. But deciding if this law really is impermeable, or has become eroded during the ravages of the Great Recession, will be one of the central tasks for any strategist.

If we look towards Jervis (2002), we can see that this very popular theory was based, at the time of publication of the paper, on these critical assumptions:

1. A 'security community' of 'great powers' has been formed. The security community consists of the United States, Western Europe and Japan. War is unthinkable between members of this community.
2. The security community is at the forefront of technological and economic organisation and is impermeable, or unbreakable.
3. Two other powers, Russia and China are not in this technological and economic position and do not have alternative models to offer.
4. There will not be another struggle for dominance in the international system.
5. Values have shifted away permanently from a focus on nationalism and the 'glory of war' towards 'compromise, consideration for the interests of others, respect for the law, and a

shunning of violence' (p. 8). These values are shared across the community.
6. The territorial claims of states are now less important.
7. The security community has acted as an example to other states, 'peacefulness' is spreading.

If we take a Western perspective, this seems to be a convenient argument, largely vindicating the seven pillars of the liberal world order.

But there are problems.

Firstly, some assumptions have not stood the test of time, particularly those regarding the technological and economic position of other states.

Secondly, the 'law' that democracies do not fight each other is in danger of being accepted as fact without rigorous analysis and debate (Doyle, 1986). After careful analysis, Layne (1994) comes to the conclusion that there is no empirical evidence to support the 'law' and it is in reality 'based on hope, not fact' (p. 66). He concludes that the world remains as it always has been. The realists reinforce this position when they say that as the world progresses away from unipolarity, it will become a more dangerous place. For example, Layne (2008) asserts that the emergence of 'new poles of power' always destabilises the geopolitical system, and he sees no reason why China's rise will be any exception. His assessment of the future is even bleaker when he posits that if the United States seeks to maintain and build its influence at least in Asia, then it will face conflict and defeat. Weitz (2011) comes to similar conclusions and sees no alternative to conflict, unless one side alters its present course and Mearsheimer (2010) gives a stern warning too, with regard to China's rise.

Even if we put to one side the issue of analytical rigour, democratic peace theory, for our purposes, possesses at least two sizeable Achilles' Heels. The first concerns the passing of time. Mearsheimer (2003) calls this the danger of 'backsliding'. In short, no democracy can be sure that, over time, another democracy will not at some point become an authoritarian state. We deal with the issue of 'backsliding' again in Chapter 6 when we present the argument that democracy is not the static end of an evolutionary cycle for a state. It can slip backwards into either anarchy or 'despotism', immediately the legitimacy of the state elite is lost. This means, applying a strict interpretation of democratic peace theory, that no one democracy can, in the long term, rely upon another. This observation is relevant to any observer interested in the future of the liberal world order, when its original architect may be in decline.

But there is a final associated problem. Democratic peace theorists, as we have seen, base their propositions on the existence of an influential and powerful 'community'. The 'community' consists, according to Jervis, of 'the most developed states in the international system – the United States, Western Europe and Japan' (Jervis, 2002, p. 1). The problem now is that the 'community', in terms of both structural and relational power, is in decline. This observation presents democratic peace theorists with a double rub. In addition to the decline of the 'community', Gilpin (1981) tells us that when states suffer a decline in power, they can become more dangerous and may turn into the villains of the peace.

So we will not find a definitive answer to our question in the literature. Perhaps Walt (2009) puts his finger on the issue when he says that we know so little about unipolar systems, how they operate and what happens when they come to the end of their lives. The only reasonable certainty that we can draw from the established literature is that conflict may ensue if the current international order, as crafted by an historically dominant power, is challenged. One of the central assumptions of democratic peace theory is that such a challenge would never occur.

We find that this perspective is echoed in the only area of agreement in the literature that focuses upon power transitions and that is that conflict will occur if the current international order (the rules of the game) is challenged. This challenge is, in Gilpin's words, the 'desire to re-craft the rules by which relations among nations work' and 'the distribution of territory among states in the system' (Gilpin, 1981, pp. 198, 186).

But our problem is that this research, much of which is based upon an analysis of conflict as far back, in some cases, as the Trojan Wars, rests upon the assumptions that, firstly, states are the only relevant actors and that, secondly, conflict is driven by concern for material gain.

Whilst this Westphalian approach may have been suitable for analytical purposes in the majority of the 20th century, it has more limited application in the 21st century, where we are concerned with a transition or, more correctly, a proliferation of power, amongst a variety of actors that range from state elites, investment banks, multinational corporations, rating agencies, central banks and religious groups through to flash mobs and even individuals. Also, the emphasis upon material gains as a premise or motivator for conflict, as implied by Gilpin's 'distribution of territory' argument, may not be relevant to all the newly empowered actors that we referred to in the last chapter, especially 'social movements', whose members may not be motivated by material gain at all. As James (2011) observes, behaviours in international politics are complex, and their interpretation may not be entirely straightforward.

We therefore need another approach that will help us to identify if a power transition, or, more correctly, power proliferation, will proceed peacefully or will be characterised by conflict. Any such approach must be capable of assimilating a whole new field of actors together with an understanding of motivation that goes beyond mere material gain, be it in economic or territorial guises.

As we have seen, the established literature assumes that actors are motivated largely by material gains. But if we look outside the international relations field, we see that people in general are motivated by more than pure material gain. In recent years, there has been an increasing interest in the application theories of social behaviour to the field of international relations, to explore a broader range of motivators. This work is still at an exploratory stage, but a notable example is the application of social identity theory by Wohlforth (2009).

Broadly, social identity theory holds that concerns for material gain (or loss), when thinking about what motivates human action, may be something of a smokescreen. There are other underlying issues to discover. Essentially, social identity theory holds that we are driven by a concern for our relative social status. Some researchers hold that humans are 'hardwired' to sense status and that perception of relative standing in 'the order of things' is an important behavioural influence. If we are content with our relative position in a defined status hierarchy, all is well. If we are unhappy, or there is ambiguity with regard to our perceived position, we will take action to correct matters. As an example, if we feel that we deserve promotion at work, but we are continually passed over and others are promoted who we believe are less deserving, then we will take action, like getting another job.

Social identity theory proceeds to say that if there is a well-defined and accepted hierarchy of status amongst actors, then the probabilities of conflict and disruption are minimal. But if the status hierarchy is ambiguous or poorly defined and not broadly accepted, then actors will start to compare themselves with others that they believe have higher status. This activity can bring actors into conflict, especially if an actor or group of actors, that feel bound together, believe they should possess equal or higher status than others who are positioned at levels above them in the status hierarchy.

Social identity theory can be used, for example, to explain the motivations behind both the First and Second World Wars. In both cases, Germany felt that its position in the international hierarchy was constrained and suppressed, which created the desire to take action in an attempt to correct matters.

So why is social identity theory relevant in a period of transition?

Firstly, past research in the field of power transitions considers only states as the relevant actors. In addition, this research is concerned purely with the presence, or absence, of military conflict. As we shall see below, in this new age of power proliferation, we will be faced with the prospect of many different types of conflict. Finally, in this research, motivation to act is driven largely by material concerns. We need a broader perspective to accommodate a wider, and more fluid, range of actors that are now entering the arena.

In this regard, social identity theory sits well to explain both the period of stability that a unipolar world has provided us with and the possible characteristics of the future transition period that lies ahead of us.

The power (both relational and structural) possessed by the United States combined with the broad acceptance of the liberal order, at least before the Great Recession, by rising actors (such as Russia, China, Brazil and India), acted to ensure stability during a period of unipolarity. Whilst some actors may have had reservations with regard to elements of the US-defined liberal order, the power gap between them and the United States precluded any conflict.

This situation is changing. New actors are now gathering the power to challenge the United States. As Wohlforth (2009) notes, a great lesson from the fall of the Soviet Union is that competing for status with a dominant power requires the commitment of real, measurable resources. Although the Soviet Union may not have possessed such resources in the 1980s, and it failed in its challenge, new and rising actors almost certainly will acquire the power to challenge the United States.

So social identity theory as applied by Wohlforth (2009) to the field of international relations can help to warn us when conditions that may be conducive to conflict emerge. We can go further and combine them with Gilpin's (1981) and Davidson's (2002) conclusions to produce the following list of early warning signals:

1. **A diminishing power gap.** As the power gap between the United States and other actors closes, status competition could increase. In this respect, 'power' should be considered in all its forms, structural, relational, soft and smart. This also relates to Gilpin's (1981) point that state elites will go to war if they feel that the benefits outweigh the costs. As the power gap shrinks perceptions of cost of conflict will reduce, that is, for the challenger. The old dominant power may face a different cost equation as it has historically shouldered the burden of maintaining stability. In short, the dominant actor's costs are higher and put it at a disadvantage.
2. **Resources.** This point is very much linked to the first, and the issue of power. If an actor feels that its access to resources is restricted and its power base is therefore threatened, conflict may ensue.
3. **Status competition.** If actors feel undervalued, or not fully recognised in the current hierarchy, they will be motivated to take action.
4. **The rules of the game.** Failure to recognise the legitimacy of the current rules of the game, the liberal order, will materially increase the likelihood of conflict. This is widely acknowledged in the literature. If the 'rules of the game' threaten access to critical resources or political, economic or social self-determination, the risk of conflict increases.
5. **Capacity and will to resist.** When challenged, the dominant actor will resist, if it believes it has the capacity to do so. Following Gilpin (1981), the dominant actor will try to defend its position whilst it feels it still can.

The possibility of conflict can be avoided if the dominant actor (a) can be persuaded to accept a downward revision in its status or

(b) is able to re-establish a significant power advantage over rising actors.

Having established the broad preconditions for peace and conflict as we leave a unipolar world behind us, we are left with the question 'if conflict does break out, what form will it take?'

Just as we have moved beyond the concept of the state as the primary actor, so we must move on from the assumption that conflict can just be a clash of army versus army or terrorist explosions. There are two other forms of conflict that will most likely characterise the future, that is cyber warfare and arguably of even more importance economic warfare. In terms of cyber warfare, Nye (2011b) makes the interesting observation that we know as little about the rules and tactics of cyber warfare as we did about nuclear warfare in the early 1950s, but in the eyes of many this is a war where the opening shots have been fired.

Moving to economic warfare, Førland (1993) defines economic warfare as 'an intensive, coercive disturbance of the economy of an adversary state, aimed at diminishing its power' (p. 151). Førland's definition includes UN sanctions and economic blockades, but here we are concerned with a more populist use of the term that embraces protectionist trade measures (such as the US–China 'chicken and tyre feet spat', Dyer & Braithwaite, 2009; Dyer, 2010) and exchange rate controls, all of which are designed to attack the first pillar of the US-led liberal order, being open markets. Again, some would say that the first shots have already been fired.

Questions, answers and a framework for the future

We are now in a position to develop a framework to conceptualise the characteristics of a world in transition, particularly the potential pathways of change and the trigger points for conflict. If we draw together the conclusions of this chapter together with those of Chapters 3 and 4, any framework to conceptualise the pathways of change must embrace:

(a) **Actors.** The inclusion of multiple actors.
(b) **Type of change.** The capacity to distinguish between first- and second-order changes and the associated pathways that first- and second-order changes may take.

92 The Era of Global Transition

(c) **Status and order dissonance**. The reflection of actors' concerns, with regard to both perceived status and the legitimacy of the current order or rules of the game.
(d) **Power**. Indication of the relative levels of power that actors hold.

Such a framework is introduced in Figure 5.3.

The vertical axis is labelled 'Dissonance'. Here we are concerned with the degree to which an actor, which could be a state elite (or its successor), a market elite or a social movement, accepts both its perceived position in the status hierarchy and the legitimacy of the current rules of the game as defined by the United States. The vertical axis is therefore a combination of two assessments, status recognition and support for the US-defined liberal order. The vertical axis runs from 'low', indicating acceptance of an actor's perceived position, or the respect it enjoys, to 'high', indicating a position where lack of perceived status and discomfort with the liberal world order prevails.

The horizontal axis captures smart power, the cocktail of all forms of power, relational, structural and soft.

The framework is like a map divided into zones. Where each actor is positioned indicates the possible action that the actor might take. At the bottom, we have either no change or only first-order change. The remaining zones describe different change scenarios. Actors can be positioned with reference to the two axes. The zones that actors are positioned in then gives an indication of potential scenarios or what the future may hold and acts as a starting point for debate.

Stasis indicates the likelihood that no change will occur. No actor is close enough in power terms to challenge the United States. All actors are close supporters of the liberal world order and are content with their perceived status. Those that could display some dissonance (potentially China and Russia) are prepared to go along with the current order for two reasons. Firstly, the current order is delivering economic wealth, fuelling its continued growth and internal stability, and secondly, they do not yet have the power to challenge the United States and win.

If, however, one very powerful actor or a coalition of less powerful actors was to be positioned in the *Incremental change* zone, then we could expect change, but this would be first-order change, only

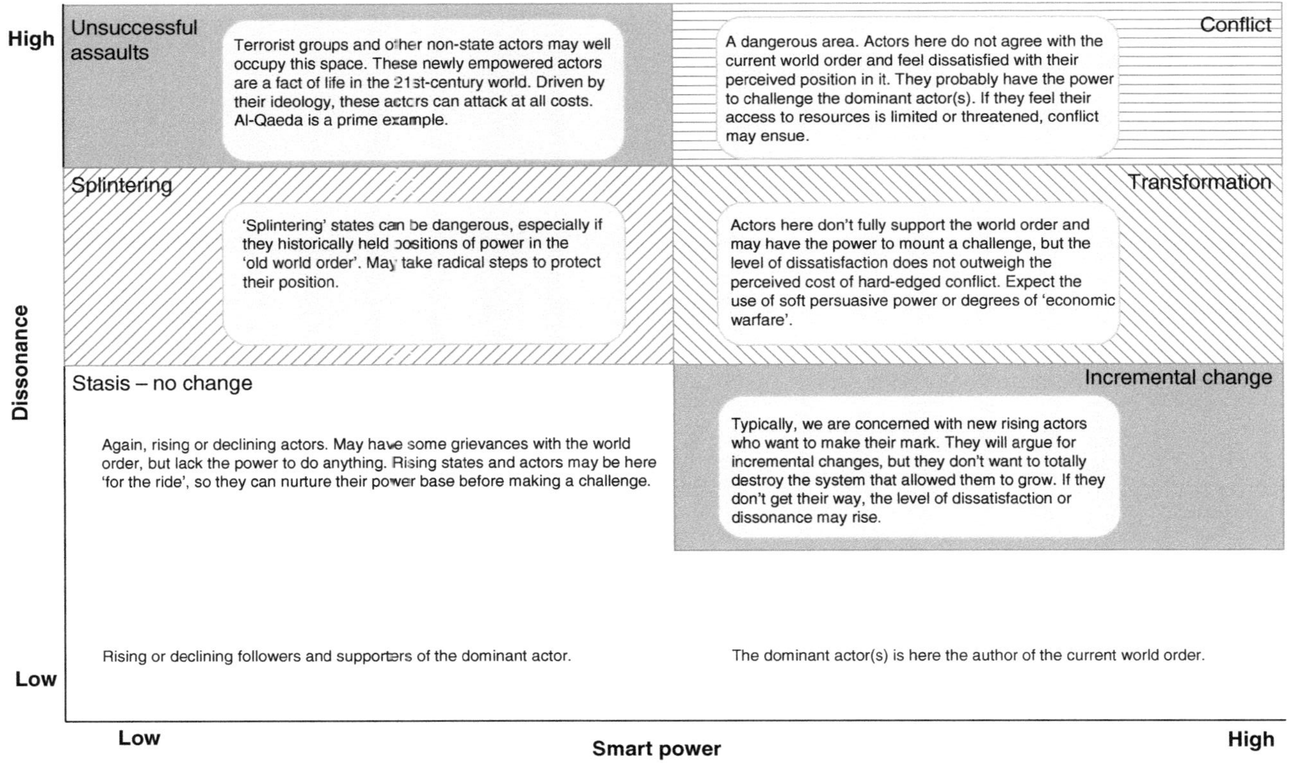

Conflict

Unsuccessful assaults

Terrorist groups and other non-state actors may well occupy this space. These newly empowered actors are a fact of life in the 21st-century world. Driven by their ideology, these actors can attack at all costs. Al-Qaeda is a prime example.

A dangerous area. Actors here do not agree with the current world order and feel dissatisfied with their perceived position in it. They probably have the power to challenge the dominant actor(s). If they feel their access to resources is limited or threatened, conflict may ensue.

Transformation

Splintering

'Splintering' states can be dangerous, especially if they historically held positions of power in the 'old world order'. May take radical steps to protect their position.

Actors here don't fully support the world order and may have the power to mount a challenge, but the level of dissatisfaction does not outweigh the perceived cost of hard-edged conflict. Expect the use of soft persuasive power or degrees of 'economic warfare'.

Incremental change

Stasis – no change

Again, rising or declining actors. May have some grievances with the world order, but lack the power to do anything. Rising states and actors may be here 'for the ride', so they can nurture their power base before making a challenge.

Typically, we are concerned with new rising actors who want to make their mark. They will argue for incremental changes, but they don't want to totally destroy the system that allowed them to grow. If they don't get their way, the level of dissatisfaction or dissonance may rise.

Rising or declining followers and supporters of the dominant actor.

The dominant actor(s) is here the author of the current world order.

Dissonance: High → Low

Smart power: Low → High

Figure 5.3 Pathways of transition

minor adjustments are made to the liberal order. The challenging actors are not overly concerned regarding their perceived status and do not mount a major challenge to the liberal order. The United States is prepared to acquiesce to their relatively minor demands. Marginal change occurs and conflict is avoided.

As we proceed into the remaining zones, we face second-order change and the possibility of conflict. Only *Transformation* offers us the opportunity to avoid conflict. If actors were plotted here, they would be dissatisfied both with their perceived status and would want to make changes to the liberal world order. If the United States is persuaded to acquiesce peacefully, change occurs without conflict. If the United States does not give way, conflict may follow, if perceived costs of conflict do not exceed the perceived benefits.

Conflict, or the prospect of conflict, is a characteristic of all remaining areas on our map.

In the case of *Splintering*, conflict, if it arises, is localised.

In a world of *Conflict*, one or more challengers appear, driven by extreme concerns, with regard to both their status and the US-defined order. The challengers have the power to confront the United States. The United States can either resist or stand aside. If the former route is chosen, then conflict ensues, and a new order, substantially different from today's world, could appear. If the latter route, standing aside, is chosen, the likely outcome is a divided world, a return to a world of 'Iron Curtains'.

Finally, in *Unsuccessful assaults*, actors appear that again have strong grievances with regard to their status and who reject the liberal order. These highly motivated actors may mistakenly believe that they have the power to overcome the United States and mount a direct attack. Terrorist groups fit into this area.

It is of course impossible to reduce the world, its actors and their motivators to one sheet of paper that can definitively predict the future, but this approach can be useful in helping to define key actors, their grievances and the likely action that they might take. In short, this approach is designed to engender discussion and reflection in respect of the item that must be near the top of the business leader's agenda, which is 'does the world face a period of first- or second-order change and if the latter, do we face conflict in any of its forms?'

Conclusion

Understanding which pathway is ahead is the central issue when looking towards the future. In many respects, it is more important than trying to guess what the world might look like in 10 or 20 years time. After all, it is the character of the change pathway that lies ahead of us that has more immediate relevance for any organisation's strategy.

Using the framework presented in this chapter presents us with a more comprehensive view of the types of change pathways or scenarios that lie in wait for us than do the more traditional, uni-dimensional economic mapping approaches that we first used in Chapter 3. These earlier approaches all seem to assume peaceful transformation, which is a big call to make.

Critically, we reviewed the conditions that must prevail if major conflict (military, cyber or economic) is to be avoided. Although there is disagreement within the international relations literature as to the preconditions for conflict, there is broad agreement within it that dissatisfaction with the 'rules of the game', as laid out by the most powerful actor (the United States), is the most likely precursor.

Chapters 3 and 4 tackled the deep assumption that looking at states and economic projections may be the best way to see a world in transition. In Chapter 5, we have gone further and challenged another deep assumption – that we have reached the end of an era of conflict. We have looked at the foundations of democratic peace theory, many of which have been shaken in the Great Recession. A critical decision for any reader is now to reassess this argument.

Chapters 3–5 have given us tools to think about the *Era of Global Transition*. In Chapters 6–8 we will continue to test our deep assumptions and finally, in Chapter 9, we will return to use our tools to think about how the future may unfold.

Reflection points

Determining the most likely pathway depends upon the answers to three major questions:

1. Do we believe that the world has matured? Will major state versus state military conflicts be a thing of the past? Or will

conflict appear in non-military forms? For the strategist, the ongoing validity of the assumptions underpinning democratic peace theory is the first key question to answer.
2. Secondly, who are the actors that will possess, or believe that they will have, the power to challenge the United States? The challenging actors could be state elites, market elites or even social movements.
3. Finally, we have to consider the issue of dissonance. In other words, which actors are dissatisfied with their position of influence and have issues with the legitimacy of the US liberal order?

Additional reading

The chapter has taken a realist's perspective, especially when debating the democratic peace theory.

For those interested in further exploring the realist perspective, John Mearsheimer's work is relevant, especially Chapter 10, 'Great Power Politics in the 21st Century' in

Mearsheimer, J., 2001. *The Tragedy of Great Power Politics*, New York: W. W. Norton.

For a view of alternative perspectives, see Chapter 4, 'Liberalism: The Basics' in

Sutch, P. and Elias, J., 2007. *International Relations: The Basics*, London: Routledge.

Finally, Pinker's work puts forward the proposition that the world is maturing and becoming more peaceful. See

Pinker, S., 2011. *The Better Angels of Our Nature: The Decline of Violence in History and Its Causes*, London: Allen Lane.

6
Solitary, Poor, Nasty, Brutish and Short?

Tearing apart the accepted

> Everybody wants democracy.
>
> A globally inter-connected world will bring growth, and growth will bring with it universally shared values.
>
> As economies grow, so the importance of religion will diminish.

These are just three of the popular assumptions that have underpinned economic globalisation.

Things that many may well hope for.

At first glance these may appear to be just commonsense assumptions that can be accepted without any further investigation or testing. Surely everyone wants democracy, to grow wealthier and to turn into brand-savvy, shop-a-holic consumers?

Or do they?

We can spend hours debating sales growth projections, customer acquisition targets, new routes to market, the re-engineering of business processes and return on investment ratios. But how long do we spend sharing, discussing and testing these deep assumptions?

Are these assumptions bedded in reality? Does 'everyone' really want democracy? Do attitudes to democracy change over time, especially when times are bad? Is the world driven by universally shared values? Will economic growth really push religion and age-old cultures to one side and produce a world of consumers? Do we all want the same type of globalisation?

98 *The Era of Global Transition*

Figure 6.1 The 21st-century quadrilemma

These are critical questions to answer, if we are to start to get to grips with the demands that could emerge both from the bottom 'Social movements' and left 'State elites' poles of our *21st-century quadrilemma* shown in Figure 6.1. Without debating and answering these questions, we cannot possibly understand a world in transition.

The aim of this chapter is to set a foundation for such a debate. We will start by questioning if globalisation has produced a universal set of values and, if it has not, is this still a reasonable aspiration? From there, we will turn to look at secularism and turn finally to democracy. We will explore how democracy is viewed across the world and question whether or not attitudes to democracy change, especially during times of crisis and economic hardship. We all know that states can progress from dictatorships to democracies, but is this not a one-way but a two-way street? Could established democracies slip back into the grasp of despots, autocrats and dictators?

We will start the debate with the quest for universal values.

All for one or all for many?

One of the underlying assumptions driving the onward march of economic globalisation is the emergence of a set of universal common values that will be shared by all across the globe. In short, as we get richer and enjoy the material fruits of economic globalisation, we all adopt the same values and standards of behaviour. The twin drivers of technology and increasing wealth will create a world united by one culture. Economic globalisation will become 'the arch destroyer of long-sedimented traditions along with accompanying artistic and cultural heritages' (Featherstone, 2010).

As Eisenstadt (2000) notes, classical theories of modernisation have all assumed that as states develop economically, their citizens will accept a common set of values, usually conceived as 'Western' values. The proposition was that as states develop and enjoy the fruits of capitalism, their citizens would turn into Westerners. Although this may seem (for some) to be a worthy aspiration, the underlying theory is untested and experiences since the Second World War have, Eisenstadt holds, demonstrated that the theory is flawed.

Whilst economic development has stimulated change, the result has not necessarily been the adoption of pro-Western values. Indeed, what has appeared is change, or modernity, but in a kaleidoscope of different forms. Rather than having one new shared set of values or 'modernity', we have, as Eisenstadt puts it, 'multiple modernities'. Eisenstadt's proposition of multiple modernities builds upon our earlier observations and findings regarding the unexpected fruits of globalisation in Chapter 3. By empowering individuals, we have in turn empowered difference. As we have seen, Gray notes:

> By enabling practitioners of different cultures who are geographically scattered to interact through new communication media, globalization acts to express and to deepen cultural differences.
>
> (Gray, 2009, p. 60)

So, although the technologies that empower individuals emanated initially in the West, they will not necessarily bring with them the wholesale adoption of Western values and ideas. As we saw in Chapter 4, we can already see that a variety of different forms of capitalism are appearing, with some countries, not just China, adopting a very much more state-centric or regulated approach than that found in the West. As Bremmer (2010) observes, by far the majority of the new economies – including Saudi Arabia, the United Arab Emirates, Egypt, Algeria, Ukraine, Russia, India, South

Africa, Brazil and Mexico – have made moves to implement forms of capitalism that are materially different from the free-market models of the old economies. The same may well be true of democracy. As Hobson and Kurki (2009) note, the moves towards democracy in the 21st century will be made in a very different environment to that which existed when the established democracies emerged, so we could well see new hybrid forms influenced particularly by religion, economic, environmental and gender concerns.

Recent studies provide support for the proposition that we are entering a world of not single but multiple modernities. Rojas and Zahidi (2010), for example, report upon research conducted jointly by the World Economic Forum and Georgetown University. This covered over 130,000 respondents and points us in the direction of Eisenstadt's (2000) multiple modernities. In this study, barely half of all respondents believed that universal values existed in the world. Of greater interest, there was a significant degree of local variance, with respondents in some countries, such as Mexico, largely accepting the proposition that universal values exist, whereas others, such as France, soundly rejecting the proposition. We can see this variance of opinions in Figure 6.2.

But just as there is both doubt about existence of universal values and local variance in opinion, there is just as much local variance

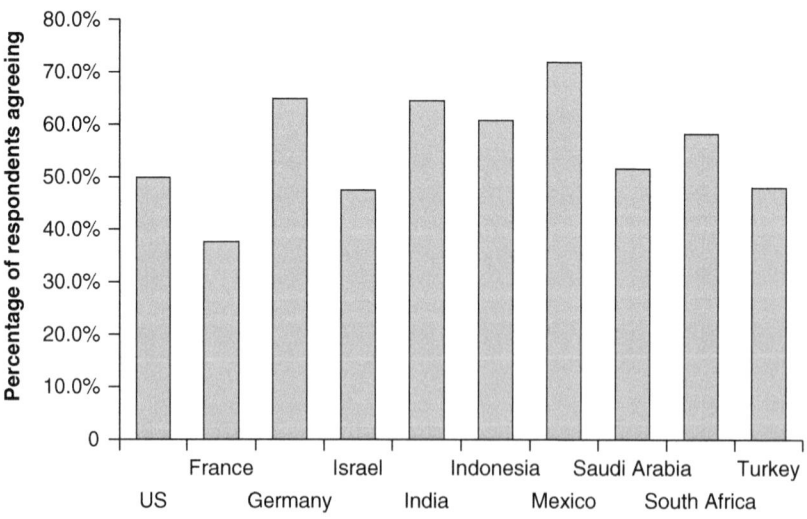

Figure 6.2 Do you believe that universal global values exist?
Source: Schwab et al. (2010).

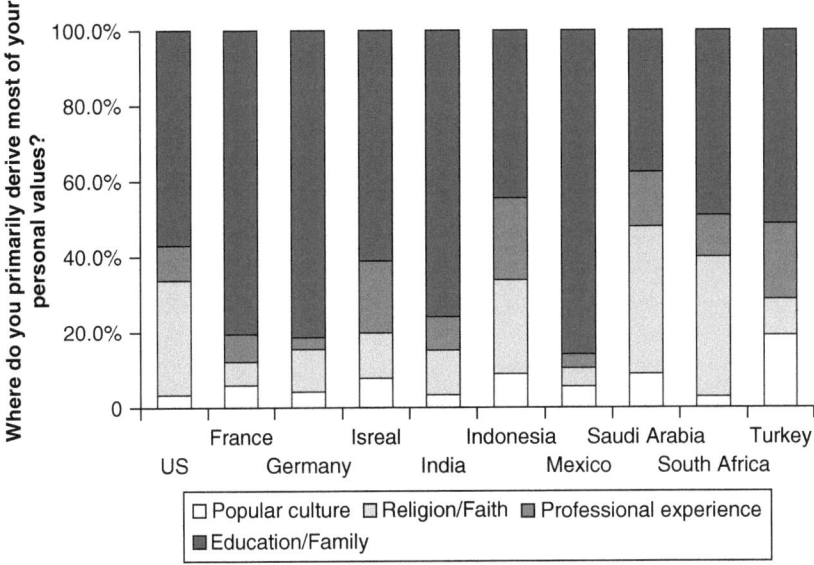

Figure 6.3 The architects of personal values
Source: Schwab et al. (2010).

on what *drives* the formation of our values. In other words, what are the key influencing forces that help to shape an individual's values? Rojas and Zahidi (2010) also examined four sources of influence in respect of the formation of values. These are (i) religion, (ii) education and the family, (iii) work and finally (iv) popular culture. The results are shown in Figure 6.3. In today's connected and consumerist environment, one may jump to the conclusion that popular culture is now the leading 'architect' of personal values. But, surprisingly, in this study, it is not the case. More traditional influences appear. Popular culture falls soundly into fourth place with overall only 6% of respondents stating that popular culture is the major influence on their values. Even if we look at the youngest age group surveyed in this study, 18- to 23-year-olds, the picture barely moves, upwards by only one percentage point to 7%.

What this study does tell us is that firstly there is a great deal of disagreement on the proposition that universal values do exist. Rather, research and opinion tells us that we should prepare for a world that is characterised not by unified values, but by increasingly localised personal values and cultures.

The great unforeseen paradox is that globalisation spawns difference, not unity. Why should individuals use a new-found power of communication to support the views and values of others rather than their own cultures? The reality that we face is that it is unlikely that a universal set of values will appear, at least in the medium term. The last hopes of any such united global culture appearing are fast sinking, as we bid farewell to a world dominated by one state and a multitude of new actors appear (Featherstone, 2010). If we look towards China, there is mixed evidence and opinion of a rapid shift to Western-style consumerism. Some note that there are 'formidable' barriers to overcome and structural changes to be made, particularly in the area of welfare reform, if the traditional propensity to save at rates of up to 50% of household income is to be overcome (Berthelsen, 2012). Others, such as Atsmon and Magni (2011), paint a different picture, saying that the Chinese 'have taken to consumerism with ease', so providing a more hopeful outlook for global consumerism.

The critical element in Rojas and Zahidi's (2010) work is that there are two really powerful influencers or architects of personal values. Firstly, education and the family, and, secondly, religion. These findings fly in the face of the commonly held view that popular culture in our socially networked world will be the architect of the values of the young. The role of religion as a powerful architect of values challenges another of globalisation's great untested assumptions.

Secularism. The assumption that economic progress will displace religion.

Secularism and a clash of globalisations

As Thomas (2000) notes, ideas of secularism and the 'modern world' are based upon the principle that all behaviours can now be explained away through the lenses of science and technology. All decisions in a globalised world will be made in an economically rational manner. Objectivity will rule in our new global society. There will be no room for the subjective, the economically unmeasurable elements of personal beliefs and the spiritual world.

This perspective is probably best summed up in the words of Fukuyama (1989), when he held that in this new world ideological struggles would be replaced by 'economic calculation, the endless solving of technical problems, environmental concerns and the satisfaction of sophisticated consumer demands' (Fukuyama, 1989, p. 18). This viewpoint best describes the foundation for the secularist argument. As democracy and wealth spreads, so will objectivity and rationality. Beliefs, spirituality, faith and religion will fade away, to be remembered only in dwindling and secluded private ceremonies, hidden away from the gaze of the population at large.

Once again, this assumption pivots on two major assumptions. Firstly, that the liberal order will deliver a fair slice of wealth to all, and, secondly, that people will value wealth over cultural values. In other words, consumerism and materialism will overturn, in a few short decades, beliefs developed over the millennia. This is a far too simplistic and presumptive view. Even if democratic capitalism did succeed in delivering a fair slice of wealth to all, why should people abandon their beliefs and culture overnight?

Perhaps Hedley Bull (Bull, 1984; cited in Thomas, 2000, pp. 817–818), writing some 30 years ago, had it right when he talked about three waves of revolt that would characterise the post-Second World War world. The first wave of revolt that he described lasted from the late 1940s to the 1960s and was characterised by a struggle against colonialism and the need for national independence. The following wave, lasting through the 1970s and 1980s, was a struggle for racial and economic recognition. But the third and final wave that Bull predicted was one of cultural liberation from the West, a drive to re-assert traditional and indigenous cultures, echoing Thomas's point that we should not see religion as a 'set of privately held beliefs', something that can be tucked away into a dark corner, but as an organising point for communities. This is a position that it has occupied in the past. In other words, religion and culture will re-emerge and be as they have been historically, a powerful architectural force and, following Shani (2002), a force that is now being reinvigorated to challenge the established Westphalian view that citizens of a state owe their primary allegiance to the state.

Although we could debate about the timing of Bull's waves of revolt (Bull died in 1985), the argument here is that we are now living within Bull's third wave, a complex struggle for religious, cultural, racial and economic recognition.

Forgetting the power of religion could have been one of the most important mistakes that scholars in the field of international relations have made, when it was assumed that the state would always be the primary organising point (Thomas, 2000). As Kaufmann (2010) holds, fundamentalist religious movements have the ability to challenge states that rely on pragmatic policies and secular nationalism.

So looking at the world through secularism's untested lenses may mean that we miss the big emerging picture (Brooks, 2003).

But let us go back and remember the secularist argument. If the liberal order could deliver:

(I) Economic growth and a fair slice of that growth to all and
(II) A universal set of values

then religion would be consigned to history.

This leads us to the question, *'Is the liberal order now perceived as having passed the two tests of secularism?'*.

In terms of the delivery of a fair slice of economic growth to all, there is a strong perception that the liberal order has produced a 'broken contract' (Packer, 2011). The contract that Packer refers to is an unwritten social contract between citizens, business and government, or between the 'elites and the masses', that guarantees that the benefits of the economic growth will result in shared prosperity. That contract, it is held, was broken when the Bretton Woods stabilising mechanisms were eroded by the neo-liberalist movement. Roubini's (2011) observation is the same. We are faced with inequality of wealth distribution in both the old and the new economies caused by 'financial liberalisation'. In the eyes of many, the free-market 'Anglo Saxon' model has failed miserably, bringing with it the legitimacy of capitalism and democracy and more importantly three of the seven pillars of the liberal order:

1. *Open markets*: That a totally open world economy is the essential foundation stone for prosperity.
2. *The social bargain.* That citizens will be protected from capitalism's booms and busts.
3. *Multilateral institutions.* The Bretton Woods institutions will ensure the integrity of the social bargain and prevent capitalism's booms and busts.

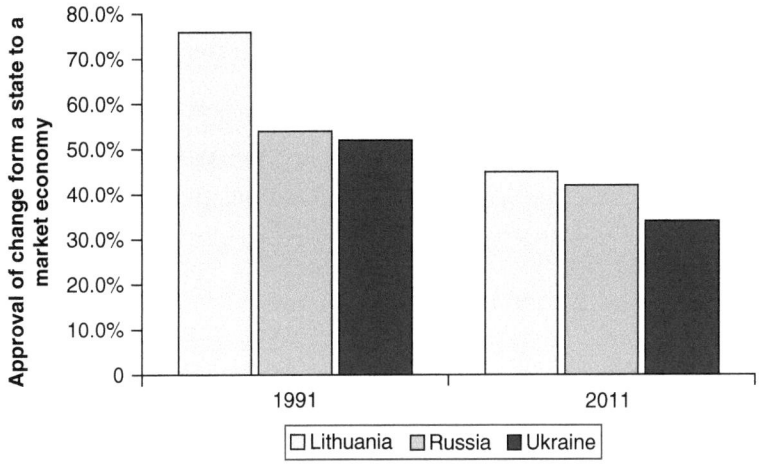

Figure 6.4 After the Soviet Union: Approval of change from a planned to a market economy
Source: Kohut et al. (2011).

There are many other voices carrying similar messages of capitalism's inequalities, including Bivens (2008) and Dewan (2008).

But these voices of doubt do not just emanate from the established economies of the West. The same image emerges if we return to the views of countries that were in the former Soviet Union, where we see approval ratings in respect of the liberal order plummeting over two decades (Kohut et al., 2011).

As we can see from Figure 6.4, in Lithuania, support for a market economy has dropped from 76% in 1991 to 46% in 2011.

These observations must be countered by many well-founded arguments that the liberal order has an enviable track record that can be enhanced, if the lessons from the Great Recession are learnt by business leaders (Barton, 2011; Bower et al., 2011). These lessons include the need to move away from the creation of pure shareholder value, to satisfying a broader range of interest groups (Bogle, 2009; Layard, 2009). Becker and Murphy (2009) make the important points that firstly, capitalism has an impressive track record, has boosted global GDP by over 140% during the period 1980 to 2007, lifting 'hundreds of millions' out of poverty; secondly, that a reformed and reinvigorated capitalism has a central role to play in the future development of poorer states and finally that eschewing capitalism risks global stagnation. But it is argued that capitalism has a potentially powerful role to play too in the rebuilding and reinvigoration of the established economies of the West. Businesses have an important role to play in the process of rejuvenation by providing investment, assisting the state in the provision of welfare, healthcare and, of course, transferring key know-how that can boost productivity in the state sector (Bisson et al., 2010).

But the coming debates and confrontations in the *Era of Global Transition* will not be won by those with the strongest economic arguments, but by those who shout the loudest and can appeal to the emotions of the majority. If we refer to the social protest movements that have arisen across Europe and the United States as an example, then there is a popular conception that the liberal order has failed. And it is the popular conception that matters, not economic reasoning. The fate of the liberal order will be decided ultimately by the electorate.

At best, we are approaching a period that we could call 'capitalism's long test'. Building on Rogoff (2011), if political systems are seen to fail to take decisive action to stimulate growth and reduce inequality, at least by the end of the 21st century's second decade, then capitalism and democracy could be overthrown. There will be no one to hear the rational cries that capitalism and the liberal order can and do work.

But what of secularism's second test, the generation of a universal set of values?

If the United States and the West set out to be seen as the exemplar of unified values, then the Great Recession has revealed, in the eyes of many, a cultural crisis of Western making.

Many are now saying that we have not just experienced an economic recession, but a recession of values and this value-based recession is far deeper and more difficult to fix than any 'normal' economic recession.

For some, this crisis of ethics, culture and values is directly attributable to the free-market economy (Betto, 2010), a system as designed by the West (Cagrici, 2010). As Betto notes:

> The market, left to its own devices, has lost sight of all ethical values and had become focused on monetary values alone, a victim of its own excess of ambition.
>
> (Betto, 2010, p.21)

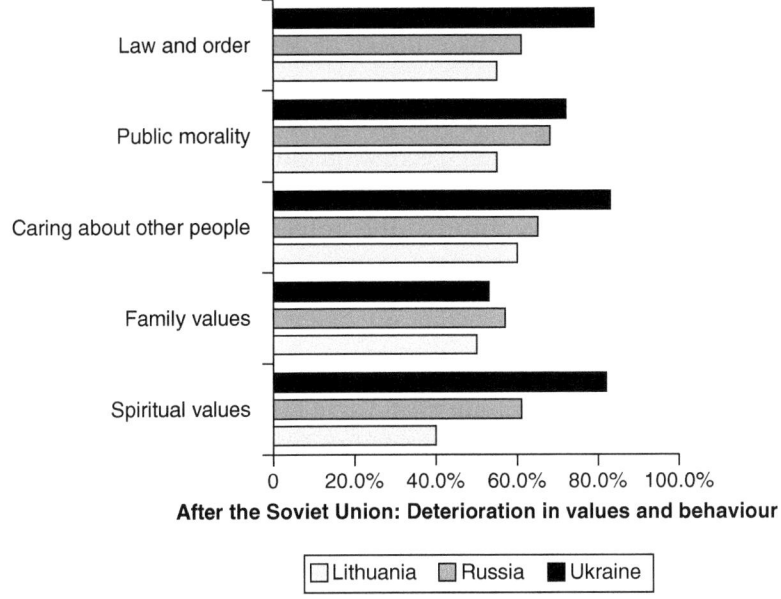

Figure 6.5 After the Soviet Union: Deterioration in values and behaviour
Source: Kohut et al. (2011).

If we turn again to look at Russia, Lithuania and the Ukraine referring to the research of Kohut et al. (2011), we see, as shown in Figure 6.5, surprisingly large numbers of people who feel that values have deteriorated during their short 20 years of life outside the planned economy of the Soviet Union. In these countries, the overwhelming majority are of the opinion that in the world of capitalism advancement can only be achieved at someone else's expense. Clear majorities believe that democracy and capitalism have had a poor impact on public morality and the way that people in society treat each other.

But is this a feeling that is peculiar to the countries of the former Soviet Union? The answer is that voices of discontent are being heard in both old and new economies alike.

Sachs (2010) holds that the United States is in the grip of a moral crisis, where a narrow short-term focus has replaced a concern for helping others. Other observers point towards a growing 'moral ambivalence' (Glauber et al., 2008) that is eating its way through society. Cagrici (2010) sees this as a direct product of 'Western modernisation' that is producing pressures for domination, self-gratification and the relentless pursuit of earning and consumption, a view shared by many others including Kirill (2010). Rather than seeing economic progress as producing unification, these onlookers see the danger that unfettered economic progress will produce division and conflict. China, for example, concerned at the influence of Western culture, has announced the implementation of a 'cultural security' programme in the light of 'hostile forces [that] are intensifying the strategic plot of westernizing and dividing China' (Wong, 2012).

Again, we are in a position that secularism is struggling to pass the test. Whilst the jury is divided, there is evidence that many feel that the liberal order has failed to deliver values and behaviours that appeal to the good in all. We must strongly consider a future where, as Brooks (2003) notes, 'Secularism is not the future; it is yesterday's incorrect vision of the future'. Finally, there is another sobering perspective to witness, the perspective of the Arab world. Prince (2011) holds that in the Arab world secularism has a bad name. Unlike the West, secularism is not associated with democracy. Rather, it is associated with repressive regimes.

But perhaps the key to understanding the dilemma that the world faces is to go back to problems, or ambiguities around the definition of the word 'globalisation'. It is clear that to many, globalisation has different goals, objectives or measures of success. For Khatami (2010), this difference in perspectives is at the epicentre of the storm. Khatami sees a Western definition of globalisation as:

> [A] uniform life style, a standardized frame of understanding and a single value system for the entire world. In this narrative, all cultural patterns are dissolved in this process of globalization, and all differences will be replaced by a single structure.
> (Khatami, 2010, p. 25)

This definition, with its focus on integration and emergence of a 'single-value system', shares some similarities with the definition that we referred to in Chapter 1:

> [T]he closer integration of countries and people of the world which has been brought about by the enormous reduction of costs of transportation and communication, and the breaking

down of artificial barriers to the flows of goods, services, capital, knowledge, and to a lesser extent people across borders.

(Stiglitz, 2002, p. 9)

The above ties in with another description that reflects a popular view of globalisation's benefits:

> Globalization is helping to give birth to an economy that is closer to the classic theoretical model of capitalism, under which rational individuals pursue their interests in the light of perfect information, relatively free from government and geographic obstacles. It is also helping to create a society that is closer to the model that liberal political theorists once imagined, in which power lies increasingly in the hands of individuals rather than governments, and in which people are free, within reasonable bounds, to pursue the good life wherever they find it.
>
> (Micklethwait & Wooldridge, 2001, pp. 341–342)

These descriptions of globalisation and its benefits focus on the power of rationality, economic growth and wealth as the great unifier.

There is however another view of what the process of globalisation should produce that has nothing to do with economic integration, rationality or wealth. This view sees technology enabling not wealth, but encouraging and appreciating cultural diversity:

> [G]lobalization means increasing diversity at the global level, and surpassing uniform and omni-focal identities.
>
> (Khatami, 2010, p. 26)

This view of globalisation focuses upon using advances in communication to value, reinforce and develop localised cultures, beliefs and traditions. From a similar perspective, Williams (2010) calls for a redefinition of growth away from consumer-fuelled materialism and economic growth towards 'growth in human capital'.

We are left with a warning that taking and pursuing economically rational definitions of globalisation will result in a period of 'fracturing and dissolution' and that what is really required is not 'economic globalisation' but 'values globalisation' (Marx, 2010; Matsunaga, 2010).

Understanding the process of transition has therefore much to do with understanding the characteristics of a dialogue that must be engaged to reconcile these two very different views of globalisation. From this perspective, the challenge that a transitioning world has to face is not the maintenance of growth or the balancing of power, but bringing together, if it is possible, two very different definitions of globalisation.

This is a dialogue that most believe has not yet started. For many, the dialogue or the effort to bridge the gap can only be led by the state (Kirill, 2010; Marx, 2010; Usmani, 2010) and faith-based organisations (Shankar, 2010) working in unison.

So everyone wants democracy?

Surely everyone (apart from current and aspiring totalitarian and authoritarian leaders) wants democracy?

Or, will the hallmark of the 21st century be a crisis of democracy? Are we facing a test of which is the best form of legitimate authority? Which is the favoured approach, a democratic system where the role of the central authority is strictly limited, or is it an Iranian religious autocracy or could it be China's single-party system (Kaplan, 2011)?

Will the unwritten assumption that everyone wants democracy be overturned?

In Chapter 4, we suggested that the future was to be found in the past. The seeds of the structure of a globalising world could be found by looking back to the Middle Ages in Europe. In a similar vein, the voices of the past may help us to make out the future.

It may be interesting to start by examining the work of the 19th-century philosopher John Stuart Mill. In his work *Considerations on Representative Government* (Mill, 1861), Mill suggests that democracy might not be the best form of government for every situation and that states go through a series of phases to reach a democratic system. In situations of total anarchy, Mill proposes that states need the iron grip rule of the despot, the autocratic leader. Once the iron rule of the despot has restored order, a 'good despot' then allows the education of the people, who in turn demand representative government (democracy).

Mill's thinking gives us a view of a 'development cycle' where states progress from uncontrolled anarchy, through the stabilising but unsavoury influence of the despot, then education through finally to democracy.

But there are other lessons too, to take from Mill's work. Firstly, the reign of the despot or authoritarian leader may be the only way to control a state in anarchy, where the rule of law and order has totally broken down. The same observation applies when a population has been violently suppressed for decades by a 'bad despot'. Rather than the immediate transition to democracy, a 'kind despot' may be required to encourage the education and development of the suppressed population. Secondly, despotism is only good for a period of time. As people become more educated or aware of the freedoms beyond their borders, they will demand more representative government, which of course is the challenge that China faces. The third, and arguably most important point, is that this is not necessarily a one-way street. When democracy is achieved, this is not the *final* position. States can retreat from democracy to despotism or even to anarchy. Mill has some interesting observations on this latter point, the retreat from democracy. Democracies are vulnerable when they become absorbed by what Mill most appropriately calls 'sinister interests'. Mill refers to sinister interests and their dangers as follows:

> One of the greatest dangers, therefore, of democracy, as of all other forms of government, lies in the sinister interest of the holders of power: it is the danger of class legislation, of government intended for (whether really effecting it or not) the immediate benefit of the dominant class to the lasting detriment of the whole.
>
> (Mill, 1861, pp. 127–128)

He then goes on to conclude that any democracy should not:

> allow any of the various sectional interests to be so powerful as to be capable of prevailing against truth and justice, and the other sectional interests combined.
>
> (Mill, 1861, pp. 129–130)

In short, democracies can fall if their dominant elites are seen to use their powers to pursue their own sinister interests and, in so doing, lose the perceived legitimacy of the majority.

This points us towards an 'chaos–order' model as shown in Figure 6.6:

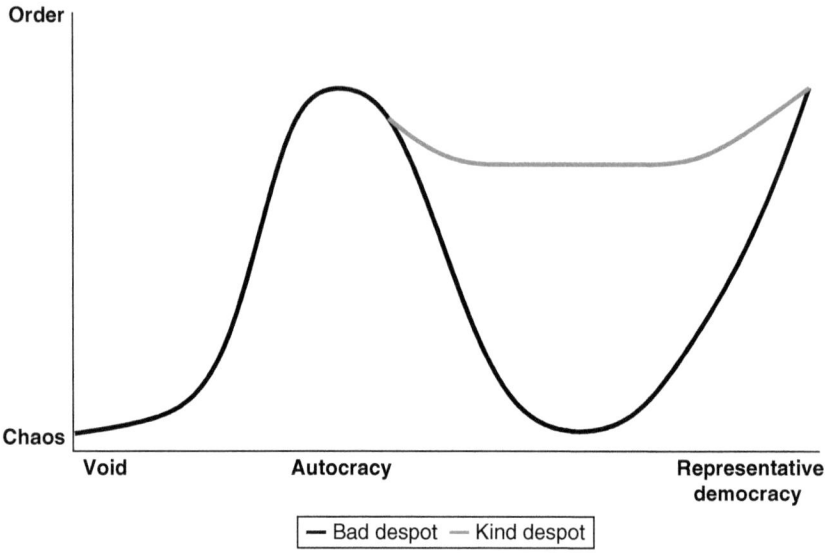

Figure 6.6 From chaos to order, from the void to representative democracy

We commence the life cycle with a state with no central authority, a void that exists in a climate of chaos. By 'chaos' we mean the world that an earlier philosopher, Thomas Hobbes, describes as a 'state of nature' (Hobbes, 1651). Without a central authority, Hobbes holds that the life of man will be 'solitary, poor, nasty, brutish, and short' (Hobbes, 1651, p. 78). In other words, without authority, humans are capable of and will do terrible things against their fellow beings. At some point, autocracy, or in Mill's words, a 'despot', takes control and rigidly imposes order. Despots can be 'bad' or 'kind'. The despot can be 'bad' and inhibit any development of the population, totally suppressing learning and communication. Alternatively, a 'kind' despot will allow these activities, paving the way for a relatively orderly transition to democracy. However, in the case of a repressive 'bad' despot, the escape from autocracy is a violent one, plunging the state into the depths of chaos, the passage to democracy then being a slow and tortuous one. The important point to remember is that this is very much a two-way street. Reaching democracy is not a fixed end point. If the elected government, the 'dominant elite' is seen by a substantial proportion of the population to be pursuing 'sinister interests', it will lose legitimacy. A backwards journey then starts. If a 'kind despot' appears, order may hold until circumstances allow a return to democracy. A 'bad despot' or no despot at all heralds, following Hobbes (1651), a nasty, brutish world.

This life cycle, or moving backwards and forwards from anarchy through to democracy and back, is similar to the J-Curve (Bremmer, 2011). Bremmer's J-Curve posits that states can be stable when they adopt two forms of leadership, either 'closed' (despotism in Mill's language) or open (democratic). The problem, from Bremmer's perspective, is that to proceed from a closed to an open state entails going through a period, and usually a prolonged one, of chaos.

There is some evidence today too to support Mill's assertion that democracy is not seen as a suitable vehicle for every situation, especially when the going gets tough.

As Chu et al. (2009) observe, within East Asia, only in Japan, the Philippines and Thailand is democracy seen as preferable to all other forms of government by a substantial majority of the population. Of even more interest, in only one of the countries surveyed, Thailand, was democracy seen as more important than economic development. Chu's work, which covers China, Hong Kong, Japan, Mongolia, Philippines, South Korea, Taiwan and Thailand, could therefore provide important pointers as to preferred forms of governance, particularly in troubled times, which leads us to seriously consider if the relatively authoritarian 'China Model' may become increasingly popular, pushing the liberal order to one side. As Chu concludes, democracy in this region may be in crisis. This could well be a trend that we see emerging in other regions, including Asia (Keidel et al., 2008), and new democracies where the democratic process is seen to be corrupt (indulging in Mill's 'sinister interests') and failing to produce both growth and an equitable distribution of wealth (Bajoria, 2008).

In Russia, the Ukraine and Lithuania, attitudes to democracy are declining. In 1991, a clear majority in all three countries approved the move from a single to a multiparty system. Now, some 20 years later, this majority has all but disappeared (Kohut et al., 2011). In these countries, capitalism is seen as having failed in its role to generate and equitably distribute wealth. Interestingly, in this study, when respondents in Russia and the Ukraine were asked to decide which was more important, a strong leader or a strong economy, 57% and 60% respectively chose a strong leader. Similarly, respondents in all three countries thought overwhelmingly that a strong economy was preferable to democracy, echoing the Chu et al. (2009) East Asian research.

These studies show evidence of support for an authoritarian leader (Mill's 'kind despot') that can guarantee that no one will be left in need in times of crisis. There is also the view that in times of economic crisis, autocratic systems are better at defending citizens, autocracies being able to move faster than democratic governments and without fear of a short-term popular backlash (Dennison, 2010). A good example of this is the speed at which China was able to put in position a range of policy responses, including a $586 billion injection, during the Great Recession, that enabled it both to maintain growth at near 9% per annum, whereas all other major economies were collapsing into recession, so cementing its position as a dominant world power (Breslin, 2011a).

The picture becomes even more confusing when we look at research that has investigated the relationship between democracy and the generation of wealth. In an early study, Helliwell (1994) found that there is, as one would expect, a tendency for citizens to prefer democratic government as they got richer, but the same study found that the introduction of democracy slowed the rate of economic growth. This leaves one wondering if citizens would reject democracy if their wealth decreased. A later analysis (Doucouliagos & Ulabasoglu, 2008), reviewing all the available research, concluded that democracy had 'zero direct effect' on economic growth, although democracy had some side benefits and disadvantages. The benefits include growth in human capital, economic freedom and levels of inflation. The disadvantages include, surprisingly, increased government spending and restrictions in international trade. However, whilst this study concluded that democracy has a zero effect on economic growth, it does enable us to rule out the proposition that democracy has a negative effect on growth. A final study, by Acemoglu et al. (2008), muddies the waters even further. This study discounts the commonly heard assumption that as states get richer, their citizens will demand democracy. This study, covering a 100-year period, found no relationship between income growth and the rise of democracy, turning conventional thinking on its head. Its conclusion was that if rising income does have a casual relationship with democracy, then the effect exists only if measured over long periods of time, that is a time horizon of over 100 years.

These observations and findings, that at the very least, challenge conventional wisdom, become even more worrying when some hold that the world is experiencing a 'democratic recession' (Corrales et al., 2009) and that authoritarian states, capable of generating economic growth, may be on the rise. Corrales et al. pick out China and Russia for particular comment. Both these countries have crafted a model that blends capitalism as a wealth-generating mechanism, with, in China's case, a single-party system and, in the case of Russia, a form of democracy where real power is centred in a tightly grouped dominant elite.

To some, all this means that the dice are becoming loaded against representative democracy (Youngs, 2009).

For many readers in established democracies, the above may appear to be a contrarian's review of outlandish, theoretical models that can be consigned to the lifetime of Hobbes (1588–1679) or even Mill (1806–1873). But it is held here that they are relevant today in developing, new and old economies alike.

Any state can travel forwards and backwards as Mill (1861) suggested. Democracy can be long in the making and quick in the losing.

Despots waiting in the wings?

One clear message to draw from the international relations literature is that dying empires or expiring great powers can be dangerous. It is not just the new actors, the upstart rising states, that can be sources of aggression and instability, declining states, even Europe or the United States, could be dangerous too; a failing economy can produce a demagogy, where leaders in their desperation appeal to populist fears and prejudices (Soros, 2011).

If we look towards the declining powers and Europe in particular, the picture is not pleasant. As Goodwin (2011) notes, popular extremist parties in Europe represent one of the most significant challenges to democracy and surprisingly large swathes of the electorate are receptive to their messages.

The Great Recession, it can be argued, has merely helped to fuel the cause of extremism (Boland et al., 2009). As both Goodwin (2011) and Mammone (2009) note, support for popular extremist parties is fuelled by a toxic cocktail of economic insecurity and a growing distrust of established mainstream political parties, which are distant from the 'grass roots' day-to-day concerns and worries of their electorate (Meikie, 2011). However, it is not just the Great Recession that has fuelled support for extreme right-wing parties and groups. Worryingly, there is a long history of embedded support for extremist thinking in Europe (Mammone, 2011), and despite the decades that have followed the Second World War, there is evidence that such views are endemic. In Germany, Rothberg (2011) holds that in 2010 there were some 15,000 incidents associated with right-wing extremist groups of which some 5% involved violence.

Such extremist parties feed upon the preservation of tradition and local culture. Globalisation is portrayed as a direct threat to historic cultures and practices. So, the continuance of globalisation and the erosion of borders act as a catalyst to fan these embedded flames. As Klau (2011) puts it, the old economies of Europe are facing a watershed. For the first time in well over 100 years, parents in Europe will no longer have the confidence that their children will grow up to enjoy a more affluent and secure existence than they did. All this fuels a toxic extremist recipe. As Klau goes on to observe:

> This transformation [globalisation] changes not only the social dynamics of Europe but affects its politics in ways most political parties have not even begun to address. The promise of a materially better tomorrow with higher incomes and better welfare provisions rings ridiculously hollow today, but most social democrats and centre-right politicians in Europe know of no other way to fight an electoral campaign. Our main political parties are choosing to deal with a historic transformation obvious to every voter by doing their utmost to suppress it from the political and electoral debate. This denial of reality is almost certainly one of the main causes of the rise of populism we are seeing in much of Europe today.
>
> (Klau, 2011)

However, the economic crisis in Europe acts to deepen this toxic cocktail of embedded divisions and financial insecurity (Sachs, 2011), producing a drive towards fragmentation and nationalism as opposed to integration. The solutions are difficult to find, but, as Sachs argues, there could be a significant role for business, especially multinational corporations, with their experience of bringing different cultures together in single workplaces.

Conclusion

We started this chapter by asking if globalisation had produced a set of globally shared values. A short answer would be 'not yet'.

The central message that we have to get to grips with, is that we are faced with a 'clash of globalisations'. The forces of globalisation have unwittingly released two opposing goals. One side has in mind a world populated by rational individuals and wealth-generating markets. The other wants the forces of globalisation to heighten differences in values, beliefs and customs and to produce a world characterised not by material wealth, but by the wealth of human capital. The real dialogue between the two sides has yet to commence.

Secularism too is a long way away. We ignore the power of religion, culture and beliefs at our peril.

Another surprise is that democracy may not be seen as a universal panacea. There are times, particularly times of economic crisis, when autocracy may be preferred, making the 'China Model' a real contender to the liberal order. The conclusion is that we should not merely see the future as a tussle between two adjacent segments of the 21st-century quadrilemma, the liberal order and state capitalism. To see the full range of potential outcomes we have to look further and consider the position of social movements.

Reflection points

We have continued the path of challenging assumptions. In this chapter we have addressed the following deeply held assumptions, from the total of nine presented in Chapter 2:

> *Deep assumption 3*: Globalisation will bring wealth, and a reasonably fair distribution of that wealth, for all.
> *Deep assumption 4*: Everyone wants to live in a democracy.

Deep assumption 5: As wealth rises, so will secularism. We will forget old cultures and beliefs and adopt the same universal, largely Western values. The importance of religion will fade away as globalisation marches on.

Deep assumption 6: Everyone wants to be a consumer.

This may be a good point for readers to consider their own verdicts.

Additional reading

The study conducted jointly by the World Economic Forum and Georgetown University referred to earlier in this chapter contains a wealth of views and opinions from faith communities:

Schwab, K. et al., 2010. *Faith and the Global Agenda: Values for the Post-Crisis Economy*, Geneva: World Economic Forum. Available at: http://www.weforum.org/issues/faith-and-religion [Accessed March 22, 2012].

For a potentially chilling and uncomfortable account of how the world could divide along cultural lines see:

Huntington, S., 2002. *The Clash of Civilizations and the Remaking of World Order*, London: Free Press.

7
Another Way

TINA – There is no alternative?

So frequently, many businesses complain about being knocked off course by totally unexpected and unplanned events.

On many occasions, these devastating occurrences are referred to as 'black swans'. The originator of the term 'black swan' (Taleb, 2008) says that these high-impact events lie outside normal perceptions, which leads us to ask the question 'is it possible to see these black swans before they hit us?'

Many of these events should of course not really be shocks. Roubini and Mihm (2011) make this point with regard to the Great Recession. These 'black swans' appear to be shocks because our own view of the outside world and the future that it holds is too restricted. This is not surprising, as many business leaders feel that too little time is spent thinking about the future and that there are shortcomings in the tools and approaches that are commonly used to aid our 'forward vision'. One research study revealed that leaders in a staggering 97% of organisations felt that they did not have access to an 'early warning system' that could alert them to future shocks. In the same research, 81% believed that their vision of the outside world needed widening (Day & Schoemaker, 2005). It is almost as if our optometrists have prescribed lenses that are too weak for our spectacles. Just having a broader, less inhibited vision than competitors could therefore be a source of real competitive advantage.

As we can now guess, many events should not be 'black swans' at all. The purpose of the *21st-century quadrilemma*, introduced in Chapter 4, is to encourage readers to explore as broad a future landscape as possible. The quadrilemma introduces a wide range of potential world orders.

Our vision or view of the future should not be limited to one or two – which would be too dangerous. Understanding a broader range of worlds will help us to avoid the shock of the new. It is now clear that the Great Recession has undermined many of the commonly held assumptions about the way the world works, from democratic peace theory, through to secularism. Change will occur, and when it does occur the swan carrying the message could be flying at very great speed.

Many will argue that there is no alternative (TINA) to free-market capitalism and the liberal order. But there are alternatives that reside across the quadrilemma. The viability of each will not be determined by rational economic thought but by the perceptions of the dominant actors, be they state elites, post-state elites, market elites or social movements. The influence of market elites may now stand fatally wounded by the Great Recession and the scramble will be to see which of the two remaining groups of actors, state elites or social movements, will win through and be the major architect of change. It might be sobering to reflect on Zizek's reminder that, following the trauma of the 2008 financial melt-down, communism could appear again on our radar screens:

> [D]o not be afraid, join us, come back! You've had your anticommunist fun, and you are pardoned for it – [it is] time to get serious once again!
>
> (Zizek, 2009, p. 157)

So we can see that the balance of power or the balance of influence may be shifting. It is time to explore the broad zones shown in Figure 7.1 where control, stability, religion and values are more highly prized than an economically rational, materialist world.

In this chapter we will venture into two alternative models to explore other parts of the quadrilemma, apart from the more familiar rationally economic perspective. The first venture reflects upon the outcome of momentous events in the Middle East in 2011 and 2012, and we consider a world where capitalism still exists, but where religious movements are the dominant actors. In this world, influence has slipped from the hands of the market elites into the hands of social movements and the state elites. Market elites have

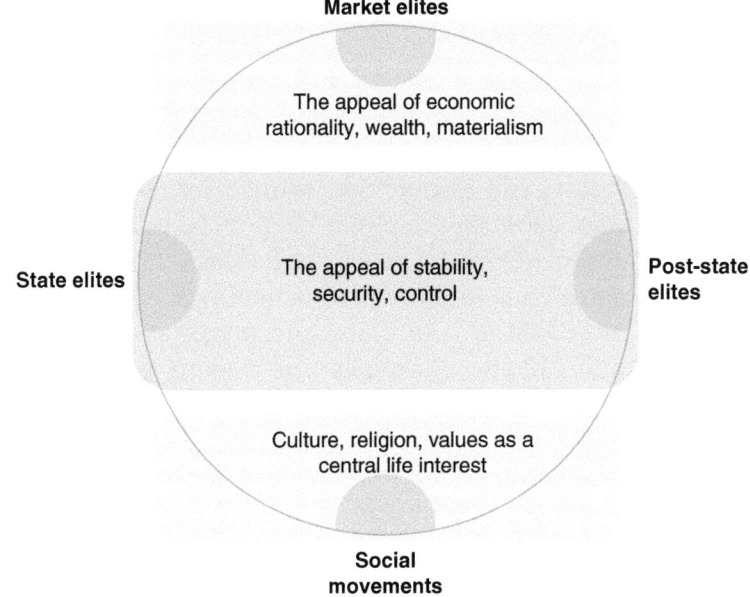

Figure 7.1 Three opposing perspectives

to get used to being a tertiary voice. The second approach that we will examine is the 'China Model', a mix of authoritarianism and state-controlled capitalism that has brought millions out of poverty. To many, this is a fully tested methodology and a worthy successor to the liberal order.

A religious capitalism?

In Chapter 2, we concluded that seeing the world in terms of states and economic growth projections obscured our vision. It stopped us from seeing what really could happen in our transitioning world. Even more importantly, if we take this economically statist perspective, we will be blind to who are the real architects of change and those fast-flying 'black swans' that may appear on the horizon. A very good example of the restricted vision that results from these more traditional approaches is provided by Thomas (2005), citing the Iranian revolution and the fall of the Shah of Iran in 1979. Established analytical tools did not predict this milestone or 'black swan' of the 20th century. As Thomas observes, the dominant thinking at that time was (and probably still is in many minds) that the world was being steadily transformed by an unstoppable wave of globalisation that will in turn produce a secularist society.

In the last chapter we presented an argument that secularism may be a relic of the pre-Great Recession world. If it is, then the sorry truth is that whilst we might know a lot about how market and states elites can re-craft the world order, we know very little, if anything, about the role that religion or, for that matter, other social movements could take in reshaping our world. What we do know, going back into the past, is that in the 17th century, state leaders succeeded in controlling and marginalising religion. As we debated in Chapter 4, we may now be approaching a new 'Westphalian moment' which begs the question 'whose turn now is it to be marginalised?'

With state leaders and financial markets facing questions of credibility, we need to shift our gaze.

Our focal point for now will be social movements and in particular religion. We need to explore how these actors may re-craft the world order. Many, for example, Kaufmann (2010) and Thomas (2005), point to a 'resurgence' in the role and influence of religion that will characterise the remaining decades of the 21st century. Thomas defines such a resurgence as:

> the growing saliency and persuasiveness of religion, i.e. the increasing importance of religious beliefs, practices and discourses in personal and public life, and the growing role of religious or religiously-related individuals, non-state groups, political parties, and communities, and organizations in domestic policies, and this is occurring in ways that have significant implications....
>
> (Thomas, 2005, p. 26)

This means that increasingly the state may have to share power with, or cede power to, actors to whom religion is the primary central life interest. The only alternative is to create a religious 'firewall'.

It is important to note that this religious resurgence does not merely apply to one religious group, in some far off land, that we can observe at a comfortable distance through our plasma TV screens. It is a process that could extend beyond religion and is occurring in advanced, emerging and developing states alike, driven firstly, as Kaufmann (2010) points out, by changing demographics and secondly, by potentially, if we suffer another economic crisis, the empty promise of consumerism and materialism. These twin drivers are particularly relevant in the established economies of the West and it is the second driver, the vacuum, that could be left by materialism and consumerism that is the most worrying. If we reflect upon the levels of youth unemployment in many advanced countries and the long-term effects of 'austerity' debt-reduction programmes, we are left wondering, what is the future of consumerism? If wealth and consumerism recede, then what will fill the void for the offspring of 'Generation X', the post-Second World War baby boomers who have known nothing but a consumer-driven life? What, for these offspring, will fill the vacuum as the lure of consumerism deflates? How will they react as this vacuum manifests itself? Will it be religion that fills the void?

For many, when the word 'religion' is mentioned, stereotypical images appear, usually associated with violence, terrorism and extremism. But this does not have to be the case as Khalaf and Saleh (2011) observe. It is time to consider what a world might look like if religion or other social movements took the driving seat, eroding the dominant influences of both the state and market elites. We will try to catch a glimpse of such a world by looking at religious capitalism, taking the possible influence of Islam as an example.

We should start our journey with Silvestri's (2007) observations. Firstly, Islam consists of many theological and legal traditions and one must therefore think of 'a multiplicity of versions of Islam'. However, despite this plurality, Muslims throughout the world identify with a single 'global community of believers'. It is this concept of a 'global community of believers' that can create a highly influential force providing, as Silvestri notes, '...enormous symbolic strength, communal identity and potential to unite for common causes' (Silvestri, 2007, p. 22).

On top of this capacity, Islam has, in common with other religious movements, the power to operate across the territorial boundaries of individual states. The one obstacle that Islam does face as Silvestri pinpoints is the absence of a common vehicle and a common voice so that it can negotiate effectively with other key architects of change.

But despite this limitation, Islam remains a powerful potential architect, waiting in the wings, especially if democracy and capitalism do lose their legitimacy. It is in such a context that Silvestri's words are sobering:

> But perhaps, in the end, the real serious challenge that Islam poses to Europe and to the West is its ability to question the validity and the effectiveness of the notions of power, authority and justice which underpin our political bargaining, structures and institutions. The transnational, religiously inspired, and civil-society-based mobilization of Muslims across the world exposes the failures of traditional forms of political participation and of representative democracy; it picks up a global message of dissatisfaction with the ability to bring about justice on earth.
>
> (Silvestri, 2007, p. 28)

Others would concur with Silvestri's sobering words. Denoeux (2002) states that the Islamist project 'provides a comprehensive critique of the existing order, challenges it and aims to change it' (Denoeux, 2002, p. 61). In Ayoob's view, the Islamist project or political Islam 'offers a more just alternative to the way that the current international order is organized' (Ayoob, 2007, p. 631).

An example of the role of religion can be found in the 'Arab Spring' of 2010–2011, where one of the most powerful driving forces against the ruling autocracies was a religious one, in the form of Islam (DePetris, 2011).

All these observations are relevant, especially when we consider the capacity for Islam to change. Some may see religious orders as immobile monoliths, but in the emerging landscape of the Middle East, Islamist political parties may prove in the future to be surprisingly flexible (Hamid, 2011) and may well support the democratic process.

In this world, we should not lose sight of the fact that religion, in the context we are examining, Islam, will assume a central role in politics (Lynch, 2010) and will probably continue to do so into the distant future (Moubayed, 2011). As Diaa Rashwan from Cairo's Al-Ahram Center for Political and Strategic Studies puts it in the context of the Middle East, 'Without Islam, we will not have any real progress' (Wright, 2011). So what is 'political Islam' or 'Islamism'? Denoeux provides us with this help:

[Political Islam or] Islamism, in short, is a form of instrumentalization of Islam by individuals, groups and organizations that pursue political objectives. It provides political responses to today's societal challenges by imagining a future, the foundations of which rest on reappropriated, reinvented concepts borrowed from the Islamic tradition.

(Denoeux, 2002, p. 61)

But when we consider what political Islam really means today for the future of capitalism, then views become divided and fall into almost two camps.

Some would argue the case for a strong regulatory approach, verging upon autocratic state style capitalism as practised in Saudi Arabia, the UAE and, pre-Arab Spring, Egypt and Algeria (Khanna, 2010; Mahbubani, 2009).

Others would take an alternative line and put the case that the picture emerging from the 'Arab Spring' is different and the last thing that we should expect to appear is another autocratic regime (Souaiaia, 2012). In many eyes, the emerging picture could well radically contradict the past. Whilst Islam is inseparable from politics, this does not mean that in practice capitalism will be dismantled (Shamoo, 2011). Rather the opposite, we may experience possibly only small adjustments to capitalism even in its more extreme neoliberal form (Prince, 2011). Examples of the type of adjustment that we might expect to see are given by Usmani (2010, pp. 52–53) who isolates four key changes relating primarily to speculative trading:

1. Money is a medium of exchange only and its speculative trading should be banned. Usmani cites lessons from the Depression of the 1930s to support his case.
2. Similarly derivatives should be banned.
3. Securitisation, collateralised debt obligations (CDOs) and the sale of debt are all, Usmani observes, 'prohibited in Islamic jurisprudence'.
4. Short sales in stocks, commodities and currencies should be prohibited.

Many of these proposals tackle the same issues that the original Bretton Woods approach was designed to focus upon to stop capitalism's excesses, so the approaches take us back to the post-Second World War financial environment.

There are two strong arguments as to why we may well not see the wholesale dumping of capitalism by political Islam.

Firstly, it must be remembered that many countries where political Islam is surfacing as a serious architectural force are faced with massive economic obstacles that include broken industrial infrastructures, poor healthcare and deep-seated corruption (Shamoo, 2011). Understandably, the electorates in these countries are looking for solutions that are economically credible. As the co-founder of Tunisia's Ennahda Party, Rached Ghannouchi puts it, 'Islam as a solution is not enough for them; people want jobs and better lives and will demand results' (Ghannouchi, 2011). Ghannouchi goes on to acknowledge that the country's unemployment levels need to be solved by investment, which in turn depends upon the need to encourage a free-market system and root out corruption.

Noland and Pack's (2004) analysis would support the perspective that capitalism has a role to play. Looking specifically at the Middle East, Noland and Pack point to a demographic bulge that in turn will produce a long-term increase in eager young people looking for work. This burgeoning workforce will demand economic growth of 5–6% annually if it is to be satisfied. Noland and Pack also hold that the disciplines of Islam may well produce a productive workforce:

> If the Middle East is able to cash in on this [demographic] dividend, future pundits may praise the disciplined 'Islamic ethic' as a contributor to development just as erroneously as they condemn it as an obstacle to growth today.
> (Noland & Pack, 2004, p. 7)

Whilst this sounds a promising future, we are left with the warning that if economic growth is not delivered, then an opportunity will be handed to the extremists.

Secondly, the concept or position that political Islam would not ride roughshod over capitalism is reinforced by the arguments of Nasr (2009) who states that the real driver of change, globally, is an emerging Islamic middle class driven by what Nasr calls an 'Islamic Calvinism'. He defines this as 'an ethic of hard work and savings, investment, and economic growth, combining strict piety with raging entrepreneurship' (Nasr, 2009, p. 247). Nasr goes on to describe this emerging force as 'a dynamic sector of society [that] dreams of democracy replacing theocracy and the rules of business trumping ideology' (Nasr, 2009, p. 255). But again, we are left with warnings. The first warning is that this emerging class is as yet too small. Secondly, the process of change will take time and may be fractious. The first iterations of a new, more capitalistic model will be 'Islamic, conservative and all too often prudish and misogynist' (Nasr, 2009, pp. 259–260).

But of all these warnings, it is Noland and Pack's (2004) that seems to be the most relevant if we look to the immediate future. What will a burgeoning young population, looking for work, do if economic growth fails? If growth does not materialise, then the door opens for others, which leads us to the role and influence of extremists.

There has always been a degree of ambiguity or uncertainty as Husain (2011) puts it, when we consider how extremists will react to the emergence of new Islamic democracies. Some are certain that extremist groups will resort to encouraging sectarian violence in order to undermine the process (Rashid, 2011). This is all part of the observation that political Islam is made up of a diverse range of groups and any process of moving towards democracy and greater acceptance of capitalism may produce a period of fragmentation, especially when Islamist parties are forced to compromise with each other when they reach power. This reveals the greatest unknown of all, which is the influence of harder line religious parties (Sabra, 2011). The real threat to peace will not come from Islamic parties confronting secular parties, but from the conflict that may emanate from efforts to reconcile the interests of a diverse range of Islamic parties (Wright, 2011). This conjures up pictures in the mind of a path towards democracy and capitalism (Nasr's 'Islamic Calvinism'), which is composed of fitful steps with extremists pushing and pulling at the edges (Topol, 2012).

In so far as the power of political Islam to create a transnational *caliphate*, Ayoob (2007) sees this as unlikely, as historically Islamic political activity is limited by a state's borders; and Sayigh (2012) takes a similar perspective, observing that there is insufficient support or resources for the emergence of such a new 'super state'.

The conclusions for the future of 'Islamic capitalism' especially in post-autocratic states could be surprising and may be summarised as follows:

1. In many post-autocratic states, power sharing and compromise will at least initially be the order of the day. Whilst, as Souaiaia (2012) points out, there are certain areas where room for compromise will be limited including the adoption of shari'ah as a main source of law, most Islamist parties, with the exclusion of those with more extremist views, will be prepared to compromise and work with secular parties.
2. The last thing that electorates want is another autocracy. There is a good possibility that democracy will be given a chance.
3. Most parties will turn to capitalism as the first choice to solve deep-seated economic and infrastructural problems.
4. The impact of political Islam on capitalism may not be as great as some fear. The types of changes proposed by Usmani (2010) are, in many cases, not too far away from the post-Great Recession measures being proposed in the West.
5. The process will be fitful and strewn with challenges. Extremist groups will want to try to derail the process and, following Nasr (2009), it is likely that Islamic capitalism will go through an evolutionary cycle, its first forms being 'conservative and all too often prudish'.
6. There is one great caveat that the post-autocratic states of the Middle East share with Europe. This is of course the failure of capitalism to produce economic growth and the distribution of a reasonable slice of such growth for all. Both in the Middle East and Europe there are plenty of extremists waiting in the wings if growth does not materialise.

So, whilst the voice of the market elites may take more of a back seat, a world with Islamic capitalism may not look too different from that we have known in the past.

But what of another emerging order, the 'China Model'?

China: Autocratic capitalism?

China's approach to the management of economic growth is gaining in popularity and is seen by many as the only viable and tested alternative to the Western economic formula, that is popularly called the 'Washington Consensus'.

The 'Washington Consensus' sums up the Western 'recipe' for economic development, a route that aspiring states can adopt or buy into to achieve growth and prosperity. It is a term first coined in 1989 and embraces the ten key policies that it was believed would help the deeply indebted countries of Latin America to find a path to sustainable growth (Williamson, 2004). Its roots or 'DNA' are of course deeply embedded within the 'seven pillars' of the liberal world order that we reviewed in Chapter 5. The main policies included within the 'Washington Consensus' are as follows:

- Fiscal discipline,
- Reordering public expenditure, to focus principally on basic healthcare, educational and infrastructure needs,
- Taxation reform,
- Interest rate liberalisation,
- Competitive exchange rates,
- Trade liberalisation (opening markets),
- Liberalisation of overseas investment (allowing foreign direct investment),
- Privatisation,
- Deregulation,
- Property – the right of individuals to buy property.

Many associate the 'Washington Consensus' with neo-liberalism and the experiments with deregulation and the minimisation of the role of the state during the Reagan and Thatcher eras. However, Williamson, the original author of the term 'Washington Consensus', is at pains to stress that the original policies did not encompass such neo-liberal excesses.

The real problem is that in the eyes of many, this approach now lacks credibility following the Great Recession and is far too rigid and prescriptive in its approach (Breslin, 2011b).

So an alternative, growing in popularity, is China's approach, dubbed the 'China Model' or the 'Beijing Consensus' (Ramo, 2004).

What exactly is the 'China Model' or the 'Beijing Consensus'?

This is a question that may be a little more difficult to answer than defining the 'Washington Consensus' as there is no clear 'set of instructions' for aspiring users.

Frequently, references to the 'China Model' and the 'Beijing Consensus' paint a picture of an autocratic variant of capitalism, based upon a rigid strategy or set of plans, the whole approach being designed towards the end of the 20th century.

This is a misunderstanding, in more ways than one. Firstly, it is not a totally rigid model. Some writers describe it as an exploratory process of learning through experimentation or 'groping for stones to cross the river' (Ramo, 2004). Secondly, the 'China Model' is held to be part of a plan that spans centuries. Barnett (1986) sees it as part of a process that can be traced right back to the mid 19th century, a process that has as its driving mission a quest for wealth, power and above all, respect in the modern world. It should therefore be seen as part of an incredibly long-term project that is beyond the planning horizons of most in the West.

The latest chapter in this pan-century quest emerged in the mid-1970s and since then, the model, or approach to national economic management, has progressed through at least two phases of development (Scissors, 2011). The first phase (that Scissors calls the 'China Reforms') focused upon stimulating growth. The first steps were granting property ownership rights and the introduction of commercial practices in China's agricultural sector. Further changes in 1992 progressed this thrust for commercialisation into the urban economy. At the same time, steps were taken to reduce the role of central government. It is this version of the 'China Model' (Scissors' 'China Reforms') that has been the most successful in generating massive economic growth delivered not through, as in the Western case, capital investment, but through a metamorphosis in terms of labour productivity (Hu & Khan, 1997).

The 'China Reforms' model came under scrutiny by China's leadership during the period 2003–2004, following concerns that progress would be unsustainable, a view reinforced during and after the Great Recession. A second phase or model then emerged that Scissors calls 'China Reverts', as it reflects an increasing role of the state. There were five major concerns that lead to the emergence of the 'China Reverts' model (Breslin, 2011a):

Concern 1: Balancing. The major worry, heightened by the 2008 financial crisis in the West, was that the model was unbalanced in terms of China's reliance upon overseas demand as opposed to demand driven by the indigenous population. In short, China needed to reduce reliance on Western consumers, which may well never reach again its pre-2008 heights. This need to drive internal demand emerged as a major issue for China. During the early lifetime of China's first model 'China Reforms', domestic consumption, Breslin estimates, was about 60% of China's GDP, but by 2007 this had plummeted to approximately 36%. Increasingly, China was becoming dependant upon demand from overseas consumers and action was deemed necessary.

Concern 2: Finance. The dependency upon overseas finance, which like overseas demand, could dry up without warning. Both this issue and the need to stimulate domestic demand reflected worries about an unwelcome web of dependency upon Western economies.

Concern 3: Inequality. A widely used measure of inequality is the 'Gini Coefficient'. This varies between 0 representing perfect equality, where everyone has the same wealth, to 1 representing total inequality, where one person has all the money! By 2008 China's 'Gini coefficient' stood at 0.47, the same as the United States. But in the early 1980s, the coefficient stood at 0.30 (Williamson, 2012), so whilst there has been a vast increase in the size of the economy, wealth distribution has deteriorated. The big worry here was emerging social instability. It should be remembered that it is estimated that there are some 200 to 300 protests a day in China (Bequelin, 2012), so the threat of instability is a constant worry. After all, the legitimacy of the ruling communist party rests upon the generation of wealth and its perceived equitable distribution.

Concern 4: FIEs or 'foreign invested enterprises'. This concerns the benefit to China of exports made within factories owned by foreign investors. In short, China wanted to retain more of the economic benefits generated by these operations rather than foreign investors taking the lion's share.

Concern 5: Local short-termism. Central government was worried that local authorities were putting concerns regarding short-term social stability before long-term economic development.

The key actions taken in response to these five concerns included:

- Continued centralised management of exchange rates.
- Loosening of monetary policy that would, coupled with a massive financial injection into the economy and tax breaks, stimulate domestic demand.

- New measures to protect domestic businesses from foreign competition.
- Increased centralisation of decision making.

In short, the current emphasis is upon decoupling from the old economies of the West, both in terms of reliance upon demand emanating from these countries and also, surprisingly, foreign investment, where the real worry was that if overseas investment continued, then China's capacity as the workshop of the world would outstrip the world's requirements!

So the focal point of 'China Reverts' is the need to build a self-reliant development model that was based upon encouraging domestic demand, as opposed to a reliance upon exports and continued overseas investment. The goal is self-sufficiency, arguably not world domination.

So what are the characteristics of the 'China Model' in its current version? We could, from a Western perspective, identify these features:

- Unlike the 'Washington Consensus' there is a strong nationalistic 'tinge'. The primary driver of economic growth is the national interest.
- Illiberal markets. There is no total liberalisation of markets. The state maintains a key role in controlling competition in the interests of indigenous businesses. Markets are not totally open and foreign entrants face hurdles and entry conditions.
- The central management of exchange rates again for the benefit of domestic businesses.
- Centralised decision making, an absence of democratic debate.
- State control of key strategic industries. In all, there are some 114,000 state-owned businesses in China, the top 121 of which are run by China's Assets Supervision and Administration Commission (Sheridan, 2012). To put this in perspective, as Sheridan observes, 40 out of the 46 Chinese companies in the 2010 Fortune Global 500 were state owned. There are strong political linkages too. All the leaders of the 130 top state-owned businesses are members of the Chinese Communist Party.

In view of its ever-changing form, this may be too rigid a classification and a better approach may be to identify what the model is *not*

(Breslin, 2011c). From this perspective, it has not historically been about abrupt short-term transitions (one should contrast this with the 'Washington Consensus' approach to the liberalisation of the ex-Soviet bloc countries), complete liberalisation, democracy and rigidly following one pre-defined solution.

But these are all characteristics of the approach from observers outside China. From inside China, the view is subtly different and Wei (2011) puts forward the following essential characteristics:

1. 'Speaking the truth through facts'. Wei describes the process of rejecting dogma and ideology, when China examined and rejected both the Soviet and Western market models.
2. 'Prioritisation of the lives of people'. The priority here is lifting people out of poverty. Therefore for China, 'human rights' are about poverty reduction, which should be contrasted with the Western human rights perspective of putting individual's political rights above all other rights.
3. The pre-eminence of the provision of stability.
4. Gradual long-term reform. This is a long distance project spanning multiple lifetimes, not one five-year plan.
5. Sequential differentiation or developing the economy in strict phases, starting, as we have noted, in the agricultural sector.
6. The 'visible hand' and the 'invisible hand', or the blending of market forces and ultimate state control, again to provide stability.
7. Looking at the outside world and selecting strong proven concepts and approaches from other economies.
8. Finally, in Wei's words, 'having a relatively neutral, enlightened and strong government'.

So is the 'China Model' unique with its emphasis on nationalism and its rejection of liberalisation?

Probably not, if we go back in time far enough. In terms at least of the protectionist elements, there are similarities between the rise of great powers in Europe and America and even the development of some Asian economies after the Second World War (Breslin, 2011b).

But could others try to copy the 'China Model'? Could it be applied anywhere?

Breslin's (2011b) conclusion is that this is a very specialised model, and in terms of its totality could only be applied to China.

Many commentators within China itself would agree with this, noting that whilst the model in its entirety cannot be emulated, it being very 'China-specific', elements of the process could well be copied and applied elsewhere.

Scissors' (2011) view is different and holds that the first version of the 'China model', 'China Reforms' with its emphasis on 'more rights for people, a smaller state and trade liberalization' is a 'superb model' for any state in any stage of development. However, the second version, 'China Reverts', he feels will result ultimately in collapse. One must be careful too regarding making claims for any broad application of the China Model in view of the 'China-specific' observation. Early successes of the China Model, some hold, are due to two country-specific one-off bonuses (Babones, 2011). The first bonus was the structural ability to urbanise its population; in other words, to bring in potential workers from the country to new factories in the cities. This explains the early spectacular economic growth rates, as workers in a manufacturing sector produce significantly more GDP per head than those employed in a traditional agrarian setting.

But the second bonus is even more China specific and that is the issue of human fertility and mortality.

For China this is a double-edged sword.

The positive side of the blade is the result of the introduction of the one child one family policy in 1979, even though fertility rates were falling. The implementation of this policy freed up women to work, rather than caring for large, young families and allowed the state to invest its limited resources in building productive capacity. Declining life expectancies also have freed a new generation of workers to go out and earn a living rather than care for an elderly family. But there is a negative, blunt side to the sword too. If fertility rates do not rapidly improve in a country that has been dubbed 'The Sick Man of Asia' (Huang, 2011) (air and water pollution alone kill over 750,000 a year) where will future generations of workers and entrepreneurs come from?

Whilst there may be problems of application in other states and many unanswered questions with regard to the medium- to long-term effectiveness of the 'China Model' in its second version, there are very great attractions in the most surprising of settings.

An obvious attraction is that it is not regarded as a 'Western' model. In many countries, memories still linger of Western dominance during both the colonial era and the 1997 Asian economic crisis when the IMF imposed strict economic reforms. By contrast to the 'Washington Consensus', the 'Beijing Consensus' appears to come with few strings and conditions attached. Importantly, it allows retention of national identity and at least superficially, national autonomy. There are no IMF rules to abide by, and protectionism is countenanced, which could well be a popular vote winning strategy in many emerging and austerity hit economies. The one major downside could be dealing with China's soft power pressures, which may be the price to pay in the longer-term for any material support China provides to aspiring states that fall within the attraction of its orbit.

Arguably, the most significant attraction is that it could, potentially, avoid the trauma of the move from autocracy to representative democracy and free-market capitalism that we observed in the last chapter. Both Mill's (1861) thoughts and the J-Curve (Bremmer, 2011) indicate a painful period following the prolonged rule of the despot. The 'China Model' offers a tempting way out of this conundrum, both for the population at large and the despot him or herself as the 'China Model', with its promise of wealth through stability, offers the 'good despot' a prolonged period in office. But one should not be mistaken at thinking that concepts such as Mill's and Bremmer's apply only to autocracies. The point that we made earlier is that both models are two-way streets and can apply even to established democracies. This latter point could be most relevant in the second and third decades of the 21st century when the established democracies, particularly in Europe, face their biggest test. If the austerity-led recovery programmes are seen to produce depression as opposed to recovery, then governments will face crises of legitimacy and exposure to extremist demands. The 'China Model' has the potential to fit well with opinions regarding the relative importance of economic stability in times of crisis that we introduced in the last chapter. Critically, electorates exposed to prolonged periods of economic stagnation may well value economic stability over democracy.

In these contexts, the 'China Model' with its emphasis on centralised control, stability and the promise of chaos avoidance may be all too attractive to resist.

This position is shown in Figure 7.2. This illustration is a development from the Mill (1861) 'life cycle approach' introduced in the

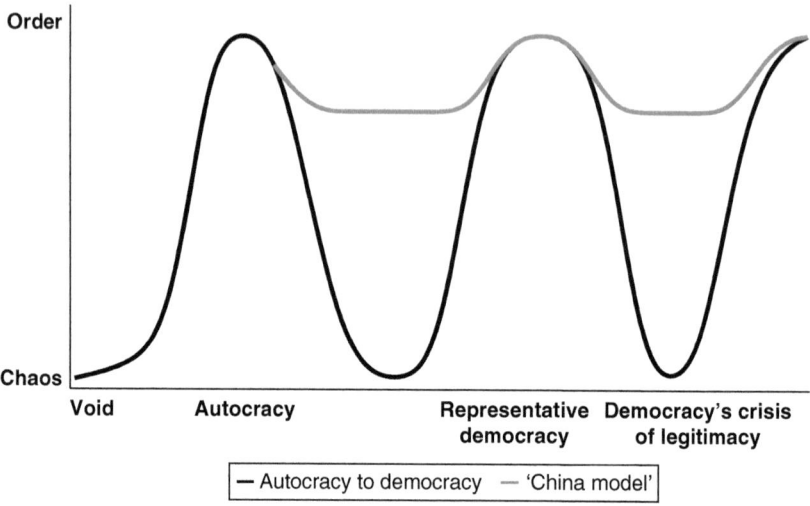

Figure 7.2 From chaos to order and democracy's crisis: The potential smoothing effect of the 'China Model'

last chapter. Here, the life cycle is extended to include a crisis of legitimacy for representative democracies that may be experienced in coming years. The attraction, in this scenario, of the 'China Model' is shown, as it offers a route to avoid the wholesale chaos that could follow a collapse of democracy's legitimacy.

In the final analysis, views on the viability of the China Model are divided. Some see the dice as firmly weighted in Beijing's favour. For example, even though elements of the model are as yet to be tested by time, China's position and opportunities for manoeuvre are so much greater than those of the United States, which is encumbered by debt, low growth prospects in the medium term and the need to re-engineer the structure of its economy. In addition, apart from the United States, there is no one prepared to stand up against China's centrally managed exchange rate policy. China too is using its influence to build a network of trade and financial relationships in Africa, Asia and Latin America and it has acquired enough soft power to demand that foreign organisations wishing to enter China's growing market share technology with China's domestic companies. For these reasons, some see us returning to a unipolar world by 2030, but this time the ruling power will be China (Subramanian, 2011). Any serious strategist, therefore, needs to consider the implications of a world dominated by the 'China Model'.

The most frequently cited stumbling block that the 'China Model' faces is the need to maintain economic growth, stability and distribution of wealth. The distribution of wealth will, it is hoped, deliver and maintain social stability. But in the shorter term, there is another testing point. China's current focus, as we have seen, is to reduce external dependencies by increasing domestic consumer demand. So the real test is if a series of centrally designed policy measures can fundamentally change consumer behaviour (Pettis, 2011).

The best way of seeing the 'Beijing Consensus' is as a model of unfolding parts. At the moment, we have only really seen parts one and two and only the first instalment, 'China Reforms', has been subject to rigorous testing. As for the second model, we shall have to see how well this deals with, or eliminates capitalism's booms and busts, particularly in China's housing sector (Chovanec, 2011). The first version of the 'China Model' has excelled in providing growth. Whether or not the second model is as efficient at allowing the state to manage growth is highly questionable. If the 'China Model' fails, then in 2020 we could well find ourselves in a situation where there is not a viable consensus at all, both the Washington and Beijing variants having bitten the dust.

We should remember that this is not communist China's first successful attempt at growth. The 'Great Leap' of 1952–1959 saw impressive gains with production rising between 14 and 18% annually (Eckstein, 1964). However, these gains vanished nearly as quickly as they had started and by the early 1960s, China was in the grips of a depression.

In the final analysis, the stunning growth rates achieved since the end of the 1970s may indicate the Achilles' Heel. Being undemocratic, the Chinese Communist Party has created a 'performance legitimacy'. In other words, it is only seen as legitimate in the eyes of the Chinese people if it can continue to deliver increased prosperity (Yao, 2010).

Conclusion

Many say that there are no alternatives to the 'Western way' or the 'Washington Consensus'. As we have seen in this chapter, this is very much a restricted view.

The issue of the viability or legitimacy of alternative models is again very much in the eye of the beholder. There are at least two models that many think could have greater legitimacy and relevance and the number of alternatives will grow the longer that the world, and particularly the West, takes to recover from the shock and aftermath of the Great Recession.

Surprisingly for many, some models of Islamic capitalism may be very close to what has been known in the West. Some may find these variants more business friendly than the autocratic 'China Model'.

But we must not leave this chapter with the view that it is only the liberal order or the 'Washington Consensus' that is questionable. The 'China Model' in its latest form is also highly questionable. Its legitimacy hangs by the thread of wealth distribution. If this thread breaks then both the model and China's dominant elite will fall.

Islamic capitalism too faces an uncertain road. Failure to deliver growth will allow the extremists to enter.

So the 'Washington Consensus', the 'China Model' and emerging Islamic capitalism all face their 'long tests'. The legitimacy of all depends on the same outcome. That is an outcome that embraces both the generation of wealth in the coming decade and, of course, the perceived fairness of the distribution of that newly created wealth.

Reflection points

1. Will the 'Washington Consensus' have to change to survive?
2. Will the emerging economies spawn their own versions of capitalism?
3. In what circumstances could the 'Beijing Consensus' become the dominant world model?
4. Could the world divide around different models and fall into the three zones of Figure 7.1?

Additional reading

For a discussion of the emergence of and challenges presented by the 'Beijing Consensus' and other variants of state capitalism, try:

Bremmer, I., 2010. *The End of the Free Market: Who Wins the War Between States and Corporations?*, New York: Portfolio.

The World Economic Forum prepared long-term scenarios following the banking crisis of 2008 – *The Future of the Global Financial System*. These scenarios include views of a world populated with different economic models. These scenarios can be accessed here: http://www.weforum.org/reports/future-global-financial-system-near-term-outlook-and-long-term-scenarios.

8
An Engine of Growth?

The excitement

It is as if the Great Recession has cleaved the world into two.

Many of the advanced economies face a long, uphill struggle for growth. But there is another world. The BRICs, composed of Brazil, Russia, India and China, are dubbed as the favourites to excel in the 21st century. The original predictions for these states (O'Neill, 2001) appear to be coming to fruition. The economies of the BRICs have grown impressively since the Goldman Sachs paper, which gave birth to the acronym, was published in 2001.

For most new and emerging economies, the Great Recession proved to be a mere 'blip' on the radar screens of growth. Research conducted by the World Bank in 2012 showed that Brazil, Russia, India and China had fared the best during the global financial crisis, especially India and China, states that had experienced no contraction whatsoever in their economies.

This, of course, was in stark contrast to the experiences of many of the advanced economies who have struggled to regain momentum and to reignite growth. These older economies now seemed to be laden down, not with opportunities, but with problems. These problems range from staggering levels of national debt, through to major questions regarding the viability of the structure of their economies (Posen, 2009; Sassen, 2009). After the banking crisis of 2008, many were quick to point out that economies, such as that of the United Kingdom, with its exposure to the banking sector, were inherently volatile and could be exposed to a 'doom loop' that threatened more distress in years to come (Johnson, 2009).

The resilience of the new and emerging economies has reinforced, in the minds of many, the expectation that the BRICs and other new economies will be the engine of growth for the remainder of this century. There are great hopes that consumer growth in these new economies will return the world to a path of sustainable economic growth. In short, the consumers in the new economies will rescue the West.

The BRICs, with several new additions, appear now to be at the epicentre of a new world, their destiny assured. These new additions include Indonesia, Turkey and Mexico, all states that could well turn in significant economic performances in future decades. One must not of course overlook Africa and the Middle East too, as potential focal points for growth.

Economic growth is, of course, one of the vital ingredients of power, an ingredient that can increase the amount of structural power (the ability to change 'the rules of the game') available to states. As we have seen, structural power should not be underestimated, as it enhances dramatically the influence that can be brought to play in the world. Critically, economic growth can give new and emerging states the ability to redefine, at the very least incrementally, the historically US-led liberal order. Flushed with success, it is only natural to expect that these states will wish to apply their own remedies to mitigate capitalism's excesses, just as the United States did in 1944.

And a challenge

Despite these hopeful signs that point towards continued growth amongst the BRICs and their new colleagues, all powers, whether growing or declining, face challenges. It is important to balance the challenges faced by the advanced economies with those facing the new and emerging economies.

A multipolar world will by definition be populated by actors looking to build power. How that power is used depends upon the question of maturity that we have introduced earlier and is of course a question that applies to old, new and emerging economies alike. Whilst there is hope, there are those who do not see the rise of new holders of power as a peaceful issue. The most notable may be Mearsheimer who argues that a by-product of economic growth will be security competition, particularly in Asia. Mearsheimer goes so far as to say that 'China cannot rise peacefully' (Mearsheimer, 2010). If we follow this line of thought, the stage is set for intensified future conflicts between states. It is a line of thought that must be followed and then accepted, moderated or rejected. That is the purpose of this chapter.

We start with a brief overview of the BRICs followed by examples of some of the challenges that may be ahead, taking Asia as our focal point. All eyes, as we have noted, do appear to be, after all, largely upon Asia.

The hopeful economies: A brief overview

Brazil is the first state to form the BRIC acronym and is the most prominent emerging economy in South America. Brazil is attractive for a number of reasons, including a sound growth record and a growing middle class. Brazil is the world's largest exporter of sugar, coffee and meat and the third largest consumer of mobile phones (The Economist, 2011). Brazil is also a biofuel innovator, being the world's second largest producer and a leading exporter (Pearson & Pfeifer, 2011). This focus on sustainable innovation has made Brazil an attractive country to invest in and it has already attracted funds from British Petroleum, who bought a majority stake in a Brazilian-based bioethanol and sugarcane producer in the spring of 2011 (Pearson & Pfeifer, 2011). There are, however, worries regarding economic freedom. Brazil was ranked number 99 in the Heritage Foundation's 2012 Index of Economic Freedom (The Heritage Foundation, 2012) and concerns were expressed in this study regarding property rights and corruption. Brazil also has a relatively active state involvement in its economy (Bremmer, 2010). There are worries too that in an attempt to sustain growth, Brazil may resort to protectionist measures (Pearson, 2012). But most importantly, Brazil is an ambitious state, keen to have its voice and views aired on the world stage. It has aspirations that see it taking a top table position at all the world's major institutions including a permanent seat at the UN's Security Council (Cardenas, 2008; Hanson, 2009). If Brazil's growth continues and the West continues to falter, Brazil could well be a potential architect of a new world order.

Russia's rise has been in large part due to its significant position as an exporter of natural gas and oil (Harding & Hearst, 2009). Soaring energy prices have, in the past, materially fuelled its growth.

Following its emergence from the financial crisis in 2008, Russia's GDP growth then plunged in the face of flagging demand for its energy abroad in the midst of the economic downturn. Some observers argue that Russia has structural problems that plague its future potential for social and economic development (Aslund, 2008, 2009). There are concerns too at the pace and direction of economic reform and Russia is positioned at 144 in the Heritage Foundation's 2012 Index of Economic Freedom (The Heritage Foundation, 2012). Aslund (2009) presents a view of the state of Russian business quite succinctly: 'Russia is suffocating from the dominance of corrupt state corporations and red tape – and oil isn't going to save it this time.'

However, what Russia does possess in its favour is its location which could make it a pivotal architect in the future. In 1904, Sir Halford Mackinder published an article entitled 'The Geographical Pivot of History' (Mackinder, 1904) stressing the strategic importance of exerting influence over 'the heartland' (or Eurasia), a vast continent-sized region, which is predominantly occupied by Russia, but stretches far west, south and east to touch Belarus, Iran and China. Russia and the United States have long been in competition over 'the heartland', both possessing military bases in the region due to the vital pipelines that run through it (Godemont et al., 2011). Vladimir Putin's quest for a 'Eurasian Union' (Buckley, 2011) is unsurprising, given the pivotal geographic position, summed up by Engdahl (2008) who holds that 'a power that dominates Eurasia would exercise decisive influence over two of the world's three most economically productive regions: West Europe and East Asia'. Such value has not gone unnoticed, China is eager to guide parts of Central Asia, which occupies a considerable proportion of 'the heartland', towards Beijing (Godement, 2011). The declining influence of both the United States and Europe could leave a power vacuum in 'the heartland' that Russia could all too easily fill (Barysch, 2010). Should Russia's influence over 'the heartland' be successful, it may give Moscow a strong stature in global trade, acting as an intermediary between Asia and Europe.

After China, India has often been regarded as the main contender to the United States, in terms of future economic dominance and there has been much speculation about India and China vying for supremacy amongst the BRICs (Badkar, 2011). According to Wolf (2010) (and the projections of the Author), the Indian economy may surpass the United Kingdom's by 2020 and be the equal of Japan's around ten years later.

One of India's assets is its population, which stands at some 1.1 billion. This figure is set to continue growing, giving India the accolade of potentially being the world's largest state in population terms by 2026 (Nelson, 2010). India also possesses approximately 50–100 million English speakers (Nye, 2011c). This is advantageous, given that many multinational corporations often look to outsource to areas where employment costs are low. India has attracted attention from notable US companies such as Coca-Cola and Ford who have made substantial investments. India's status as an established democracy has helped develop its international reputation and the fact that it shares a border with China is both a blessing and a curse. The proposed superhighway, stretching over a thousand miles from Kolkata to the Yangtze River basin, has been a cause for optimism amongst believers in 'Chindia', the idea that China and India could have a cooperative relationship over the next century and grow alongside one another (The Economist, 2006). However, historical disputes over the national borders may cast a shadow over the possibility of India forming a special relationship with China, an issue that we will look at later.

With its burgeoning population, India looks set to join the top table of the world's architects. But, in common with Brazil and Russia, the state has a heavy involvement in the business sector through state-owned operations. There are concerns too as to whether India's infrastructure can support future growth at historic levels (The Heritage Foundation, 2012).

Then, of course, there is the contender that has frequently been promoted as the one that will soon overtake the United States and become the world's largest economy, China. China has the largest army out of all of the BRICs and ranks, in military expenditure (Stockholm International Peace Research Institute, 2012), second only to the United States, which is set to reduce its military investment in years to come (Hille, 2011). China has seen its economy achieve a 10% compound annual growth rate over the last 20 years, adding credibility, as we have seen, to the 'Beijing Consensus'. China also has developed a monopoly on rare earths, substances that are used to produce sophisticated pieces of technological equipment and are difficult to mine (BBC News Business, 2012). China accounts for about 97% of total global production of rare earths (BBC News World, 2012), an issue that we will turn to look at later in this chapter.

In addition, China has increased both its sphere of influence and access to the resources that it will need to secure its future growth (Follath, 2010; Moran, 2010).

It is for reasons such as these that China has often been tipped to eclipse the United States as the world's leading superpower and, if it wishes, it could well be the architect of the next world order. Unlike any of the other contenders that we have reviewed, it may in the foreseeable future have the power to do this and, in many eyes, it already possesses a tested model that is very different from the seven pillars of the US liberal order.

Challenges everywhere

Although all these new aspiring contenders have ideas that are different, in varying degrees, to the US order, they do share one characteristic in common with the advanced economies. The future is not clear cut and there are challenges ahead.

The challenges are of course distinctly different. For the advanced economies, the challenge is one of economic restructuring and reinvigoration to solve, especially the lingering spectre of youth unemployment. For the emerged and emerging economies, it is different. It is one of securing the infrastructure and resources to maintain an impressive track record of growth.

Historic rivalries and a problem of borders?

Whilst it has been popular in recent years to hope that issues of territorial boundaries are assuming less importance in international affairs (this is one of the assumptions referred to by Jervis (2002), when reviewing the democratic peace theory), there is some evidence to suggest that this issue may well flare up again in the coming years.

China and India's prospects of future mutual growth have been placed in the hands of the 'Chindia' concept (The Economist, 2006); the belief that there is a real possibility that China and India could form a special relationship akin to that of the United Kingdom and the United States. However, commentators such as Joseph Nye (2011c) have observed flaws in this hopeful theory by looking at previous flashpoints that have occurred between these states, specifically over territorial issues. Relations between India and China had been on a knife edge ever since Prime Minister Nehru provided shelter for the 14th Dalai Lama after an unsuccessful Tibetan uprising against Chinese forces in Tibet during 1959. Furthermore, many Tibetans who took part in the attempted uprising were trained by the CIA and Indian armed forces (Emmott, 2009). Emmott (2009) also observes that siding with Tibet and sheltering the Dalai Lama made Beijing view India as an ally of the enemy. In 1962, the two states met head-on at the Himalayan border to dispute land, which both claimed as their own. The result was humiliation for India, as the Chinese dominated the ill-equipped and unprepared Indian troops in a brief but brutal conflict (Gokhale, 2010).

In 2009, the territorial issue resurfaced when India erected new military bases on the Himalayan border. Beijing responded furiously and flexed its muscles to show its military might. A communication from the Communist Party asked India to 'consider whether or not it can afford the consequences of another potential confrontation with China' (Smith, 2009). The message that China has consistently projected is not a simple claim to territory, but rather a forewarning: India cannot afford to clash with China (Emmott, 2009). The belief within China is that it is progressing and gaining strength, and it will not falter in the face of any who stand to challenge its interests and ideology (Godement, 2009). This has been the case with Japan and could quite possibly be the case with India. There are two essential and yet basic observations that we can take away from this very brief historical analysis. Firstly, China and India are essentially the two closest rivals in the BRICs and they both occupy the upper echelon of this group, so increasing the likelihood of competition. To supplement this competition, confidence within these states is increasing, leading, in turn, to a growing feeling of confidence in their own ideologies (Hailin, 2010). Secondly, confrontations concentrating upon the Sino-Indian border and Tibet have occurred on multiple occasions and resurfaced again only recently. If both India and China are set to compete for hegemony and influence in the 21st century, such tensions are likely to resurface with more at stake, challenging the hope of a 'Chindia' world.

India has also had serious political and military conflicts with another state that it shares a border with, Pakistan. Since the partition of British India after the Second World War, the two states have engaged in a series of conflicts, being either conventional military conflicts or the so-called 'proxy wars' where terrorists occupy the limelight. In total, three official wars were waged between India and Pakistan in 1947–48, 1965 and 1971 (Reuters, 2010).

Most recently, relations between the two states have been plagued by terrorist 'proxy wars' (Chidambaram, 2009). As India grows, it may well present terrorists with a higher-profile target and therefore an opportunity to attract more attention and potentially cause more devastation. Tension between Pakistan and India assumes more interest too, when we consider a growing relationship between China and Pakistan (Lamont & Bokhari, 2011). In return for China's assistance, Pakistan has avoided opposing China's 'core' interest areas, including Taiwan, Tibet and the South China Sea (Kabraji, 2011).

The nature of the relationship between Pakistan and India is worth grasping if we are to uncover what future conflicts may occur and the effects that they may have. As we have seen, relations between India and Pakistan have been volatile since the establishment of Pakistan in 1947. More recently, India has accused Pakistan of unofficially provoking tension by supporting terrorist groups such as Lashkar-e-Taiba who have carried out serial attacks in Indian cities (Desai & Kuusito, 2010). Indian security has been plagued by terrorism, with more than 6,000 terrorist attacks recorded between 1970 and 2010 (University of Maryland, 2012). Should these events escalate, they would pose a great threat to India's growth ambitions.

Both India and Pakistan have nuclear weapons capabilities, which raise the stakes considerably. India achieved nuclear capability after successful tests in 1974, whereas Pakistan did not achieve nuclear status until 1998 (Bokhari, 2006). From this position, Pakistan has often claimed its nuclear ambitions are purely defensive. Despite that, it is Pakistan that has often been labelled as the prime nuclear threat. In the past Pakistan has refused to sign a 'no-first strike' agreement (Tharoor, 2011) with its neighbour and has even threatened to use its weapons against India in 2002 (Astill, 2006). The fear amongst those in India is directed towards who has control over Pakistan's nuclear arsenal. Could lack of stability in

Pakistan mean its nuclear capabilities could fall into the hands of terrorists or other rogue elements (Tharoor, 2011)? In light of such volatility, Indian officials have previously stressed that the lack of safety surrounding Pakistan's nuclear weapons is of global concern (ANI, 2012).

Afghanistan is an issue that may be set to only add fuel to the fire between Pakistan and India. Pakistan has traditionally enjoyed a close relationship with Afghanistan, but it has started to regard India as a rival to its 'strategic depth' in Kabul, Afghanistan's capital. New Delhi has made significant outreaches and investments in Afghanistan since the demise of Taliban leadership in 2001 (Nelson, 2011). India is worried about Islamic extremism, given the history of terrorist attacks within its borders and it is therefore in its interest for a post-NATO Afghanistan to be at least a moderately stable state.

The future of a post-NATO Afghanistan is ambiguous, not least because India and Pakistan are competing for influence there, but because the numbers of Taliban insurgents have increased dramatically since the war began in 2001, rising four fold between 2006 and 2009 (AlJazeera, 2009). The assassination of Burhanuddin Rabbani, the Afghan government's chief negotiator with the Taliban makes it increasingly difficult to believe that Afghanistan will become a stable state in the near future (Bajoria, 2011).

The South China Sea

The South China Sea, which stretches from Singapore to Taiwan, has all the makings of a future conflict area. There are nine states that touch the South China Sea, all of which are considerably smaller than China both in economic and hard-edged military terms. Some of these states have, in the past, looked towards the United States to preserve security, but with the prospects of the power of the United States in decline, these days could, despite the recent strategic review, in the long-term, be numbered.

The South China Sea is host to ample resources, which may well serve as catalysts for conflict. The seabed promises oil, with estimates stating that there is potentially as much as 213 billion barrels available (EIA, 2008). As the economies that border on the South China Sea grow, so too will fuel and gas consumption, making these reserves all the more valuable. In addition, the South China Sea is a crucial highway for naval fleets. More than half the world's annual merchant tonnage travels through it and a third of all maritime traffic uses the space (Kaplan, 2011b).

Not surprisingly, China declares the largest claim to the South China Sea, despite being geographically less central than other nations such as Vietnam (Roughneen, 2011).

Military spending in China has increased in line with its economic growth, and many defence analysts argue that China's real military expenditure exceeds its official military budgets (Buckley, 2012). Naval investment receives more than a third of the official military budget in China, and the South China Sea is the main priority for the People's Liberation Army Navy, the name given to China's naval forces (Richardson, 2010). With two aircraft carriers planned to be in place by 2015, the Chinese navy represents a potent force, able to challenge the United States (Richardson, 2010).

Despite the obvious economic power and influence that control over the South China Sea could give the Chinese government, Kaplan (2011b) argues that there is a simpler but deeper motivation, nationalism: 'The South China Sea is an obvious arena for the projection of Chinese power.' Beijing has referred to the South China Sea as a core national interest. This terminology has been used with regard to Taiwan and Tibet in previous years and essentially means that China has interests that it will enthusiastically protect (Kurlantzick, 2010). The feeling amongst many in China is that the South China Sea, like Taiwan, was taken away when China was weaker (Richardson, 2010) and the time may come when China wishes to reassert what it sees as its rightful ownership.

Such developments have not gone unnoticed by China's rivals: Vietnam, Indonesia, Singapore and Malaysia have all greatly increased defence expenditure (Defence Intelligence Organisation, 2010). The potential unease surrounding the ambitions of China has raised concerns amongst Western states and Western-allied states too; Australia's military expenditure has increased amidst such fears. Furthermore, US marines have been permanently deployed in Northern Australia and the United States' use of naval ports in Australia has also been expanded. In fact, the United States has had a presence in the South China Sea for 60 years and people in many of the states which occupy the area have regarded the United States as an entity that has the ability to tame the ambitions of China and act as a potential defence screen (Kurlantzick, 2010).

The South China Sea could well prove to be a test case. National interests and old-fashioned hard-edged power may eclipse diplomacy as the deciding factors in how the South China Sea is treated: 'The balance of power itself, even more than the democratic values of the West, is often the best safeguard of freedom' (Kaplan, 2011b).

A problem with the basic staple of life?

Water is a resource, which is a natural necessity, but it is also difficult to manage, which is why it may divide the world. Brazil, India, China and even the United States have all faced difficulties in dealing with water: drought, flooding and lack of sanitation have all become concerns of a commodity that many take for granted and industrialisation is tapping underground water supplies at an alarming rate (Richardson, 2012).

The political friction surrounding water may become a real issue as the effects of climate change continue to escalate. Many water transportation networks travel across national boundaries and political disputes could erupt:

> Played wrong, trans-boundary water – or unequal water resources – can be a source of mutual anxiety and tension. While the concept of 'water wars' may be overdone, national security sensitivities over water are acute.
>
> (Emmerson, 2011)

Water, an essential aspect of life may become a flashpoint.

The governments of both India and Pakistan are facing each other when it comes to water, a commodity which is set to become more crucial to development amongst the emerging economies. To support its expected growth, India has planned to undertake numerous hydroelectric power projects on rivers that cross into Pakistan. These water sources irrigate 80% of Pakistan's agricultural land. The rivers concerned also help power half of Pakistan's hydroelectric power capabilities (Desai & Kuusito, 2010). The fear from within the Pakistani border is that India's control over these rivers could be used to instigate a flood or drought. Such possibilities would have catastrophic effects on Pakistan's economy and severely damage hopes of its own economic progression.

Issues of water, rivers and power also come into play when we consider relationships between India and another neighbour, China. It is estimated that the amount of water annually produced in and around the Himalayas is set to decline by almost 275 billion cubic metres (Strategic Foresight Group, 2010). The main reasons for this are water usage in agricultural projects in China, India, Nepal and Bangladesh as well as declining levels of rainfall. This would directly concern, not only India and China, but also Nepal and Bangladesh. Water scarcity and the subsequent effects it would have on food availability are estimated to give rise to the migration of 50 to 70 million people in the four states (Strategic Foresight Group, 2010). China has expressed a desire to build a dam of epic proportions, which effectively diverts water flow from the transboundary Brahmaputra River away from India and towards the north of China. As Chellany (2011) notes, China now has over half of the world's 50,000 large dams and is fast emerging as a 'hydro-hegemon with no modern historical parallel', a position that could well have ramifications for all of China's neighbours.

Rare earths and persuasion

One of China's strengths is that it owns a dominant monopoly on the production of rare earths. Rare earths are used in the manufacturing of a wide range of electrical equipment, from mobile phones and tablet PCs to hi-tech missiles and components in nuclear power stations (BBC News Business, 2012). Demand for such materials has obviously risen dramatically. As demand has risen, China has continued to tighten its grip and limit supply. The notable danger is that shortages may ensue, affecting developments in technology outside China, which produces 97% of these resources (BBC News World, 2012). The reality would be that as demand for products that are made from rare earths expands, prices for products like mobile phones and LCD screens could skyrocket, having a devastating effect on already fragile Western consumer markets. In light of this, the United States, Japan and the European Union filed a complaint to the World Trade Organisation (WTO) that China has been illegally restricting exports of rare earth metals and asked for the WTO to reprimand China (Foley, 2012). The dispute over rare earths is all the more fascinating, as it represents the collision of the free-market economies and a rising China. By deliberately creating a scarcity of these materials, China would effectively corner international manufacturers and make them move their production to its shores (Foley, 2012). 'We want our companies to build those products, here in America' (Obama, 2012) was the manner in which President Obama expressed the United States' attitude.

The rare earths issue illustrates another emerging problem, the use of resources as tools of persuasion. This is a very real issue and events have already unfolded, which emphasise this. In September 2010, China cut off its supply of rare earths to Japan, when tensions erupted in the East China Sea, which borders on the South China Sea (Bradsher, 2010). Rare earths are naturally an essential ingredient for Japan's economy: just as one example, rare earths are used in the electric motors of the Toyota Prius (Gillis, 2010).

Management and resolution

Both the old and the new worlds face challenges, albeit of a different kind. These challenges present subtly different threats to both worlds too.

For the old, advanced economies, the challenge is a race to restructure economies, to reduce reliance upon the more volatile sectors of a services-based economy, to build tangible exports and to overcome a dangerous spectre of long-term unemployment, particularly youth unemployment. Failure to meet this challenge brings the threats of political instability, extremism and protectionism.

But the emerged and the emerging economies have their challenges and their threats too. It cannot be taken for granted that their growth will continue and be the engine of a prolonged global economic recovery.

We have used Asia as our focal point in this brief analysis. As Emmott clearly points out, 'Asia's rivalries are bitter and are keenly felt, for both historical and strategic reasons' (Emmott, 2009). Much now depends upon how these rivalries are managed and resolved. We have tried to illustrate a few of the potential flashpoints, firstly looking at territorial issues, including of course the contentious problem of the South China Sea. There are many other geographic flashpoints including the future of Afghanistan when NATO withdraws. If Afghanistan destabilises, will that destabilisation spread to Pakistan and beyond?

Asia also faces a resource challenge and the biggest test may come over ownership and distribution of that most basic of staples of human life, water.

Reflection points

In many scenarios, the issue of resilience raises its head as a major strategic issue for debate. This debate can embrace at least:

1. The loss of a market, if economic warfare breaks out.
2. The robustness of globally stretched value chains.

Additional reading

For discussion of Asia's challenges, try:

Bardhan, P., 2010. *Awakening Giants, Feet of Clay: Assessing the economic rise of China and India*, Princeton: Princeton University Press

Emmott, B., 2009. *Rivals: How the power struggle between China, India and Japan will shape the next decade*, London: Penguin.

9
The Long Test

Into practice

The purpose of this book is to provide approaches and ideas that will help readers to develop their own views of the opportunities and challenges that a world in transition brings. This final chapter will not therefore recommend one view or future scenario. Constructing a forward-looking perspective is, like the whole process of strategy making, a very personal matter, something that should be shared with and crafted at least by the key decision makers in any organisation. Building views of the future creates many strategic benefits. Reading other people's scenarios or views of the future can be helpful, but deeply held assumptions are challenged, minds are changed and innovation appears as we develop these forward-looking pictures for ourselves.

In this final chapter, we will explore a process that can be used to craft forward-looking views of a world in transition. We will use both the approaches introduced in Chapters 2–5, and the debates presented in Chapters 6–8. The process that we will use, and that readers are encouraged to apply, takes the form of the following four steps, which are summarised in Figure 9.1:

Step 1: Deep assumptions or deep pitfalls? In Chapter 2 we introduced the nine deep assumptions that are infrequently debated but have a strong subliminal influence on our decisions. We will revisit these in the light of the observations made in earlier chapters and debate whether or not acceptance of such deep assumptions could be the biggest mistake that one could ever make when thinking about a world in transition.

Step 1: Deep assumptions or deep pitfalls?
- Assumptions born in a period of unipolarity may now be flawed.
- Testing deep assumptions challenges the 'mental maps' that stop us seeing a new emerging world.
- The process of testing deep assumptions helps to build a cohesive top team with a common focus.

Step 2: Looking forward
- Identifying the key actors.
- The liberal order – support or dissonance? How will actors' views change?
- Who will be the dominant actors? State elites, market elites or social movements?
- Unity? Fragmentation? Conflict?

Step 3: Rethinking globalisation
- Economic wealth or human values?
- Unity or diversity?
- Globalisation as a journey to unity through fragmentation?

Step 4: Revisiting strategy
- Stakeholders or shareholders?
- Short-term or long-term?
- Cost leadership and technology versus technology and people?
- Options in an uncertain world?

Figure 9.1 Developing a future view: The process

Step 2: Looking forward. The power maps, the dissonance matrix and the 21st-century quadrilemma developed in Chapters 3–5 will all be applied to develop two possible outlooks for our world in transition.

Step 3: Rethinking globalisation. This third step in the process is to rethink what 'globalisation' is all about. In earlier chapters, we presented two descriptions of globalisation that reflected popular Western views of what globalisation is, how it works and, of course, the perceived benefits. Now is the time to revisit these definitions. Perhaps we have to think of globalisation from new perspectives to better understand the future.

Step 4: Revisiting strategy. If our assumptions change, new sources of influence appear and the purpose of globalisation shifts, then every organisation must revisit its strategy, how it gains competitive advantage in its marketplaces. To explore how strategy may evolve in a new transitioning world, we will revisit the fictional insurance organisation that we introduced in Chapter 2, and examine the reaction of its leaders.

The process, ideas and approaches described here can be used by any organisation, large or small to think about the future. A resources section is included at the end of the chapter to help readers do just this.

Step 1: Deep assumptions or deep pitfalls?

Chapter 2 introduced nine deep assumptions that are frequently taken as 'fact'. Of course they are fact, aren't they? It is almost too embarrassing to raise them for debate at a management meeting. But it is important to spend time, a long time, looking at these deep assumptions. They were, after all, formed in a world that has passed. That world was very different to the one that we now stand in and the worlds that lie ahead of us.

All may not therefore be as it would appear. We must not let our assumptions, our perceptions and 'mental maps' get in the way of seeing a new, unfolding reality.

It is impossible therefore to start to constructively think about a world in transition without a debate that challenges deep assumptions. Such a debate must distil fact and opinion, grounded in constructive discussion, from a mirage of convenient dreams or outdated rules. The results of this distillation process may not be totally benign, but it is better to face up to the unpleasant rather than ignore it. There are two other by-products of this process. The first is the puncturing of the 'artificial bubbles' we referred to in Chapter 2. The second is the construction of the cohesive, change-focused top-level management team that is a prerequisite for success in uncertain times.

We will now revisit each of the nine assumptions here and reflect upon them. Many of the conclusions presented may be found to be provocative. They are designed to be so, to encourage debate and reflection.

Deep assumption 1: The state-centric world

> The world will always consist of a network of states or countries. Looking at the world in this manner and judging the importance of each state by the size of its economy and economic growth rate, is the best way of seeing the future world.

This may look like an obvious statement, but it provides a misleading vantage point from which to view the future. It hides the real forces, or more correctly actors, who will be the most influential architects in any future world.

There is far more to the era of transition than the mere consideration of the effect of a decline in the relative dominance of the United States' power, be that power measured by economic growth projections or in terms of military spending. There may be some comfort in looking at the future in this way, because this vantage point can infer that the future, at least for the next decade or so, will be very much like the past. There will be nothing too much to fear. Things will carry on as they have always done. Economies will continue to enjoy steady growth. The system will remain intact. The broad shape of the world stays the same.

But this misses the crux of the matter. There are other interests at work, interests that have been unintentionally empowered, as our engine of globalisation has grown and gathered pace.

The central point is that, almost unwittingly, globalisation has unleashed an assault upon the state's or, more correctly, the state's ruling elite's powers of self-determination. This has exposed the state and its leaders to an attack from two different camps, social movements on the one hand and market elites on the other.

State elites now find themselves at a critical junction.

The signpost at this junction points two ways.

In one direction, the signpost points towards the cession or sharing of power. Following this route is not simple, as there is another immediate fork in the road ahead if we take this direction. The most difficult choice for states, or their successors, post-state elites, will be who to share power and influence with? For many, and particularly the old states of the West, one choice is the renewal of a long

158 *The Era of Global Transition*

relationship with the market elites. But the problem is that the legitimacy of the market elites may have been fatally flawed during the Great Recession and its prolonged aftermath. The only alternative partners for power sharing are the 'new kids on the block', social movements. Many may dismiss social movements, as they have yet to articulate 'a better way'. But possibly all they need is a little more time. Or another recession.

If we stop walking down this road of power sharing and turn around, we remember that the signpost pointed in another direction. We walk up to the signpost. The writing on the sign is old and faded, but we can just make out the word 'nationalism'. This path forces us to abandon the dream of a unified world and takes us back into the past, a world where states (or blocs of states or networks of cities, for example) maintain a tight, dominant grip on power. After all, this is not the first time that globalisation has come to an abrupt halt. Its last efforts foundered in the early 20th century.

These are the very broad choices that our 21st-century quadrilemma sets out. There are three broad families or groups of worlds that await us as we show in Figure 9.2. Firstly, is a world of material gain and growth, or a return to the world before the

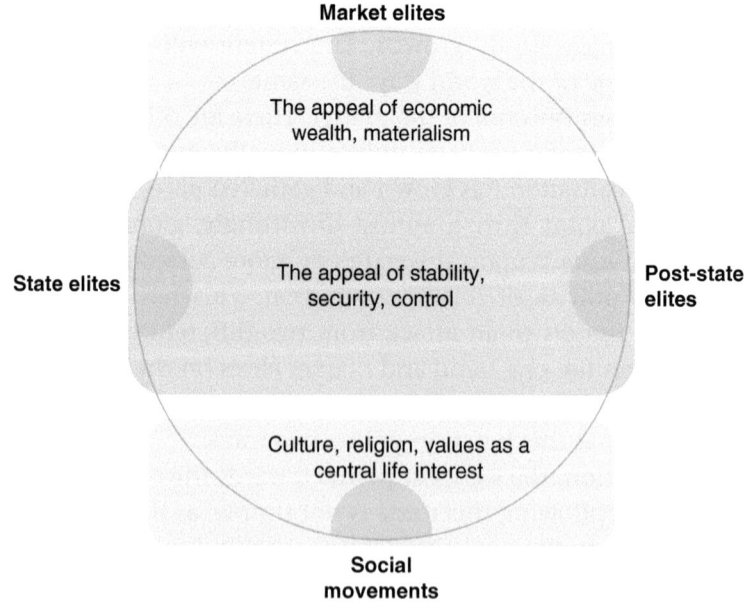

Figure 9.2 Future choices: Which world or worlds?

Great Recession. Secondly, is a world where stability is valued above everything else and where power is tightly held by state elites or post-state elites. This is a world of nationalism, or even regionalism. Finally, we have a world where, arguably, spiritual growth is valued above material growth.

Who will win in this three-way competition? Who will be the most powerful?

The powerful will be those who have acquired the smart power to alter 'the way things are done', just as the United States flexed its muscles after the Second World War to craft the liberal order.

And of course, in today's and tomorrow's world, it is not just states and their elites who can wield smart power.

Instead of seeing the future in terms of states and GDP trend lines, the best way of conceptualising the era of transition is to think that the end of a unipolar world has opened the door to a struggle, not just between states and their leaders, but between four groups of actors. The challenge is to see which voices will win through and where, in the quadrilemma, we will travel to.

Deep assumption 2: An unstoppable force

> Globalisation is an unstoppable force, driven increasingly by technology.

This is a frequently heard argument. Globalisation is just unstoppable. After all, surely everything that has been invested in trying to tie the world together over the last three decades, from the Internet to globally stretched value chains, cannot be undone? That would take decades, it is unthinkable.

The sorry truth is it can be undone and undone very quickly. There have been other failed attempts at globalisation. It is worth remembering that globalisation's last collapse, in the early 20th century, was destroyed by a determination, or belief, that the forces of globalisation should serve business, not people and societies (Jones, 2008). Could history be repeating itself?

Much depends on economic progress, or lack of such progress, over the coming decade. Lack of progress will, in all probability, spell the end of the rule of economically rational decision making. Power and influence will ebb away from the market elites. This is why the concept of capitalism's and the liberal order's long test, introduced earlier, is so important. If the world faces a second recession in a decade, or if a recovery, particularly in the old economies of the West, is truncated and is both socially and geographically inconsistent, then the seductive pull of protectionism will be all too difficult to resist. Electorates will demand such a route. The doors may also open to the extremists. This is why the next decade, the decade of the long test, is so important.

A very likely outcome, of failure to pass the long test, is that what we will face is not traditional military confrontation, but economic warfare in the form of 'beggar thy neighbour' 1930s-style protectionism. This will make the US–China 'Tyres and Chicken Feet' spat of 2009–2010 (Dyer & Braithwaite, 2009; Dyer, 2010) and Brazil's attempts to defend its manufacturing sector (Pearson, 2012) look like the mere ranging shots that precede a fully fledged artillery barrage.

Everything hangs on the outcome of the long test and everything can be undone.

Deep assumption 3: Wealth for all

> Globalisation will bring wealth, and a reasonably fair distribution of that wealth, for all.

There is no doubt that globalisation, or the seven pillars of the liberal order, has brought millions out of poverty. That progress is irrefutable. There are, however, two major problems. The first is that there is an alternative approach to the liberal order that too has plucked many from poverty. This of course is the 'China Model' or the 'Beijing Consensus', reviewed in Chapter 7. The second problem is that there are at least perceptions that the liberal order, particularly in its late 20th-century neo-liberal form, has not done a particularly good job at distributing wealth, and more importantly in creating jobs for the less well educated, not even in its homeland, the United States (Dewan, 2008; Gapper, 2012; Jacobs, 2012).

The perceived equitable distribution of wealth is therefore part of capitalism's and the liberal order's long test too.

Deep assumption 4: The universal appeal of democracy

> Everyone wants to live in a democracy.

Well, in the best of times the answer is an unequivocal 'yes'. But in the worst of times, this may not be the case. People in economically challenging and uncertain times may well opt for a strong leader or, using the language of Chapter 6, a 'kind despot'.

There are three associated issues that we need to consider as well. Firstly, the role of economic growth as a driver of democracy. It sounds a common sense statement that surely as people get wealthier they will demand democracy. Research would tend to support this, but with one major caveat. It takes a long time for economic growth to have such a democratising effect. An economically driven, peaceful transition to democracy should be measured in many decades; it is by no means an instantaneous process. The second reservation is an associated point. The transition from 'despotism', or autocracy, to democracy is a long, tough, challenging and frequently violent road. Anything faster than a slow, progressive transition could have disastrous global implications, especially when we consider the position of China as the world's second (and maybe by 2030, first) ranking superpower, and of course its now pivotal role as the world's workshop. A collapse of the world's workshop would have catastrophic implications.

Finally, we must remember that the road to democracy is not a one-way street. Democracies can 'backslide' too into autocracies. It might be easier for democracy to lose its legitimacy than we think.

Again, much hangs upon the long test.

Deep assumption 5: Universal values

> As wealth rises, so will secularism. We will forget old cultures and beliefs and adopt the same universal, largely western values. The importance of religion will fade away as globalisation marches on.

There is a wealth of research that would tell us that this is not the case. In fact, the Great Recession has, if anything, fuelled a counter-argument. The cold reality is that this is an argument that is convenient for those who support life at the top of our quadrilemma. It may not be convenient for anyone else.

In common with democracy, if this argument does hold, then any transition away from old cultures and beliefs will take many decades and of course, if the economic going gets tough, then there is always the possibility of 'backsliding'.

Deep assumption 6: Consumerism

> Everyone wants to be a consumer.

Undoubtedly, we do all want a more comfortable existence. But everyone is different. Will we all want luxury watches? How well does this assumption fit within a world with finite resources? If we all do want to be consumers, how long will the transition take and what happens if growth slows? What will fill the vacuum left by consumerism?

This assumption is closely linked to the issue of the economic growth fuelling democracy. We must be careful not to underestimate the time needed for old habits to change.

Deep assumption 7: Perpetual peace

> We have reached the end of an era of conflict. There will be no more major state versus state conflicts. Prosperity and democracy will bring peace.

If global economic growth recovers and mature decisions are made when the world faces up to future resource shortages, then we might *just* get away with this one. It is worth remembering that when the concept of 'democratic peace' emerged, seven critical assumptions were made:

1. A 'security community' of 'great powers' (the United States, Western Europe and Japan) exists. War between members of the community is unthinkable.
2. This community is at the forefront of technological and economic innovation.
3. No other states will achieve this technological and economic position.
4. There will be no viable alternative to the liberal order. Therefore, there will not be another struggle for dominance.
5. Values have shifted away permanently, from a focus on nationalism and violence, towards concern for the welfare of others.
6. The territorial claims of states are now less important than they have been in the past.

7. The 'security community' acts as an example to other states, 'peacefulness' will therefore continue to spread.

When we look at this list, we can see the most sobering outcome or by-product of the Great Recession. Each assumption now looks highly questionable. The 'security community' is in at least medium-term economic decline, its reputation as an exemplar is rather tarnished. Others are taking a technological lead, some noting a rapid increase in China's capacity to innovate (Huang, 2010). There is at least one apparently viable alternative to the liberal order, nationalism may be appearing again on the horizon (Ferguson, 2011, holds that nationalism has 'gone viral' in China) and territorial issues may rise to the fore as resources become increasingly scarce (as an example of what might happen, see The Resource Wars of Tomorrow, 2010).

Deep assumption 8: Asia as the engine of growth

> In the medium term, Asia will drive the next round of consumer-fuelled growth. This growth in turn will fuel a sustained global recovery.

As we have seen, Asia is not unlike the rest of the world. It has its own challenges, mixed within a complex web of historic rivalries, resource competition and the need to maintain both growth and political stability. Is it just too much to expect that populations in rising economies will undertake an almost overnight metamorphosis to save the West?

Deep assumption 9: Innovation-fuelled growth

> We will innovate and find solutions to resource, energy and environmental concerns.

We probably will. Our capacity to innovate should not be underestimated and a notable example from the early years of the second decade of the 21st century is the discovery of vast shale gas deposits (Crooks, 2011).

The only uncertainty is how freely the fruits of new found innovations will be shared.

So, in a world in transition, assumptions can be dangerous things. The conclusions in respect of each of the nine deep assumptions are summarised in Table 9.1.

Table 9.1 Deep assumptions – The verdict

Deep assumptions	Verdict
1. The State-Centric World	Viewing the world as a network of states, with power defined in economic and military terms, is very much a 20th-century position. It is blind to powerful new actors who can rival states and use both soft and smart power to achieve their objectives.
2. Globalisation as an Unstoppable Force	Globalisation has failed before. The perception that globalisation benefits business as opposed to society could bring globalisation's current advances to a halt.
3. Wealth For All	The liberal order and capitalism (the 'Washington Consensus') have to prove, even in the United States, that they are efficient creators and distributors of wealth. The same criticism applies to the 'Beijing Consensus'.
4. Universal Appeal of Democracy	In a crisis, strong leadership may be valued more highly than democracy. In addition, the transition to democracy is a dangerous and elongated process. Democracies can lose legitimacy and 'backslide' into autocracy.
5. Emergence of Universal Values	Unlikely in at least the medium term. We are now faced with a 'clash of two globalisations'. One favours the development of universal values, the other the celebration of historic cultural identities.
6. Consumerism	It is unlikely that citizens across the world will transform themselves into Western consumers overnight. Like democracy, the transition, if it does occur, will take time.
7. Perpetual Peace	This is the proposition that democracies will not fight each other. Although most, if not all, of the assumptions underpinning this popular late 20th-century theory have disappeared, we can hope that the world has matured enough to avoid major conflict between powerful states. Economic warfare remains a distinct possibility.

8. Asia as an Engine of Growth	Quite possibly, but Asia's challenges, in terms of rivalries, resource competition and political stability, must not be ignored.
9. Innovation-Fuelled Growth	Our capacity to innovate must not be underestimated. Shale gas extraction is a recent example of how energy worries can be overcome. But the question is how widely will the fruits of innovation be shared?

Step 2: Looking forward

In this section, we will use power maps, the dissonance matrix and the 21st-century quadrilemma to chart potential future pathways. We will do this by looking at two different sets of outcomes for the long test. The first assumes that capitalism and the liberal order pass the long test. The second outcome looks at a bumpier, more challenging road ahead.

Outcome 1: Passing the long test

'Passing the long test' includes these expectations:

- In general, the old economies of the West enjoy a sustained recovery.
- No further significant economic disturbances occur. There is no repeat of the Great Recession.
- The world returns to a period of consistent economic growth averaging, in real terms, over 3% per annum.

A quick glance through these expectations will probably bring a sigh of relief to many readers. Superficially, these appear to be signposts to life as it was before the Great Recession and a rubber stamp ratification of the liberal order.

A closer inspection may prove otherwise, especially if we look at the possible reactions of all actors. There are many great opportunities in this outlook, but the picture might not be quite so straightforward as one would initially imagine.

Figure 9.3 provides us with an overview of who the leading states are and how their position could change during the period 2010–2030, using the more conventional power maps that we introduced in Chapter 3. The illustrations in Figure 9.3 focus upon the G8 states, or by GDP, the top eight states in the world in each year of analysis. In these power maps, we combine growth rates, relative economic size and military spending to give a

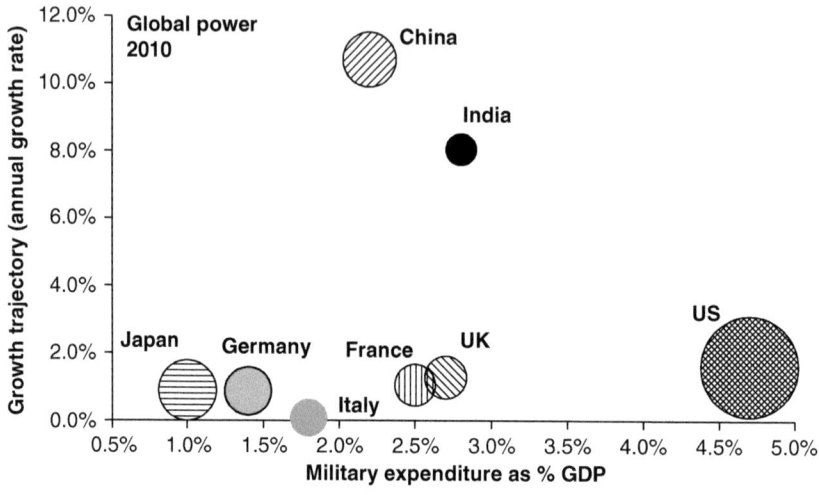

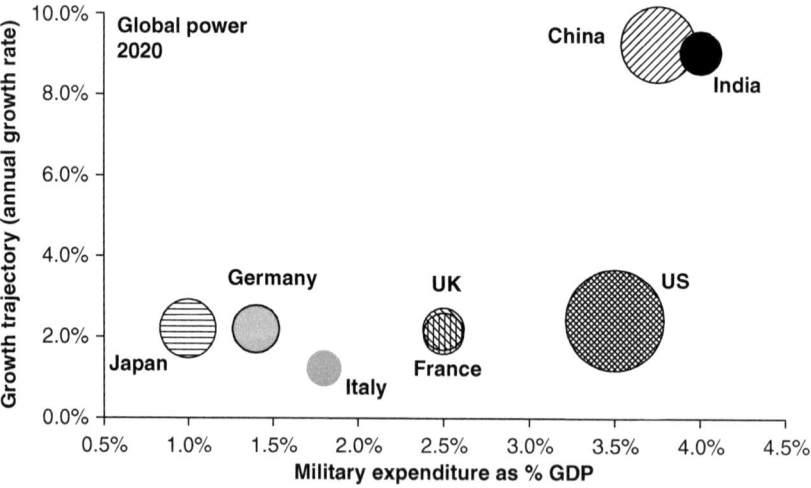

Figure 9.3 Passing the long test: Power maps (2010–2030)

Notes: Real GDP calculated at 2005 US$ values. With the exception of China, India and Brazil, military spending is assumed to decline due to sovereign debt pressure.
Sources: Historic GDP – the United Nations. Historic military spending information from the Stockholm International Peace Research Institute (SIPRI) http://www.sipri.org/databases/milex. Other projections – the Author.

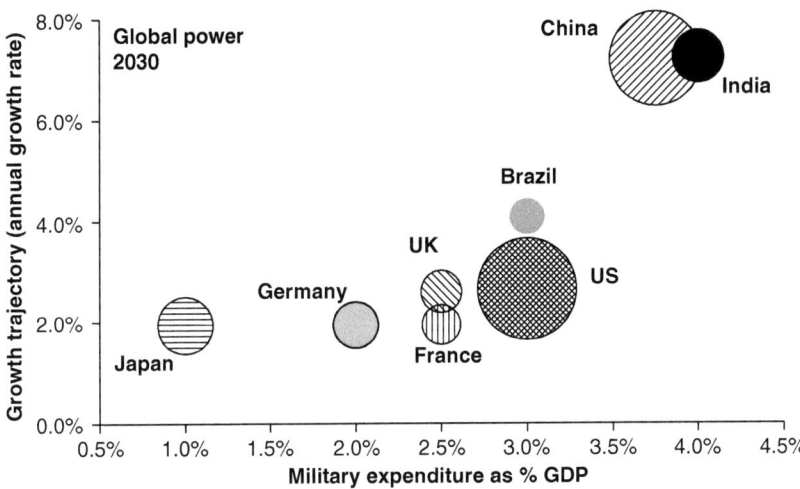

Figure 9.3 (Continued)

view of who holds 'hard-edged' power. Looking at these maps, 'growth trajectory', tells us where these states may be going in the future in terms of economic growth. This is shown on the vertical axis, as the compound annual growth rate over the preceding decade. A measure of 'hard-edged' power, military spending, is presented along the horizontal axis. The bubbles in the power maps show the relative size of each economy in the year of analysis.

Figure 9.3, which shows power maps in 2010, 2020 and 2030, paints a predictable picture of two worlds. The old economies, led by the United States, appear fractured, laden down by slow growth and debt, both of which restrict military spending. The other new world is comparatively buoyant, led by China and India whose growing economies can support higher levels of military spending (for an example of this argument, see Hoyos & Hille, 2012). By 2020, the United States is increasingly isolated and the spectre of confrontation with a fast-growing, high-spending China emerges. By 2030, domination appears complete and the United States seems to be on a journey to the bottom left of the power map to join other expiring empires.

But there is more to explore in this outlook than our rather conventional power maps reveal. We have to think about other forms of influence than just 'hard-edged', military or relational power. We have to consider the more relevant, 21st-century source of influence, smart power discussed in Chapter 3. Smart power is that cocktail of relational power, structural power (the ability to alter 'the way things are done', especially the management of the global political economy and its institutions) and, interestingly, soft power (getting the outcomes one wants without resorting to coercion or payment). Smart power does not appear in the power maps of Figure 9.3. These power maps also take a very Westphalian or statist view. We need, therefore, to include the three other groups of architects: the market elites, who were so influential in the three decades before the Great Recession, post-state elites and social movements, a group that may well emerge to take the place of market elites, as the formative architect of the future. Another big problem with the use of power maps is that we cannot see the characteristics of the transition paths that lie ahead. Critically, it is difficult to use these to predict conflict.

To include these observations and perspectives, we will use the dissonance matrix introduced in Chapter 5. Figure 9.4 summarises this rather different approach to looking at a future world and the points to look out for, especially if we want to try to see who may be a disruptive force in the future. Looking at Figure 9.4, on the vertical axis we have 'Dissonance', which encapsulates the key motivators for conflict that we examined in Chapter 5. In summary, the two key motivators for conflict are the following:

1. **The rules of the game.** Failure to recognise the legitimacy of the current rules of the game, the liberal order, will materially increase the likelihood of conflict. This is widely acknowledged in the literature. From the perspective of a state, if the rules of the game threaten access to critical resources or its powers of political, economic or social self-determination, then the risk of conflict increases dramatically. Access to natural resources may prove to be a critical flashpoint in future decades.
2. **Status competition.** This is where actors feel under-valued, or not fully recognised in the current order of things. If this is the case, they will be motivated to take action to correct the position.

These are the two factors that determine the positioning with reference to the vertical dissonance axis. As dissonance increases, so will the probability of conflict.

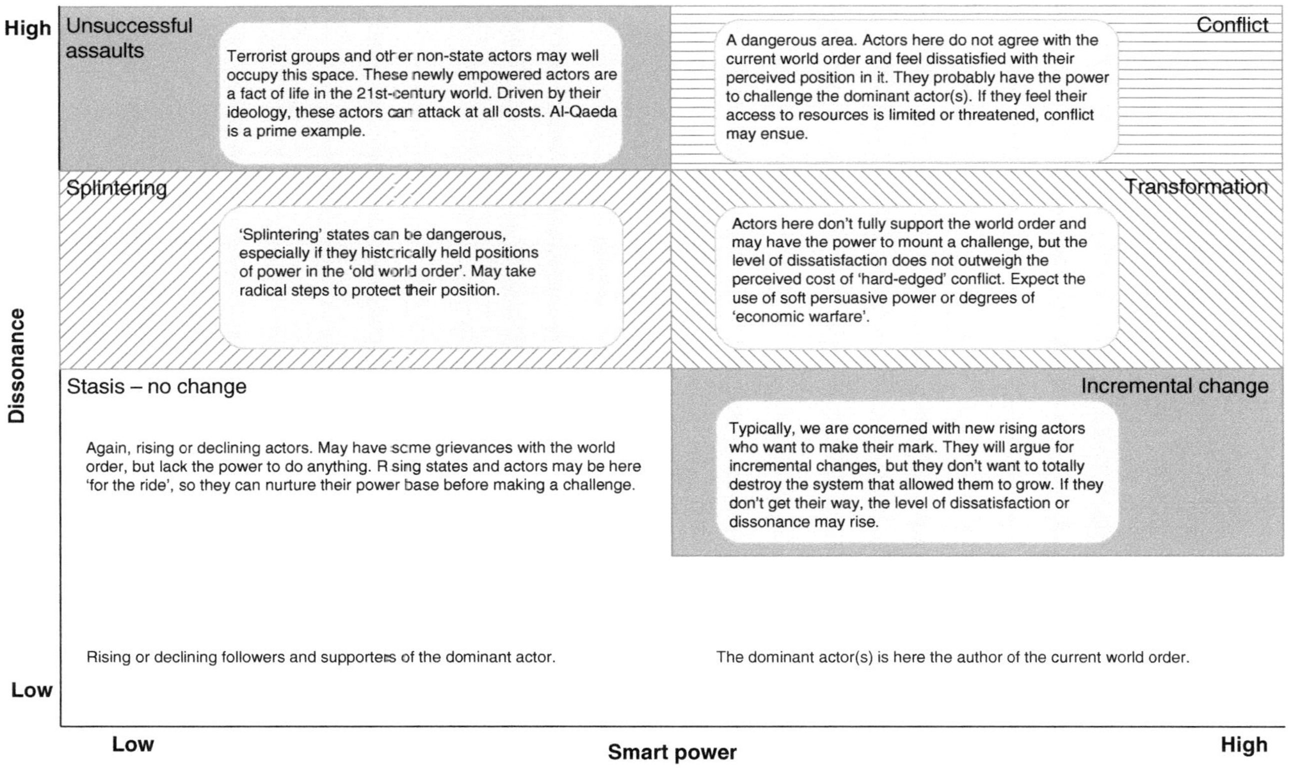

Figure 9.4 The dissonance matrix

Dissonance: High

- **Unsuccessful assaults** (Low smart power): Terrorist groups and other non-state actors may well occupy this space. These newly empowered actors are a fact of life in the 21st-century world. Driven by their ideology, these actors can attack at all costs. Al-Qaeda is a prime example.

- **Splintering** (Mid smart power): 'Splintering' states can be dangerous, especially if they historically held positions of power in the 'old world order'. May take radical steps to protect their position.

- **Conflict** (High smart power): A dangerous area. Actors here do not agree with the current world order and feel dissatisfied with their perceived position in it. They probably have the power to challenge the dominant actor(s). If they feel their access to resources is limited or threatened, conflict may ensue.

Dissonance: Mid

- **Transformation** (High smart power): Actors here don't fully support the world order and may have the power to mount a challenge, but the level of dissatisfaction does not outweigh the perceived cost of 'hard-edged' conflict. Expect the use of soft persuasive power or degrees of 'economic warfare'.

Dissonance: Low

- **Stasis – no change** (Low smart power): Again, rising or declining actors. May have some grievances with the world order, but lack the power to do anything. Rising states and actors may be here 'for the ride', so they can nurture their power base before making a challenge.

- Rising or declining followers and supporters of the dominant actor.

- **Incremental change** (High smart power): Typically, we are concerned with new rising actors who want to make their mark. They will argue for incremental changes, but they don't want to totally destroy the system that allowed them to grow. If they don't get their way, the level of dissatisfaction or dissonance may rise.

- The dominant actor(s) is here the author of the current world order.

Smart power: Low → High

The horizontal axis refers to power. We are not just concerned with 'hard-edged' relational power (as measured in Figure 9.3) but to *smart* power. Some states' capacity to use soft power in addition to military power (most notably China) will boost their position against the United States.

We can map the position of each actor who we think may be influential by judging both the degree of acceptance or rejection of the US liberal order, perceptions of status and the smart power the actor possesses. Where an actor is positioned in the dissonance matrix can give us clues as to the action that actor might take. It can be seen that Figure 9.4 is divided into six zones to help us conceptualise the characteristics of the transition paths that might lie ahead. These paths are as follows:

Stasis: There is no change to the current dominant world order. The liberal order continues to be broadly accepted. Those that may be mildly uncomfortable with its assumptions and methods do not have the power to mount a successful challenge.

Incremental change: Actors demand incremental adjustments to the liberal order. They want to put their 'stamp' on it. Challenging actors wish to avoid the costs of conflict; peaceful negotiation is their goal.

Transformation: One or more actors are dissatisfied with both the world order and their perceived status. Their power may approach or exceed that of the dominant actor (the United States). Challenging actors wish to avoid, in the first instance, conflict. If the dominant actor acquiesces, there will be no conflict. Negotiation is still the preferred route. In short, the level of dissonance does not justify the costs of conflict.

Conflict: The level of dissonance on the part of challenging actors is so high that they are prepared to risk the use of force to change the world order, that is if the dominant power offers resistance and fails to acquiesce.

Splintering: Actors are dissatisfied, but lack the power to mount a direct challenge. Actors may try to go their own way. 'Splintering states' that once held power and influence can be dangerous and may make radical moves to defend their dying position. This area can be a source of problems.

Unsuccessful assaults: Actors have major grievances with the world order, its principles and the recognition they receive. Actors may well overestimate their power. The level of dissonance drives a series of failed assaults. Al-Qaeda is an example of such an actor.

When interpreting the matrix it is worth bearing in mind the following points:

(a) When power gaps close, the likelihood of conflict increases.
(b) A reducing power gap is linked to perceptions of the cost of conflict. As the gap closes the costs reduce (especially for the aggressor). The dominant power (in the current context, the United States) faces a bigger cost burden as it has taken on the role of the world's policeman. This might put the dominant power at a disadvantage.
(c) When challenged, the dominant actor will resist, *if it believes it has the capability to do so.*
(d) Dying empires may be dangerous; they may act irrationally to defend their ground. This is why we have to watch 'splintering states'.

Although it is impossible to reduce pictures of complex future worlds and their flashpoints to one sheet of paper, this approach provides a foundation for thought, debate and reflection. Building dissonance matrices is well within the capacity of any organisation.

Figure 9.5 depicts one view of the world in 2020 based upon the assumptions underlying our first outlook, which are as follows:

- In general, the old economies of the West enjoy a sustained recovery.
- No further significant economic disturbances occur. There is no repeat of the Great Recession.
- The world returns to a period of consistent economic growth averaging, in real terms, over 3% per annum.

Although a superficial examination of global economic growth in this outlook, at an average of over 3% per annum, may indicate a return to the halcyon days before the Great Recession, a deeper analysis, reflecting upon who are the actors that will shape the world, their access to smart power and their satisfaction with the liberal order, presents a very different picture, one with great opportunities, but some challenges.

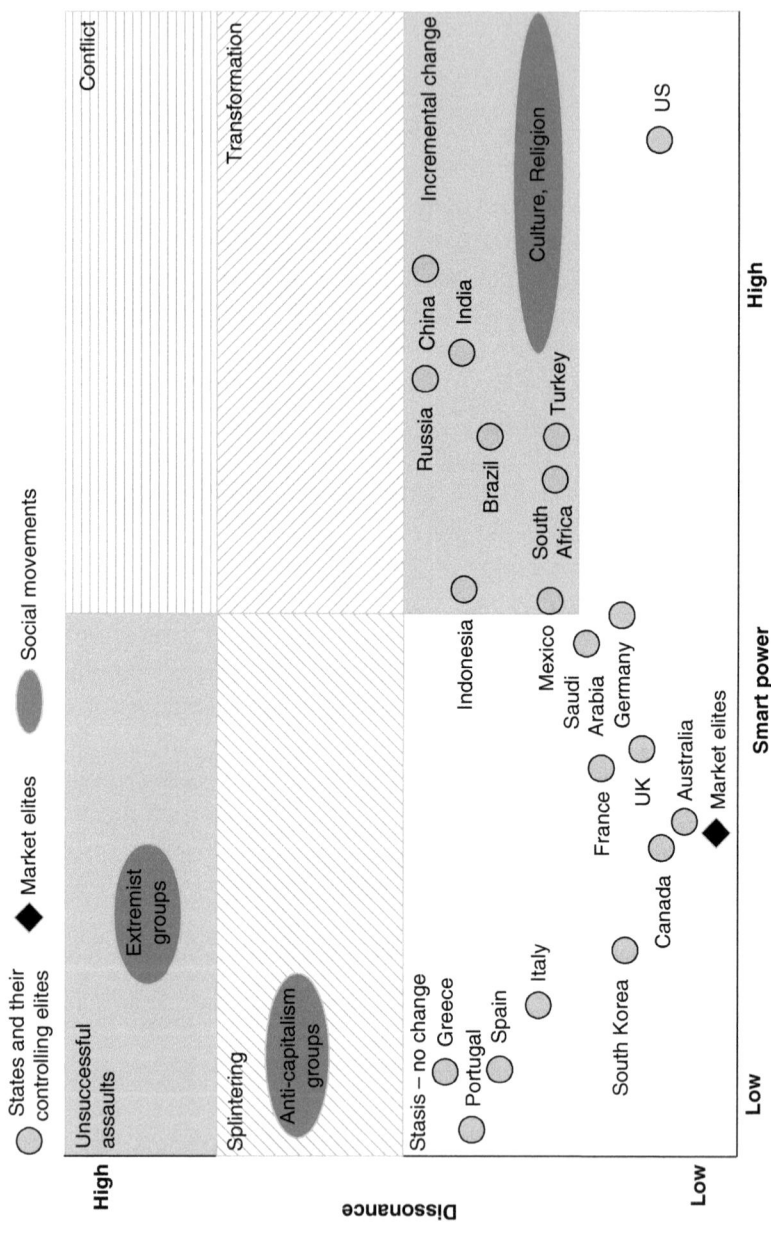

Figure 9.5 Dissonance and smart power 2020 – Passing the long test
Source: The author

Figure 9.5 represents one interpretation of the world in 2020. We can make out not one unified world, but five different worlds, all existing in different degrees of harmony. The three groups of influential actors are included in Figure 9.5. These are state elites in the form of the 'G20' (the potential top 20 economies in 2020), market elites and social movements.

Along the bottom of Figure 9.5 in the area labelled *Stasis – no change*, we can see the United States with its old friends and allies, all of whom are in relative economic decline. This is the first of five worlds. We find here that the power of the market elites has been dented during the Great Recession and its aftermath, but they still enjoy a material degree of influence. Their challenge will be getting used to working with new masters in the second world. All the actors in this bottom area of Figure 9.5 continue to support the liberal order, so there will be no threats emanating from here.

Moving upwards in Figure 9.5 to *Incremental change*, we see a group of new, emerged states, their smart power buoyed by their relative economic success. This is the new, powerful, second world. The quest of those in this world is not revolutionary change, but recognition of newly found status, by taking the seats occupied by the old friends of the United States at the world's key institutions. These new emerged states want to proffer their own brands of re-engineered capitalism. They are joined by social movements, disturbed by the neo-liberal quest for materialism and universal values. But here we are concerned with incremental, negotiated change, not revolutionary change.

If we move upwards and left to the third of our worlds, we see that the anti-capitalist groups exist, but without the power to enforce their views. As in the earlier decades of the 21st century, the world still remains exposed to terrorist groups, located in the very top left section, in the fourth world, *Unsuccessful assaults*.

But there is a fifth world too, if we move down to the top left of the *Stasis – no change* area. These arguably are the real, lingering casualties of the Great Recession, the old economies of Europe that have endured a decade of recession and an elongated recovery.

In this analysis, the United States, China, possibly Russia too, are all winners to one degree or another. The United States maintains a sphere of influence; it has enough smart power to ensure that its voice is still heard across the globe and it could well take on the role of the 'wise old sage'. But it has to share influence with the real winners in China, and, possibly, Russia. China, especially in its capacity to attract and wield soft power, finds itself in a position that now approaches that of the United States. While an analysis of China's military capabilities indicates that it will probably still be no match for the United States in 2020 (Friedman, 2012), if we add in China's soft power base, the picture can change significantly. In this outlook, China basks in the light of a great victory. By securing another decade of growth, the 'China Model' has demonstrated its resilience; it is now an equal, if not a superior, model to the 'Washington Consensus'. But China wants stability, not full confrontation. So long as the United States (or another rising power) does not challenge the access to the resources that China needs for continued growth, all is well. China's objective in this scenario is not to replace the United States as the world's dominant power and policeman; it wants the ability to run its corner of the world its way, without interruption from anyone. And the same just may be true of Russia too.

This is not a world where capitalism is consigned to the recycling bin. It is a world where others want the right to run their own variations of capitalism. In the long term this is a unifying world too. The success of the 'China Model' provides a platform for a slow, controlled move to democratisation in China. This transition will be lengthy, if it is to be peaceful. One of the lessons from the past is that to avoid conflict and economic collapse, the path to democracy is not a short, sudden one, but a well-managed gradual transition.

We can also look at the world using the quadrilemma as shown in Figure 9.6, which shows a subtly different change in the locus of power and influence. In this story, the world does return to a form of the liberal order in future decades, but not without first a journey towards increasing authoritarianism and the control of the state. Over decades, increasing wealth drives the spread of democracy and the world returns to the liberal order. The arrow in Figure 9.6 represents the first part of this journey, where power shifts firmly to the state elites.

So what seems to be a benign world, one where the old ways would probably re-emerge, may not quite end up that way. The journey may be a little different to the one we had originally envisaged.

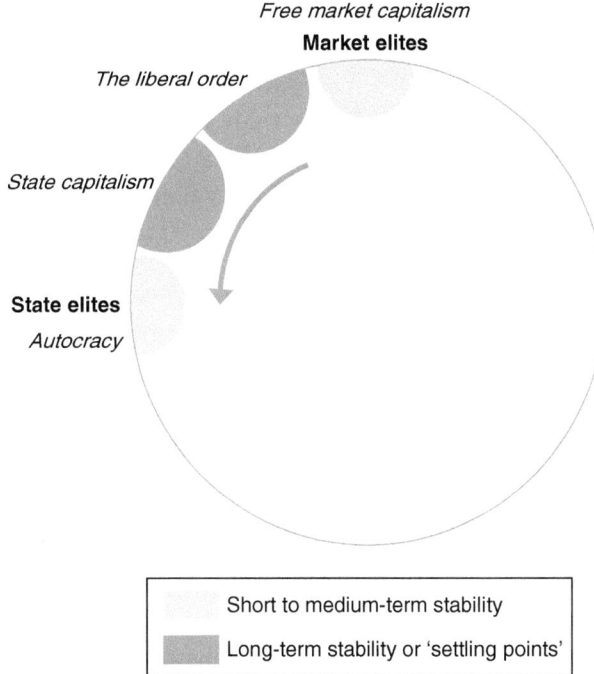

Figure 9.6 The year 2020 – A change in influence

But we have another road to explore, an equally plausible one, a road where the liberal order and capitalism stumble and fail the long test.

Outcome 2: The challenging road

In this outlook the expectations are as follows:

- The old economies of the West face a slow and inconsistent recovery after the Great Recession.
- An energy price spike triggers a global economic contraction commencing in 2017. The established economies enter a period of recession. China struggles, during this period, to maintain a 2% annual growth rate.
- The world then enters a long-term low-growth phase, growth averaging just over 2% per annum.

We start our exploration again with Figure 9.7 that uses the more conventional power maps to profile this alternative world.

176 The Era of Global Transition

Growth rates have slowed, but this world looks deceptively similar to the one we have just examined. But the gap between the United States and China appears to be visibly closing. In 2010, China's military spending was less than 10% of that of the United States. Now, in 2020, it stands at around 50%. Could China, in this outlook, be the great threat, tempted to challenge the United States,

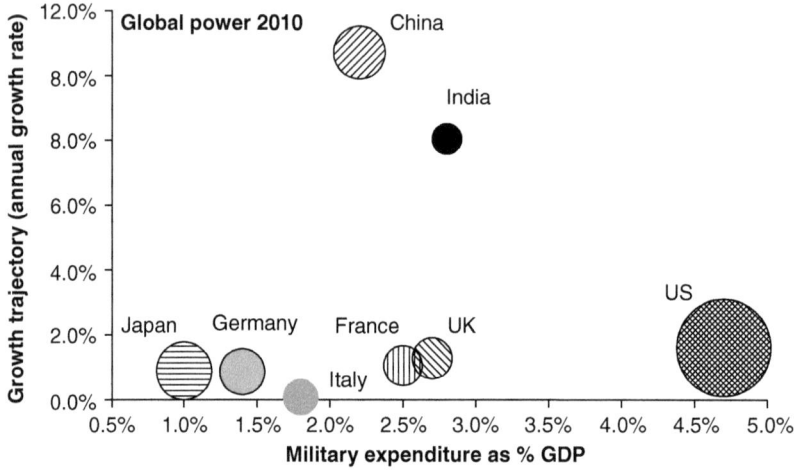

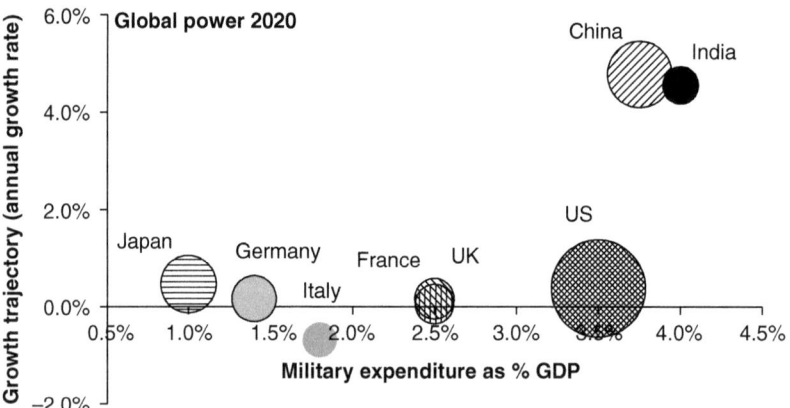

Figure 9.7 The challenging road – Failing the long test

Note: Real GDP calculated at 2005 US$ values. With the exception of China, Brazil and India, military spending assumed to decline due to sovereign debt and economic pressures.

Source: Historic GDP – UN. Historic military spending information from the Stockholm International Peace Research Institute (SIPRI) http://www.sipri.org/databases/milex. Other projections – the author.

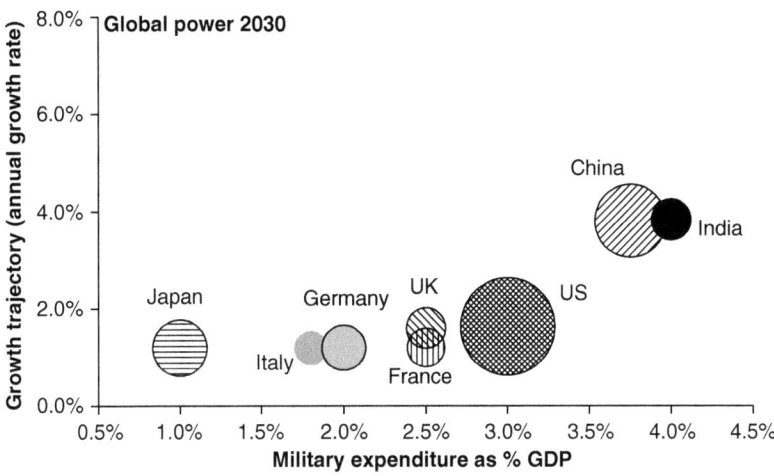

Figure 9.7 (Continued)

a state now further economically weakened by a second recession within a decade? To answer this question, we need to look more broadly. In the next illustration, Figure 9.8, we examine one possible interpretation of *The Challenging Road* using the dissonance matrix.

Figure 9.8 is one potential interpretation of this world and it carries with it the following messages:

- The second recession damages the power base of the United States, in terms of hard relational power, structural power and soft power. It struggles with the burden of economic contraction, unemployment, internal unrest and the costs of being the world's policeman. In common with many states in this outlook, thoughts turn to nationalism and isolationism.
- In terms of pure relational power, China has rapidly caught up with the United States and could easily overtake it. By 2020, its military spending will be half that of the United States. If we add China's soft power capabilities amongst the states that it has formed trade relationships with, then by 2020 China is in a position at least to defend what it sees to be its sphere of influence. This position will become unquestionable two decades later when China's military spending will have overtaken that of the United States.

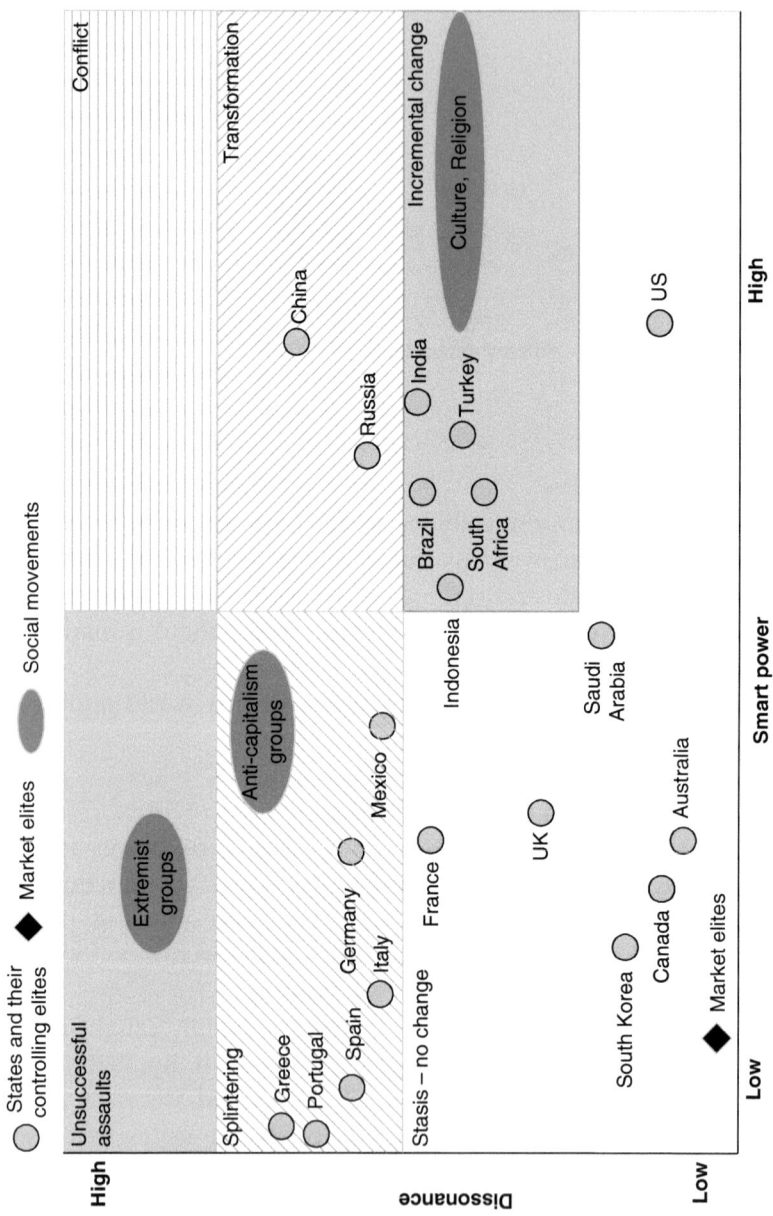

Figure 9.8 Dissonance and smart power 2020 – The challenging road
Source: The author

- Maintaining stability, security and access to resources (even water, especially in Asia Chellaney, 2011) are key issues. Access to resources is therefore again a potential source of major conflict.
- Human rights in this world focus upon security, not political freedom. Security is more important too, for some, than economically rational decision making.
- Those states that can, seek to establish their zones of stability and influence. China and Russia are best positioned to take this route. India and particularly Turkey may well too take this path. These states may have the support of influential social movements.
- Contrary to conventional thinking, a material dip in China's growth rate may not lead to internal instability, although this remains a point for debate. For the second time in a decade, it is one of the few major economies to avoid contraction while others have floundered. It will also have established a zone of influence that secures much of its thirst for resources. In relative terms, China might look like a safe place to be in this scenario.
- The influence of market elites has collapsed. This is a world where the state and emerging post-state elites are the dominant actors. By 2030, over 35% of the GDP generated by the then top 20 economies could come from those states that are sympathetic to more autocratic state capitalism.
- We can think of this as a world consisting of three distinct and gated segments. The first is led by the United States but with fewer friends. The second segment is made up of states trying to establish their own zones of stability and influence. Within these zones, it will be the post-state elites and social movements who are the dominant voices. The third segment consists of 'splintering states', typically the advanced economies of the past who have endured years of decline and austerity. It is within these states that we can expect more extreme reactions, experiments with the politics of the past, even communism.
- For businesses, this is a world where segments have to be selected carefully. This is a world of reactive, 'beggar they neighbour' economic warfare. Work in one segment and you may be unable to work in another.

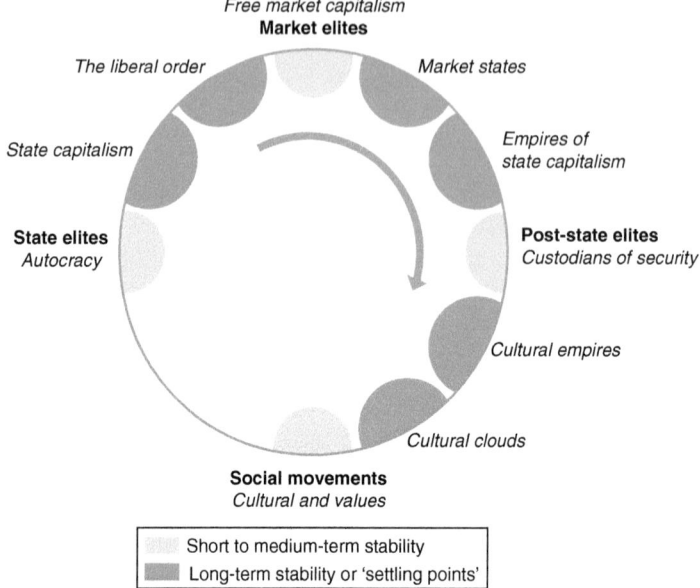

Figure 9.9 A shift of influence – Failing the long test

If we look at our 21st-century quadrilemma (as shown in Figure 9.9), this heralds a new world where social movements and post-state elites vie for control and influence. This is a world too where influence slips from the the familiar top-left of the quadrilemma to the right-hand side. It is a fractious world too, where extreme forms of organising could be explored.

Step 3: Rethinking globalisation

Over the course of this book, we have considered three definitions, or descriptions, of globalisation.

Two of these look at the unifying powers of globalisation and the promise of economic wealth that such unification can generate:

> Fundamentally it [globalisation] is the closer integration of the countries and peoples of the world which has been brought about by the enormous reduction of costs of transportation and communication, and the breaking down of artificial barriers to the flows of goods, services, capital, knowledge, and (to a lesser extent) people across borders.
>
> (Stiglitz, 2002, p. 9)

Globalization is helping to give birth to an economy that is closer to the classic theoretical model of capitalism, under which rational individuals pursue their interests in the light of perfect information, relatively free from government and geographic obstacles. It is also helping to create a society that is closer to the model that liberal political theorists once imagined, in which power lies increasingly in the hands of individuals rather than governments, and in which people are free, within reasonable bounds, to pursue the good life wherever they find it.

(Micklethwait & Wooldridge, 2001, pp. 341–342)

The first stresses integration, unity driven by increasing economic efficiency. Although the second emphasises empowered individuals, we are left with a picture of an economically rational world, driven by material wealth. Whilst these descriptions may have reflected, very accurately, the goals of many in the late 20th and early 21st centuries, these are perspectives that sit very comfortably in only one small segment of our 21st-century quadrilemma.

But we have also been presented with a third definition:

[G]lobalization means increasing diversity at the global level, and surpassing uniform and omni-focal identities.

(Khatami, 2010, p. 26)

This is the antithesis of the first two definitions. In this third perspective, we see a desire for the forces of globalisation to both encourage and value difference.

The best way of looking at the pathways of transition that lie ahead of us is to think that the bell may well have tolled, at the very least for the next decade, for the messages conveyed in the first two descriptions. If we are going to get anywhere peacefully, we have to realise that in any outlook or scenario, we must allow space for plurality and experimentation. The third description of globalisation wants to be heard and there may be trouble if it is stifled.

One of the most powerful by-products of globalisation has been empowerment. Individuals, our state and market elites and, of course, social movements will all want to experiment with their newly gained power. We need to allow this period of experimentation and plurality to run its course, before we can

182 *The Era of Global Transition*

return again to the task of unification. We should not therefore be surprised if we experience a period of disaggregation before we can attempt to unite around common goals.

Step 4: Revisiting strategy

Chapter 2 included a fictitious insurance company and we looked at their strategy for the future. The strategy and its underlying assumptions are summed up in the following illustration (Figure 9.10):

Figure 9.10 Stability–change: A view of the future

This is a strategy based on growth, stability and the emergence of the global consumer. It is also a strategy that sees the organisation as a machine that must maximise its economic efficiency in order to deliver value. The two central elements of the strategy were as follows:

(a) Ongoing relentless cost reduction driven by technology. Customer interaction moves from traditional face-to-face local offices to technology-driven web and mobile telephone contact routes. The expensive human element in processes had to be minimised.
(b) Real growth was to be found only in Asia and Africa as burgeoning middle classes appeared.

But how might this strategy change in the light of the journey through this book? The Chief Executive sets out the challenge to colleagues in the 'Memo to the Leadership Team' (see Figure 9.11).

In this memo the CEO makes these points:

(a) In view of levels of uncertainty regarding the course of 'the long test', portfolio resilience must be created. The organisation must be able to deal with a protectionist scenario, being locked out of one market previously targeted for growth. Here, the CEO is requesting that the organisation becomes 'shock proof'. This is a task for the concept of the 'stable organisation' that we introduced in Chapter 2.
(b) A 'new equation applies'. The CEO now wants to see how the organisation can make a more direct contribution to the markets or societies that it operates in. This is increased direct engagement, where both the societies and the organisation benefit and goes beyond traditional corporate social responsibility programmes. The CEO refers to this as 'human capital'. For more on this issue, see Porter & Kramer (2011).
(c) Three major areas for research, exploration and experimentation are identified. The first is the issue of how consumer demand will change in a low-growth world. The second is the 'power of closeness', getting closer to customers by blending new technology with more traditional customer contact channels. The final exploration area is the whole issue of building the 'new equation'.

> **Memo from the chief executive to the leadership group**
>
> 'It is clear from our forward-looking work that if we stick with our current strategy, we will only be fit to compete in yesterday's world. If we we don't change our ideas on what strategy really is and must deliver, we will be in trouble and very quickly. It is clear to me that we have to respond to these challenges:
>
> 1. Uncertainty. We cannot say with any confidence which of our markets will present the best long-term profit potential. In the course of the next five years, the new economies will face as many challenges as the old. For this reason, we need to keep a careful balance of opportunities in old and new markets alike.
>
> 2. The Portfolio. This leads me directly to our market portfolio. If we do face, for example, a protectionist war, then we could lose access to at least one market. I would like to see a market portfolio plan that is resilient in these circumstances.
>
> 3. Lower growth. In a low growth world we have to think about profitability in terms of year-on-year consistency rather than growth. The goal of consistency must drive change across the organisation, from our sales teams through to our remuneration packages. We also have to consider how consumer demand will change in a low growth world. What will we seek to protect if luxury goods fall out of vogue? This must be one of three areas for research and exploration.
>
> 4. The power of closeness. We need to continue our plans to base service delivery on mobile phone technology, but I am worried that in an uncertain and possibly autocratic world, this could leave us isolated and divorced from our customers. We need to consider how we blend this technology with a human interface. This is the second area for research and exploration. We need to blend new technology with our historic customer relationship capabilities.
>
> 5. The challenge of human capital. It is clear that the days are numbered for our cost leadership strategy. I am deeply worried that our plans to dramatically reduce costs still further through process virtualisation and outsourcing may count against us in many of our markets. In the scenarios we have developed, this type of action could, at best, be socially unacceptable. At worst, our offerings could be shunned. Costs, that is operating efficiently, will always be an important part of any organisation's strategy, but I would like to see your recommendations on how we can use other routes to differentiation, in addition to just lower costs and better offerings. We need to consider how we can engage our local markets more closely and deliver more than offerings and better service. We need to think beyond our current Corporate Social Responsibility plans. The challenge is, how do we help to directly develop human capital within each of the markets we operate in? This is the third area for research and exploration.
>
> 6. The new equation. The new equation sums up how strategy is changing. We use our markets to produce profit. That is one side of the equation, the old side. The other new side of the equation is how we can, in turn, add to the markets directly through our presence.
>
> I look forward to receiving your proposals to tackle each of these six key points.'

Figure 9.11 Memo to the leadership team

There are now only two deep assumptions. Not nine. The first assumption is that we are entering a period of plurality, not unification. The second is that above all stability and security will be valued above material gain. From these assumptions, the strategy shifts as shown in Figure 9.12.

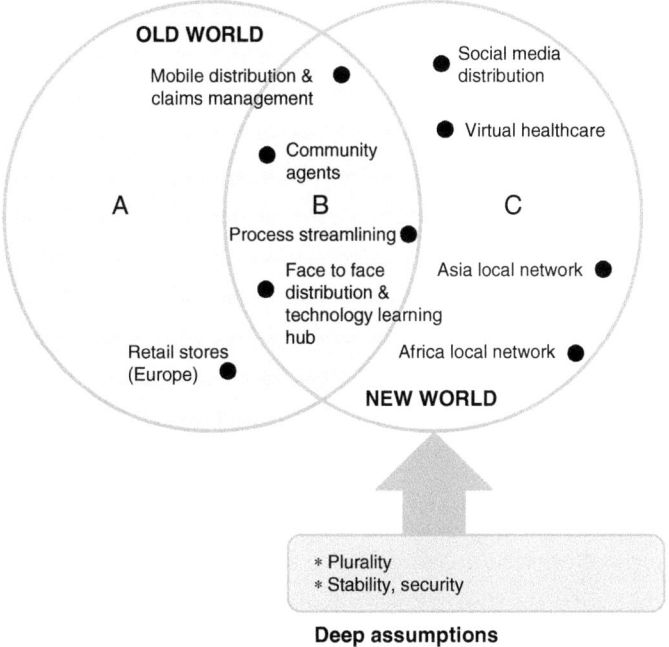

Figure 9.12 Stability–change: A second look

Firstly, this is not a time to consider quitting old markets and making bold assumptions about growth in new markets. Until capitalism and the liberal order have either passed or failed the long test it is impossible to make anything that would approach a confident prediction. Rather, this is a time to create a portfolio of potential market opportunities, knowing that some will succeed and others may fall by the wayside. In the worst scenario, if capitalism and the liberal order do fail the long test, it may be impossible to extract investments in some markets.

It is a time too to reflect on what drove the successes of the past and not to place reliance on one popular but hopeful trend. We have to confront the possibility that the world may well shift away, for a period of time, from democracy to autocracy. In a difficult, autocratic world, relying on Internet and particularly mobile technology as a marketing and distribution tool may create vulnerabilities. In a less confident world too, human interaction may once again become a powerful differentiator. This is why we can see from Figure 9.12 that the revised strategy includes blending both new technologies and what has been learnt from the past in terms of local personal distribution and contact networks. Blending these new and old technologies becomes a new area for research and experimentation.

The strategy recognises too that there are more stakeholders to serve than just shareholders. Cost minimisation and short-term shareholder value maximisation are not the only tools and recipes in this new world, where growth may slow and social movements have a far more influential say.

In a new world, strategy can be thought of as a two-way equation. A business uses its marketplace to create profits. That is one side of the equation. The other, newer side is how a business, through its presence in each marketplace, can help to directly create human capital, not only in terms of material wealth, but also social well-being and security.

This complex world

We have created a complex world, one that may be too complex. The one thing that we can be sure of is that a complex world will not progress in a rational straight line. The ideas that we had at the end of the 20th century of the progress of globalisation as a straight line belong to that past century. It is far better to think of the future as a period of disaggregation where the newly empowered want to try things their way. Only when they have tried, succeeded or failed will we be able to return to a single road.

This picture of disaggregation is present, in differing degrees, in each of the two scenarios we have looked at in this chapter. But the real value in using the approaches introduced here comes from using them to develop, with your colleagues, your own perspectives of the future.

Reflection points

1. What is your verdict in respect of the nine *Deep Assumptions*?
2. Will market elites retain their dominance? If not, who will be the key actors?

3. Are we entering a period of fragmentation or unity?
4. Is the strategy equation changing?

Resources

Economic projections and scenarios

The Carnegie Endowment: The World Order in 2050
This study provides two growth scenarios. Available at: http://carnegieendowment.org/2010/04/21/world-order-in-2050/1mjg

Goldman Sachs: BRICs
Resource page for the creator of the acronym. Available at: http://www.goldmansachs.com/our-thinking/brics/index.html

World Economic Forum: The Future of the Global Financial System – Navigating the Challenges Ahead

Prepared in 2009 after the 2008 banking crisis. Presents four scenarios. Available at: http://www.weforum.org/reports/future-global-financial-system-navigating-challenges-ahead

Democratic and economic freedom

The Heritage Foundation: Index of Economic Freedom
An index covering ten dimensions, from property rights to entrepreneurship. Available at: http://www.heritage.org/index/default

Freedom House: Freedom in the World
Annual assessment of political and civil freedom. Available at: http://www.freedomhouse.org/report-types/freedom-world

Alternative perspectives from the field of international relations

Gray, J., 2009. *False Dawn: The Delusions of Global Capitalism*, London: Granta.

Ikenberry, J., 2011. *Liberal Leviathan: The Origins, Crisis, and Transformation of the American World Order*, Princeton: Princeton University Press.

Reflections

A slow death for the neo-liberal project?

The continuing global financial crisis has been often described as the crisis of neo-liberal capitalism or neo-liberal ideology more broadly. While the public dimension of the neo-liberal dogma appears to have survived the financial meltdown, at least in economic and policy-making circles in the Anglo-Saxon countries, the private and regulatory elements of the neo-liberal architecture of the world economy were irreversibly shaken by the financial implosion. Indeed, two years after the crisis first shattered the world markets, the tone of the debate within the economics profession suggests that neo-liberal ideology has not been dented as severely as one would expect. The economics of neo-liberalism have changed, and with it, we believe, has the fate of neo-liberalism as the dominant ideology of global governance.

Ambitious plans and announcements at international gatherings such as the G-20 rarely tend to amount to concrete policy or institutions. Although at first sight the global credit crunch has destroyed the last foundations of the neo-liberal project, the reality of the post-crisis world is clearly more complex. For instance, while many commentators foresee an imminent China-orchestrated demise of the dollar as the world currency, China itself is caught in many dilemmas. It has invested heavily in US Treasuries and in the quasi-nationalised agency bonds (such as Fannie Mae and Freddie Mac) and thus has a clear interest in maintaining the US dollar at some level. At the same time, reliance on US consumers is a problem for China and there are already signs of a shift towards an endogenous mode of development inside the country. Yet generally, it seems unlikely that China will let the United States repeat the Japanese experience of sliding into a prolonged recession.

The nuances of the evolving post-crisis financial regulatory are also suggestive. The current and forthcoming regulatory proposals of the European states, led by France and Germany, are setting the tone for a series of far more comprehensive rules and regulations in finance. Yet at the same time, as a result of the post-crisis banking reform, American banks appear to be stronger and more competitive than their European counterparts, many of which are still sitting on 'toxic' securities. Moreover, all major players have a clear and unambiguous interest in the health of the US economy (yet far less in the health or success of the City of London). Also, while the tone and language of many post-credit crunch initiatives appear to have departed from earlier dogmas of the efficient market theory of finance, it is likely that few of them would materialise into effective tools for dealing with systemic risk in a very near future.

Against this background, the shift of power away from the Anglo-Saxon core to Europe and East Asia is evident. It is also clear that the global credit crunch has been a catalyst in this process. Emboldened by the green shoots of recovery, Anglo-Saxon governments are resisting deep changes to the international architecture of finance, and the current crisis of the Eurozone is conducive to this political stance. However, it appears increasingly unlikely that European or East Asian governments will be prepared to continue subsidising the Anglo-Saxon economies and support their commitment to neo-liberalism. It appears, therefore, that the neo-liberal project, reigning supreme in the 1980s and 1990s, is in retreat under the pressures of profound and far-reaching transformations in the global political economy.

Dr Anastasia Nesvetailova
Reader in IPE
Director, MA in Global Political Economy
Department of International Politics
City University, London
Anastasia.Nesvetailova.1@city.ac.uk

How capitalism must change to avoid a repetition of the 2008 economic crisis

A major issue that has been exposed since the beginning of the most recent economic crisis starting in 2007 has been the matter of 'Moral Hazard'. A range of businesses, supporters of the self-regulating free-market economy, have made past profits – and have championed the benefits arising from the innovations and risk taking of successful capitalism. Individuals and well-placed capitalists (claiming the rewards for entrepreneurs) have made substantial profits and gained substantial shares of the national wealth. When, however, the innovations and risk taking is unsuccessful the costs are passed to the wider taxpaying community meanwhile the profits have been retained by the Capitalist 'risk takers'. In times past Britain had the concept of the Commonweal – actions taken for the common good and contributions to the 'Common Wealth'– which not only developed the limits on the power and privileges of the wealthy and powerful and increases in the political power of the common people but also to the community benefits of social housing (such as the Peabody Trust), safe drinking water and sewage systems and fairly impartial justice. The challenge of the capitalist system is to develop systems that are recognised as being contributors to the Commonweal not as parasites on the wealth and well-being of the wider community.

For new economies the challenges include being willing and able to adapt to maintaining a balanced economy with consumption and investment in education and services to their populations, not just export orientation and investment in physical assets – or exploitation of physical assets. Cheap money from the United States and the European Union/the United Kingdom (from Quantitative Easing) has enabled Foreign Direct Investment and has improved productivity but also has built property bubbles in many of these emerging economies. There are certainly opportunities for recognising the worth of young people who can contribute to extra higher added value production as well as to the general development of their countries and wider society.

Western consumerism has already spread across the new economies – particularly among the younger people and for elites. The youth and urban residents of the coastal cities of China, for example, share the liking (or love) of consumerism and brands with the youngsters of London and New York. The power of fashion, shopping and spending are major factors in the emerging economies, which will see a shift from the frugality, savings orientation and thoughts of the future, which drove (for good or ill) the earlier generations in these societies.

Price and product will remain important parts of business strategy but Corporate Social Responsibility and business ethics will remain issues in the background, which may be used by xenophobic groups as support for protectionist stances and as means of blaming foreigners (with different standards of ethics/work practices/environmental impact) as the causes of declining relative power and wealth in the mature economies of the West.

There are certainly tensions ahead between the 'haves' and 'have nots' within and between societies. Within rich countries (with some exceptions such as commodity-rich states) there will need to be a revision of attitude to the balance between work and leisure – many resources are going to support those who are not working – old but capable, ill (but can do some work) and unemployed but choose not to work. In emerging economies the percentage of economically active adults is far higher than that in mature economies – in part due firstly to poverty and lack of educational opportunities and secondly the absence of a wide social security net. It might be expected that the superior medical services and access to more healthy lifestyles would provide greater workforce participation in mature economies. It is likely that as mature economies are squeezed in financial terms not only the wealthy and powerful elites will be challenged but also the weaker groups in societies who are seen as not contributing as well as they could to the wider community and 'paying their way'. The taxpayers in attacking those who have taken advantage of 'Moral Hazard' may also harm those at a disadvantage with all sorts of hazard to common morality.

Dr Wes Harry
Visiting Fellow
Cass Business School
City University, London

The rise of large economies in the 21st century

It was only yesterday that we seriously debated the possibility of the state 'withering away' under the pressures of an ever-expanding global market, only to have woken up to the current realities of the 21st century. The world scene today is dominated by giant political–economic organisations, the United States, the European Union,

China, soon to be joined by India, Brazil and possibly one or two other large state-market complexes. It appears that population and territorial size have emerged as the decisive factors in contemporary world politics. Why is that? In one way, the emergence of these giants to a position of prominence in the 21st century should not come as a surprise. Large, populous states, with sizeable internal markets were dominant throughout human history. But key to state power was always a combination of ingredients: territorial and population size played an important role since ancient times and size mattered only when combined with logistical and organisational capacities to match. The decisive factor, therefore, was the fateful decision of China, India and Brazil to adopt a capitalist road to economic growth, and develop a governance structure of the economy that emulated many of the techniques of market organisation that were developed by the European states and the United States. This is correct, but this theory does not explain the link between globalisation and size of economies. Indeed, it may be argued that one of the key functions of the WTO is to ensure that territorial or population size do not matter, because states of whatever size have equal access to markets of their neighbours.

A set of theoretical propositions known as the 'competition state' theory that were developed in the 1990s (Cerny, 1990; Palan and Abbott, 1996; Stopford and Strange, 1991) offers an alternative explanation for the rise of these giants. Competition state theory suggests that contemporary states are far less interested in the traditional bilateral geopolitical relationships, and instead are gearing themselves towards competition for market share and particularly high-valued industries. In Palan and Abbott (1996), we have argued that states have adopted myriad competitive strategies, including techniques such as the Asian developmental states, the European welfare states, the Anglo-Saxon regulatory states, tax havens and regional organisations such as the North American Free Trade Association (NAFTA) and the European Union. The combined impact of these competitive strategies was to enhance further expansion of the very legal, political and organisational infrastructures that have supported globalisation.

One problem with all these strategies, however, but crucially save the last one, was that in doing so states placed themselves in a difficult position vis-à-vis mobile capital. On the one hand, competition states sought to adopt 'business friendly' policies such as low taxation, removal of 'red tape', that is, regulations, low inflation, balanced budgets and so on. At the same time they sought to provide the necessary but expensive modern infrastructure of quality education and health systems, stable politics and excellent communication and transport infrastructure. It proved to be a very difficult balancing act.

The largest economies, however, were not caught by the same dilemma. They are not caught in a 'beauty contest' over mobile capital. On the contrary, as any CEO of any big business with global aspirations knows all too well, while they could afford to ignore small or even middle-size economies run by awkward regimes, they do not have the luxury of not having a presence in the largest-markets configuration of the United States, the European Union, China or India, however awkward the governments of these countries may be. The largest economies do not have to compete for capital and business but vice versa capital and big businesses have to adapt their strategies and tactics to conform to the wishes of the very large economies. At the same time, because of their sheer size and their strategic advantage of not having to compete ferociously for mobile capital as smaller economies do, large economies have another great advantage in the modern world: they are in a position to shape the rules of global investment, accounting, law, taxation and finance in a way that smaller states can never hope to achieve. Furthermore, they have done so in bilateral negotiations among themselves in ways that benefited their economies and businesses. Being a member of such a large-size economy, whether as the governments of sizeable states with large population, or as a governing organisation of regional organisations such as the European Union that pools together smaller states into a larger organisation, offers, therefore, a distinct advantage in the age of mobile capital. Competition state theory suggests, therefore, that there are good rational reasons for rise of the great giants of the 21st century.

Professor Ronen Palan
Department of Political Science and International Studies
University of Birmingham
r.p.palan@bham.ac.uk

References

Cerny, P. (1990) *The Changing Architecture of Politics: Structure, Agency, and the Future of the State*, London and Newbury Park: Sage

Palan, R. and Abbott, J. (1996) *State Strategies in the Global Economy*, London: Pinter

Stopford, J. and Strange, S. (1991) *Rival States, Rival Firms: Competition for World Market Shares*, Cambridge: Cambridge University Press

The changing role of soft power

When the concept of soft power was first introduced by Joseph Nye over 20 years ago, it was offered as an alternative to hard power: another way to control one's environment using co-option rather than coercion. Hence, as America – and subsequently nominated superpowers – began to lose faith in the agency of guns and money post-Vietnam, it began to appreciate and then build up its other vehicles of global influence, including its arts and culture, life style products and value memes. There's no doubt that this has been successful for the United States: even as it loses its monetary and military dominance of the globe, there are no challenges to its hold on our collective imagination.

Unlike hard power which is force, soft power is attraction – a means of drawing others into your worldview. It is less useful in countering an aggressor in full flow. Does that mean that soft power is less effective as a tool to guarantee our security in the future? No, in many ways it will be more effective but only within a shifting paradigm of global relations.

In his book *The Better Angels of Our Nature*, Steven Pinker has done a good job of evidencing the steady decline of violence across the world over the past 2000 years. As increasingly complex humans we have chosen to outlaw violence at every level to the best of our ability, establishing institutions and laws that make it increasingly difficult to use force without very good cause. Nevertheless, we still seek agency and security as fundamental individual and social needs. Soft power is a means to that end.

Soft power is relationship potential. If you have it, others want to trade with you, visit you, invest in you and protect you. Without it, you will be distrusted, and even with copious resources at your disposal, you will find it hard to thrive. China has done well to open its doors to global trade. However, its poor human rights record continues to offend the global community, severely limiting its ability to shape a popular global agenda. Norway, on the other hand, through its consistent development of intranational peace partnerships and initiatives – including the establishment of the Nobel Peace Prize – is no. 7 in the global soft power index, 13 places higher than China. We are more likely to become peace warriors than adopt Confucianism for the time being.

For many the ascendency of soft power will be a pipe dream, although smart power – the judicious balance of hard and soft power – may be conceded. This is because the dominant global culture within which this discussion takes place is hard powered: competitive, dualistic, macho even. Superpowers vie with power blocs to dictate the terms of trade, development and environmental health for all. Globalisation is still a dangerous word because multinationals and financiers remain predatory in a vulnerable world. Under a hard umbrella, even softness is largely self-interested and manipulative.

However, the tools of soft power – technology, networks, friendship, anything that makes relationship possible – are transforming the underlying global culture day by day, creating a space for cooperation and shared vision amongst global citizens that has not existed before. It may take a generation, even two, but if Steven Pinker is right and we continue to evolve towards a more complex, cooperative world, our experience of globalisation will change. Smart power within a soft powered culture gives quite a different role to hard power: instead of the aggressor it becomes the vehicle for clarity, assertiveness, structure and boldness to complement an otherwise fluid-soft-range of possibilities. Where smart power today is a compromise, the smart power of tomorrow is pure dynamism.

Indra Adnan
Director, Soft Power Network
IA@softpowernetwork.com

What challenges do the new economies face as they move forward? (By Prof. Marcelo F Simon)

I remember when my mother many years ago showed me the textbook for her economy class (she was a Chartered Public Accountant). She was born in 1933 and studied in the mid-50s.

That book included Japan as one of the poorest countries on the planet.

By the 1960s and 1970s Japan was competing globally, in the 1980s it was a threat to the global powers in terms of global leadership and – despite more than ten years of recession since the fall of the Berlin Wall (1989), earthquakes and tsunamis – Japan enjoys today one of the highest living standards in the world.

Will China return to the place of economic leadership it had until the beginning of the Industrial Revolution in Europe? Will it be followed by India, other Asian countries and Latin America? Will the 21st century be the time of an awakening Africa? Judging from the economic trends, there will be several success stories such as the Japanese. The process of global integration is irreversible.

There are two main challenges I identify in the development of the emerging world:

1. Moderate the increasing inequality (Gini): With few exceptions the general increase in global human development (HDI – Human Development Index) has been matched by growing inequality (Gini). That is, the poor are less poor, but their distance from the rich has increased. On one hand poor people may be somewhat happier due to their improved quality of life, but they are even unhappier due to the perception of injustice for being so much farther from the life standard of the rich.
2. Harmonisation of long-term planning: Democracy is the best political system designed by man. However, the limited time spent by political leaders in their jobs (e.g. presidential elections every 4 years in the United States with only one chance for reelection) means that the planning horizon of the politician is in general shorter than that of other community leaders. The politician prioritises measures that increase his/her popularity and his/her chances of winning the next election... but the most popular decisions are not always the most efficient ones. To further complicate this matter, Gary Hamel (Harvard) has identified how economic instability, technological acceleration and changes in organisational culture have affected the process of planning and generate the emerging challenge of adjusting strategic planning to that increasingly dynamic environment in which organisations perform.

To conclude, I extend these two recommendations to the more developed economies. The successful country of the future will have to harmonise growth of the Gini and HDI indexes and will have to design and follow action plans that prioritise the important matters, plans that are well-designed and adaptable to the changing environment.

Professor Marcelo F Simon (PE, MBA)
UADE – Buenos Aires, Argentina
E-mail contact marcelo@multimake.com

What challenges do the new economies face as they move forward? (By Prof. José Mauro Hajaj Gonzalez)

Everybody in Brazil nowadays is busy trying to cope with an increasingly complex environment. Brazil moved very fast from a low self-esteem third-world country to a centre-of-attention rising star BRIC member. We used to refer to ourselves as 'the giant that sleeps'. Now the giant has apparently woken up. But he is still trying to figure out what is going on. Inflation is under control, the political environment is stable, the doors are finally open to the world and emerging social classes with significant purchasing power as well as exports of commodities to a world in need of food and minerals are keeping companies busy. Multinational companies are investing more and more in the country, trying to take advantage of a heated market. On the other hand, infrastructure – that is, roads, ports, airports, transportation, energy sources – is insufficient, corruption is common and education is bad. The giant clearly has limits. It will take more than will and effort to overcome these obstacles. It will take competence in managing priorities and creativity in proposing new solutions. The recently established democracy and a tropical sense of humour are advantages in this sense: they help the civilised debate between different viewpoints and the treading of new paths.

Prof. José Mauro Hajaj Gonzalez
Associate Dean at BSP
Business School São Paulo
jose.gonzalez@bsp.edu.br

Bibliography

Acemoglu, D. et al., 2008. Income and Democracy. *American Economic Review*, 98(3), pp. 808–842.

Aitken, C. and Keller, S., 2007. The CEO's Role in Leading Transformation. *The McKinsey Quarterly*, 19–26.

AlJazerra, 2009. US: Taliban has Grown Fourfold – Americas – Al Jazeera English. *AlJazerra*. Available at: http://www.aljazeera.com/news/americas/2009/10/20091091814483962.html [Accessed March 28, 2012].

Allchin, J., 2010. Burma 'Hosting India's Greatest Security Threat'. *Eurasia Review*. Available at: http://www.eurasiareview.com/201008 317577/burma-hosting-indias-greatest-security-threat.html [Accessed September 2, 2010].

Altman, R., 2011. We Need not Fret Over Omnipotent Markets. *FT.com*. Available at: http://www.ft.com/cms/s/0/890161ac-1b69-11e1-85f8-00144feabdc0.html#axzz1fHKcTLBn [Accessed December 2, 2011].

ANI, 2012. India Expresses Concern Over Safety of Pakistan's Nuclear Arsenal. *Yahoo! News India*. Available at: http://in.news.yahoo.com/india-expresses-concern-over-safety-pakistans-nuclear-arsenal-121128219.html [Accessed March 28, 2012].

Applegate, L. and Harreld, B., 2009. *Don't Just Survive – Thrive: Leading Innovation in Good Times and Bad*, Boston: Havard Business School.

Arrata, P., Despierre, A. and Kumra, G., 2007. Building an Effective Change Agent Team. *The McKinsey Quarterly*, 4, p. 4.

Aslund, A., 2008. 10 Reasons Why the Russian Economy will Falter. *Moscow Times*. Available at: http://www.themoscowtimes.com/opinion/article/10-reasons-why-the-economy-will-falter/370643.html [Accessed March 28, 2012].

Aslund, A., 2009. Take the R Out of BRIC. *Peterson Institute*. Available at: http://www.piie.com/publications/opeds/oped.cfm?ResearchID=1445&utm_source=feedburner&utm_medium=%24%7Bfeed%7D&utm_campaign=Feed%3A+%24%7Bupdate%7D+%28%24%7BPIIE+Update%7D%29&utm_content=My+Yahoo [Accessed December 10, 2009].

Astill, J., 2006. Too Much for One Man to do: A Survey of Pakistan. *The Economist*, (8 July).

Atsmon, Y. and Magni, M., 2011. China's Confident Consumers. *McKinsey Quarterly*. Available at: https://www.mckinseyquarterly.com/Marketing/Sectors_Regions/Chinas_confident_consumers_2879 [Accessed February 8, 2012].

Augustine, N., 1995. Managing the Crisis You Tried to Prevent. *Harvard Business Review*, (November–December), 147–158.

Ayoob, M., 2007. Challenging Hegemony: Political Islam and the North-South Divide. *International Studies Review*, 9, pp. 629–643.

Babones, S., 2011. The Middling Kingdom. *Foreign Affairs*, (September/October 2011). Available at: http://www.foreignaffairs.com/articles/68207/salvatore-babones/the-middling-kingdom?page=show [Accessed January 10, 2012].

Badkar, M., 2011. Race of the Century: Is India or China the Next Economic Superpower? *Business Insider*. Available at: http://www.businessinsider.com/are-you-betting-on-china-or-india-2011-1 [Accessed March 24, 2012].

Bajoria, J., 2008. Democracy Troubles in Southeast Asia – Council on Foreign Relations. *Council on Foreign Relations*. Available at: http://www.cfr.org/publication/17980/democracy_troubles_in_southeast_asia.html [Accessed December 15, 2008].

Bajoria, J., 2011. The Taliban in Afghanistan. *Council on Foreign Relations*. Available at: http://www.cfr.org/afghanistan/taliban-afghanistan/p10551 [Accessed March 28, 2012].

Bajoria, J. and Bruno, G., 2011. Backgrounder: al-Qaeda (a.k.a. al-Qaida, al-Qa'ida). *Council on Foreign Relations*. Available at: http://www.cfr.org/terrorist-organizations/al-qaeda-k-al-qaida-al-qaida/p9126 [Accessed November 20, 2011].

Barnett, A., 1986. Ten Years After Mao. *Foreign Affairs* (Fall). Available at: http://www.foreignaffairs.com/articles/41394/a-doak-barnett/ten-years-after-mao [Accessed January 11, 2012].

Barton, D., 2011. Capitalism for the Long Term. *Harvard Business Review* (March), 84–91.

Barysch, K., 2010. Eastern Europe's Great Game. *oDRussia*. Available at: http://www.opendemocracy.net/katinka-barysch/eastern-europes-great-game [Accessed July 22, 2010].

BBC News, 2011. BBC News – Trader was Not a Hoaxer, Says BBC. *BBC News Business*. Available at: http://www.bbc.co.uk/news/business-15078419 [Accessed October 16, 2011].

BBC News Business, 2012. US, EU and Japan Challenge China on Rare Earths at WTO. *BBC*. Available at: http://www.bbc.co.uk/news/business-17348648 [Accessed March 28, 2012].

BBC News World, 2012. What are "rare earths" used for? *BBC*. Available at: http://www.bbc.co.uk/news/world-17357863 [Accessed March 28, 2012].

Becker, G. and Murphy, K., 2009. Do not let the "cure" Destroy Capitalism. *FT.com*. Available at: http://www.ft.com/cms/s/0/98f66b98-14be-11de-8cd1-0000779fd2ac,dwp_uuid=ae1104cc-f82e-11dd-aae8-000077b07658.html [Accessed March 20, 2009].

Beer, M. and Nohria, N., 2000. Cracking the Code of Change. *Harvard Business Review* (May–June), 133–141.

Bequelin, N., 2012. Legalizing the Tools of Repression. *The New York Times*. Available at: http://www.nytimes.com/2012/03/01/opinion/legalizing-the-tools-of-repression.html [Accessed March 1, 2012].

Bergsten, F., 2009. A Blueprint for Global Leadership in the 21st Century. Available at: http://www.piie.com/publications/papers/paper.

cfm?ResearchID=1323&utm_source=feedburner&utm_medium=feed& utm_campaign=Feed%3A+peterson-update+%28Peterson+Institute+ Update%29&utm_content=My+Yahoo [Accessed November 16, 2009].

Bernhard, M., 2011. The Leadership Secrets of Bismarck. *Foreign Affairs*. Available at: http://www.foreignaffairs.com/articles/136540/michael-bernhard/the-leadership-secrets-of-bismarck?page=show [Accessed October 21, 2011].

Berthelsen, J., 2012. Can China's Consumers Save West? *The Diplomat*. Available at: http://the-diplomat.com/2012/01/04/can-china%e2%80%99s-consumers-save-west/ [Accessed January 4, 2012].

Betto, F., 2010. Values in the Post-Crisis Economy. In K. Schwab et al., eds. *Faith and the Global Agenda: Values for the Post-Crisis Economy*. Geneva: World Economic Forum, p. 21.

Bisson, P., Kirkland, R. and Stephenson, E., 2010. The Market State. *McKinsey Quarterly*. Available at: https://www.mckinseyquarterly.com/The_market_state_2628 [Accessed February 8, 2012].

Bivens, J., 2008. Everybody Wins, Except for Most of us. *Economic Policy Institute*. Available at: http://www.epi.org/content.cfm/books_everybody_wins [Accessed November 25, 2008].

Bobbitt, P., 2003. *The Shield of Achilles: War, Peace and the Course of History*, London: Penguin.

Bobbitt, P., 2008. *Terror and Consent: The Wars for the Twenty-First Century*, London: Penguin.

Bogle, J., 2009. Enough Period. *Knowledge at W P Carey*. Available at: http://knowledge.wpcarey.asu.edu/article.cfm?articleid=1811 [Accessed September 10, 2009].

Bokhari, F., 2006. Pakistan "cannot afford nuclear race with India." *FT.com*. Available at: http://www.ft.com/cms/s/0/2b49cb1c-017a-11db-af16-0000779e2340.html#axzz1qPNXpUg2 [Accessed March 15, 2012].

Boland, V., Steen, M. and Escritt, T., 2009. Far Right Exploits Rising Insecurity. *FT.com*. Available at: http://www.ft.com/cms/s/0/6a31f716-5454-11de-a58d-00144feabdc0.html [Accessed June 9, 2009].

Bone, J., 2011. The Humble Fruit Seller whose Fight for Justice Created History. *The Times*. Available at: http://www.thetimes.co.uk/tto/news/world/middleeast/article3269979.ece [Accessed January 21, 2012].

Bower, J., Leonard, H. and Paine, L., 2011. Global Capitalism at Risk. *Harvard Business Review* (September), 105–112.

Bowley, G., Schwartz, N. and Story, L., 2011. Italy Pushed Closer to Financial Brink. *The New York Times*. Available at: http://www.nytimes.com/2011/11/10/business/global/italy-pushed-closer-to-financial-brink.html?pagewanted=1&_r=1 [Accessed November 17, 2011].

Bradsher, K., 2010. China Still Bans Rare Earths for Japan, Executives Say. *The New York Times*. Available at: http://www.nytimes.com/2010/11/11/business/global/11rare.html [Accessed March 25, 2012].

Bremmer, I., 2010. *The End of the Free Market: Who Wins the War Between States and Corporations?*, New York: Portfolio.

Bremmer, I., 2011. The J-curve Hits the Middle East. *FT.com*. Available at: http://www.ft.com/cms/s/0/82973086-3a04-11e0-a441-00144feabdc0.html#axzz1iW0bfjKy [Accessed January 4, 2012].

Breslin, S., 2011a. China and the Crisis: Global Power, Domestic Caution and Local Initiative. *Contemporary Politics*, 17(2), pp. 185–200.

Breslin, S., 2011b. The "China Model" and the Global Crisis: From Friedrich List to a Chinese Mode of Governance?. *International Affairs*, 87(6), pp. 1323–1343.

Breslin, S., 2011c. The Chinese Model and the Global Crisis. Available at: http://www.rsis.edu.sg/nts/article.asp?id=188 [Accessed January 11, 2012].

Brooks, D., 2003. Kicking the Secularist Habit: A Six-Step Program. *The Atlantic Monthly*. Available at: http://www.theatlantic.com/magazine/archive/2003/03/kicking-the-secularist-habit/2680/ [Accessed December 21, 2011].

Buckley, C., 2012. China to Unveil Military Budget after U.S. Asia "pivot." *Reuters*. Available at: http://www.reuters.com/article/2012/03/02/us-china-defence-idUSTRE8210D320120302 [Accessed March 2, 2012].

Buckley, N., 2011. Putin Sets Sights on Eurasian Economic Union. *FT.com*. Available at: http://www.ft.com/cms/s/0/a7db2310-b769-11e0-b95d-00144feabdc0.html#axzz1VNURHttF [Accessed August 18, 2011].

Bull, H., 1984. The Revolt Against the West. In H. Bull & A. Watson, eds. *The Expansion of International Society*. Oxford: Clarendon Press.

Bull, H., 1977. *The Anarchical Society: A Study of Order in World Politics 2nd Ed*, Houndmills: MacMillan.

Bunderson, J., 2003. Team Member Functional Background and Involvement in Management Teams: Direct Effects and the Moderating Role of Power Centralization. *Academy of Management Journal*, 46(4), pp. 458–474.

Buzan, B., 2010. Culture and International Society. *International Affairs*, 86(1), pp. 1–25.

Cagrici, M., 2010. Spiritual Values in the Face of Global Problems. In K. Schwab et al., eds. *Faith and the Global Agenda: Values for the Post-Crisis Economy*. Geneva: World Economic Forum, pp. 23–24.

Callinicos, A., 2010. *Bonfire of Illusions: The Twin Crises of the Liberal World*, Cambridge: Polity.

Cannella, A., Park, J.-H. and Lee, H.-U., 2008. Top Management Team Functional background Diversity and Firm Performance: Examining the Roles of Team Member Colocation and Environmental Uncertainty. *Academy of Management Journal*, 51(4), pp. 768–784.

Cardenas, M., 2008. Global Financial Crisis: Is Brazil a Bystander? – Brookings Institution. Available at: http://www.brookings.edu/opinions/2008/1015_financial_crisis_cardenas.aspx?rssid=global [Accessed October 16, 2008].

Cerny, P., 2006. Restructuring the State in a Globalizing World: Capital Accumulation, Tangled Hierarchies and the Search of a New Spacio-Temporal Fix. *Review of International Political Economy*, 13(4), pp. 679–695.
Cerny, P., 2005. Terrorism and the New Security Dilemma. *Naval War College Review*, 58(1), pp. 11–33.
Cerny, P., 2010. The Competition State Today: From Raison d'Etat to Raison du Monde. *Policy Studies*, 31(1), pp. 5–21.
Chakravorti, B., 2009. Creative Entrepreneurship in a Downturn – HBS Working Knowledge. *HBS Working Knowledge*. Available at: http://hbswk.hbs.edu/item/6118.html [Accessed February 24, 2009].
Chellaney, B., 2011. The Water Hegemon. *Project Syndicate*. Available at: http://www.project-syndicate.org/commentary/chellaney20/English [Accessed November 4, 2011].
Chidambaram, P., 2009. Increase in Infiltration from Pakistan. *The Times of India*. Available at: http://timesofindia.indiatimes.com/home/india/Increase-in-infiltration-from-Pakistan-Chidambaram/articleshow/5122821.cms [Accessed October 14, 2009].
Chovanec, P., 2011. China's Real Estate Bubble May Have Just Popped. *Foreign Affairs*. Available at: http://www.foreignaffairs.com/articles/136963/patrick-chovanec/chinas-real-estate-bubble-may-have-just-popped?page=show [Accessed January 10, 2012].
Chu, Y. et al., 2009. Asia's Challenged Democracies. *The Washington Quarterly*, 31(1), pp. 143–157.
Clark, I., 2000. A "Borderless World"?. In G. Fry & J. O'Hagan, eds. *Contending Images of World Politics*. Houndmills: MacMillan, pp. 79–90.
Clark, I., 2011. China and the United States: A Succession of Hegemonies?. *International Affairs*, 87(1), pp. 13–28.
Clinton, W., 1992. The 1992 Campaign: Excerpts From Speech By Clinton on US Role. Available at: http://www.nytimes.com/1992/10/02/us/the-1992-campaign-excerpts-from-speech-by-clinton-on-us-role.html [Accessed October 28, 2011].
Clinton, W., 1993. Remarks to the 48th Session of the United Nations General Assembly in New York City. *The American Presidency Project*. Available at: http://www.presidency.ucsb.edu/ws/index.php?pid=47119#axzz1RzjR0s5a [Accessed July 13, 2011].
Cohen, S. and DeLong, J.B., 2010. *The End of Influence: What Happens When Other Countries Have the Money*, New York: Basic Books.
Cooper, R., 2004. *The Breaking of Nations: Order and Chaos in the Twenty-First Century*, London: Atlantic Books.
Corrales, J. et al., 2009. *Undermining Democracy: 21st Century Authoritarians*, Washington: Freedom House.
Crandell, R., 2011. The Post-American Hemisphere. *Foreign Affairs*, 90(3), pp. 83–95.
Crooks, E., 2011. US Shale Gas Bonanza: New Wells to Draw on. *FT.com*. Available at: http://www.ft.com/cms/s/0/067a0a38-ef39-

11e0-918b-00144feab49a.html#axzz1eATqxoPy [Accessed November 21, 2011].

Davidson, J., 2002. The Roots of Revisionism: Fascist Italy, 1922–39. *Security Studies*, 11(4), pp. 125–159.

Day, G. and Schoemaker, P., 2005. Scanning the Periphery. *Harvard Business Review*, (November), 135–148.

Defence Intelligence Organisation, 2010. Defence Intelligence Trends in the Asia-Pacific. *Australian Government Department of Defence*. Available at: http://www.defence.gov.au/dio/documents/DET_10.pdf [Accessed March 28, 2012].

Dennison, S., 2010. A Crisis of Values? *European Council on Foreign Relations*. Available at: http://ecfr.eu/content/entry/commentary_a_crisis_of_values/ [Accessed September 9, 2010].

Denoeux, G., 2002. The Forgotten Swamp: Navigating Political Islam. *Middle East Policy*, 9(2), pp. 56–81.

DePetris, D., 2011. The Power of Political Islam. *Foreign Policy In Focus*. Available at: http://www.fpif.org/articles/the_power_of_political_islam [Accessed November 30, 2011].

Desai, S. and Kuusito, M., 2010. Why India and Pakistan will Continue to Struggle for Common ground. *Foreign Policy Blogs*. Available at: http://eurasia.foreignpolicy.com/posts/2010/07/20/india_and_pakistan_struggle_for_common_ground [Accessed March 28, 2012].

Dewan, S., 2008. Wage Inequality Is a Global Challenge. *Center for American Progress*. Available at: http://www.americanprogress.org/issues/2008/11/wage_inequality.html [Accessed November 28, 2008].

Dikhano, Y., 1999. A Critique of CIA Estimates of Soviet Performance from the Gerschenkron Perspective. In A. Heston & R. Lipsey, eds. *International and Interarea Comparisons of Income, Output, and Prices*. Chicago: University of Chicago Press, 271–276. Available at: http://www.nber.org/chapters/c8394.pdf [Accessed March 27, 2012].

Doucouliagos, H. and Ulabasoglu, M., 2008. Democracy and Economic Growth: A Meta Analysis. *American Journal of Political Science*, 52(1), pp. 61–83.

Doyle, M., 1986. Liberalism and World Politics. *The American Political Science Review*, 80(4), pp. 1151–1169.

Dyer, G., 2010. China to Impose Duties on US Chicken. *Financial Times*. Available at: http://www.ft.com/cms/s/0/105a0522-1208-11df-b6e3-00144feab49a.html#axzz1ns7flkgj [Accessed March 2, 2012].

Dyer, G. and Braithwaite, T., 2009. US tyre Duties Spark China Clash. *FT.com*. Available at: http://www.ft.com/cms/s/0/f67c6fe6-a024-11de-b9ef-00144feabdc0.html [Accessed September 14, 2009].

Eckstein, A., 1964. On the Economic Crisis in Communist China. *Foreign Affairs*, (July 1964). Available at: http://www.foreignaffairs.com/articles/23625/alexander-eckstein/on-the-economic-crisis-in-communist-china?page=show [Accessed January 10, 2012].

EIA, 2008. U.S. Energy Information Administration (EIA). *U.S. Energy Information Administration*. Available at: http://205.254.135.7/countries/regions-topics.cfm?fips=SCS [Accessed March 28, 2012].

Eisenstadt, S., 2000. Multiple Modernities. *Daedalus*, 129(1), pp. 1–29.

Emmerson, C., 2011. Worlds of Water. *The World Today*, 67(6), pp. 4–6.

Emmott, B., 2009. *Rivals: How the Power Struggle Between China, India and Japan Will Shape the Next Decade*, London: Penguin.

Engdhal, F.W., 2008. Russia, Europe and USA: Fundamental Geopolitics. Available at: http://www.globalresearch.ca/index.php?context=viewArticle&code=ENG20080904&articleId=10062 [Accessed September 5, 2008].

Evans, M. and Whittell, G., 2010. Cyberwar Declared as China Hunts for the West's Intelligence Secrets. *The Times*, p. 23.

Falk, R., 2000. A "New Medievalism"?. In G. Fry & J. O'Hagan, eds. *Contending Images of World Politics*. Houndmills: MacMillan, pp. 106–116.

Featherstone, M., 2010. Possible Futures for a Global Culture. *World Politics Review*. Available at: http://www.worldpoliticsreview.com/articles/7146/possible-futures-for-a-global-culture [Accessed December 3, 2010].

Ferguson, N., 2011. The West and the Rest: The Changing Global Balance of Power in Historical Perspective. Available at: http://www.chathamhouse.org/sites/default/files/19251_090511ferguson.pdf [Accessed March 3, 2012].

Foley, S., 2012. Showdown in Rare Earth Row with China. *The Independent*. Available at: http://www.independent.co.uk/news/business/analysis-and-features/showdown-in-rare-earth-row-with-china-7578260.html [Accessed March 25, 2012].

Follath, E., 2010. The Dragon's Embrace: China's Soft Power Is a Threat to the West. Available at: http://www.spiegel.de/international/world/0,1518,708645,00.html [Accessed August 25, 2010].

Førland, T., 1993. The History of Economic Warfare: International Law, Effectiveness, Strategies. *Journal of Peace Research*, 30(2), pp. 151–162.

Friedman, G., 2012. The State of the World: Assessing China's Strategy. *Stratfor Global Intelligence*. Available at: http://www.stratfor.com/weekly/state-world-assessing-chinas-strategy?utm_source=freelist-f&utm_medium=email&utm_campaign=20120306&utm_term=gweekly&utm_content=title&elq=dcfd0063f6d642caaeab94bb076ada9c [Accessed March 6, 2012].

Friedman, T., 2006. *The World Is Flat: The Globalized World in the Twenty-First Century*, London: Penguin.

Friedrichs, J., 2001. The Meaning of New Medievalism. *European Journal of International Relations*, 7(4), pp. 475–502.

Fry, G., 2000. A "Coming Age of Regionalism"?. In G. Fry & J. O'Hagan, eds. *Contending Images of World Politics*. Houndmills: MacMillan, pp. 117–131.

Fry, G. and O'Hagan, J., 2000. Contending Images of World Politics: An Introduction. In G. Fry & J. O'Hagan, eds. *Contending Images of World Politics*. Houndmills: MacMillan, pp. 1–18.

Fukuyama, F., 1989. The End of History? *The National Interest* (Summer), 3–18.
Gapper, J., 2012. Business Should Help the Heartland. *Financial Times*. Available at: http://www.ft.com/cms/s/0/0178c402-679d-11e1-b6a1-00144feabdc0.html#axzz1oXtj9OfE [Accessed March 9, 2012].
Ghannouchi, R., 2011. A Conversation on Tunisia's Future with Rached Ghannouchi. Available at: http://www.carnegieendowment.org/2011/12/01/conversation%2Don%2Dtunisia%2Ds%2Dfuture%2Dwith%2Drached%2Dghannouchi/8org [Accessed December 18, 2011].
Gillis, C., 2010. China's Power Play. *MacLean's*. Available at: http://www2.macleans.ca/2010/11/09/armed-and-dangerous/ [Accessed March 24, 2012].
Gilpin, R., 1981. *War and Change in World Politics*, Cambridge: Cambridge University Press.
Glauber, R., Oxley, M. and Vasella, D., 2008. Ethics in Globalization. Available at: http://www.hbs.edu/centennial/businesssummit/business-society/ethics-in-globalization.html [Accessed July 19, 2009].
Godemont, F. et al., 2009. *China and India: Rivals always, Partners Sometimes*, London: European Council on Foreign Relations. Available at: http://ecfr.eu/content/entry/ecfr_and_asia_centre_publish_latest_issue_of_china_analysis [Accessed October 7, 2010].
Godemont, F. et al., 2011. *China Analysis: The New Great Game in Central Asia*, Available at: http://www.ecfr.eu/content/entry/china_analysis_the_new_great_game_in_central_asia [Accessed October 16, 2011].
Gokhale, N., 2010. India Readies for China Fight. *The Diplomat*. Available at: http://the-diplomat.com/2010/07/06/india-readies-for-china-fight/ [Accessed March 28, 2012].
Goodwin, M., 2011. *Right Response: Understanding and Countering Populist Extremism in Europe*, London: Chatham House.
Gray, J., 2009. *False Dawn: The Delusions of Global Capitalism*, London: Granta.
Greenwood, R. and Hinings, C., 1988. Organizational Design Types, Tracks and the Dynamics of Strategic Change. *Organization Studies*, 9(3), pp. 293–316.
Guzansky, Y. and Berti, B., 2011. The Arab Spring's Violent Turn. *The National Interest*. Available at: http://nationalinterest.org/commentary/the-arab-springs-violent-turn-6254 [Accessed December 16, 2011].
Hadar, L., 2010. Dump All Those Paradigms: It's Nationalism, Stupid! *Cato Institute*. Available at: http://www.cato.org/pub_display.php?pub_id=12204&utm_source=feedburner&utm_medium=feed&utm_campaign=Feed%3A+CatoRecentOpeds+%28Cato+Recent+Op-eds%29&utm_content=My+Yahoo [Accessed October 14, 2010].
Hailin, Y., 2010. As China Rises, its People Grow Arrogant. *People's Daily Online*. Available at: http://english.peopledaily.com.cn/90001/90780/91345/7128339.html [Accessed March 28, 2012].

Hamid, S., 2011. The Muslim Brotherhood's New Power in Egypt's Parliament. *Brookings*. Available at: http://www.brookings.edu/opinions/2011/1223_muslim_brotherhood_hamid.aspx?rssid=LatestFromBrookings&utm_source=feedburner&utm_medium=feed&utm_campaign=Feed%3A+BrookingsRSS%2Ftopfeeds%2FLatestFromBrookings+%28Brookings%3A+Latest+From+Brookings%29 [Accessed January 5, 2012].

Hanson, S., 2009. Brazil on the International Stage. *Council on Foreign Relations*. Available at: http://www.cfr.org/publication/19883/brazil_on_the_international_stage.html [Accessed July 22, 2009].

Harding, L. and Hearst, D., 2009. Europe Fears Winter Energy Crisis as Russia Tightens Grip on oil Supplies. *The Guardian*. Available at: http://www.guardian.co.uk/world/2009/sep/13/russia-oil-exports-eu [Accessed March 14, 2012].

Harvey, D., 2010. *The Enigma of Capital and the Crises of Capitalism*, London: Profile Books.

Helliwell, J., 1994. Empirical Linkages Between Democracy and Economic Growth. *British Journal of Political Science*, 24, pp. 225–248.

Hille, K., 2011. China to Boost Military Spending. *FT.com*. Available at: http://www.ft.com/cms/s/0/6525224c-462f-11e0-aebf-00144feab49a.html#axzz1FT1nrJj7 [Accessed March 4, 2011].

Hobbes, T., 1651. *Leviathan or the Matter, Forme, & Power of a Common-wealth Ecclesiasticall*, London: Andrew Crooke. Available at: http://socserv.mcmaster.ca/econ/ugcm/3ll3/hobbes/Leviathan.pdf [Accessed March 22, 2012].

Hobson, C. and Kurki, M., 2009. Democracy and Democracy-Support: A New Era. *Open Democracy*. Available at: http://www.opendemocracy.net/article/idea/democracy-and-democracy-support-a-new-era [Accessed March 23, 2009].

Hoyos, C. and Hille, K., 2012. Chinese Defence Budget Set to Double by 2015. *Financial Times*. Available at: http://www.ft.com/cms/s/0/7b58ac0a-5592-11e1-9d95-00144feabdc0.html#axzz1nzIUmSgj [Accessed March 2, 2012].

Hu, Z. and Khan, M., 1997. Economic Issues 8 – Why Is China Growing So Fast? *International Monetary Fund*. Available at: http://www.imf.org/external/pubs/ft/issues8/index.htm [Accessed January 10, 2012].

Huang, K., 2010. From Imitators to Inventors: China's Changing Innovation Landscape. *Knowledge at SMU*. Available at: http://knowledge.smu.edu.sg/article.cfm?articleid=1309 [Accessed September 1, 2010].

Huang, Y., 2011. The Sick Man of Asia. *Foreign Affairs* (November/December 2011). Available at: http://www.foreignaffairs.com/articles/136507/yanzhong-huang/the-sick-man-of-asia?page=show [Accessed January 10, 2012].

Huntington, S., 2002. *The Clash of Civilizations and the Remaking of World Order*, London: Free Press.

Husain, B., 2011. Radical Changes. *The New York Times*. Available at: http://www.nytimes.com/2011/12/02/opinion/magazine-global-agenda-radical-changes.html?pagewanted=1&_r=3 [Accessed December 18, 2011].

Ibarra, H., 1992. Homophily and Differential Returns: Sex Differences in Network Structure and Access in an Advertising Firm. *Administrative Science Quarterly*, 37(3), pp. 422–447.

Ikenberry, G.J., 2011. *Liberal Leviathan: The Origins, Crisis and Transformation of the American World Order*, Princeton: Princeton University Press.

Jacobs, E., 2012. *In the Wake of the Great Recession, Don't Lose Sight of the Big Picture*, Washington: Brookings. Available at: http://www.brookings.edu/~/media/Files/rc/papers/2012/0315_economy_jacobs/0315_economy_jacobs.pdf [Accessed March 24, 2012].

James, H., 2011. International Order After the Financial Crisis. *International Affairs*, 87(3), pp. 525–537.

Janis, I., 1972. *Victims of Groupthink: A Psychological Study of Foreign-Policy Decisions and Fiascoes*, Boston: Houghton, Miffin.

Jervis, R., 2002. Theories of War in an Era of Leading-Power peace. *American Political Science Review*, 96(1), pp. 1–14.

Johne, A. and Davies, R., 1999. Approaches to Stimulating Change in Mature Insurance Companies. *British Journal of Management*, 10, pp. S19–S30.

Johnson, S., 2009. Is the Financial System Condemned to a "Doom Loop"? *Peterson Institute: Real Time Economic Issues Watch*. Available at: http://www.piie.com/realtime/?p=1052&utm_source=feedburner&utm_medium=%24%7Bfeed%7D&utm_campaign=Feed%3A+%24%7Bupdate%7D+%28%24%7BPIIE+Update%7D%29&utm_content=My+Yahoo [Accessed November 19, 2009].

Jones, G. ed., 2008. Historical Roots of Globalization. In *The Centennial Global Business Summit*. Harvard Business School, p. 4.

Judah, B., 2011. Sovietology's 10 Lessons for Europe. *European Council on Foreign Relations*. Available at: http://ecfr.eu/blog/entry/sovietologys_lessons_for_europe [Accessed December 17, 2011].

Kabraji, R., 2011. Pakistan: All Weather Friendship?. *The World Today*, 67(12), pp. 7–9.

Kaplan, R., 1994. The Coming Anarchy. *The Atlantic*. Available at: http://www.theatlantic.com/ideastour/archive/kaplan.html [Accessed August 2, 2011].

Kaplan, R., 2011a. John Stuart Mill, Dead Thinker of the Year. *Foreign Policy* (December), 94–95.

Kaplan, R., 2011b. The South China Sea Is the Future of Conflict. *Foreign Policy*. Available at: http://www.foreignpolicy.com/articles/2011/08/15/the_south_china_sea_is_the_future_of_conflict [Accessed March 28, 2012].

Kaufmann, E., 2010. *Shall the Religious Inherit the Earth: Demography and Politics in the Twenty-First Century*, London: Profile Books.

Keidel, A. et al., 2008. How East Asians View Democracy – Carnegie Endowment for International Peace. *Carnegie Endowment*. Available at:

http://www.carnegieendowment.org/events/index.cfm?fa=eventDetail& id=1219&prog=zch [Accessed November 20, 2008].

Khalaf, R. and Saleh, H., 2011. West "should not fear Islamist movements." *FT.com*. Available at: http://www.ft.com/cms/s/0/c2178ab8-1b71-11e1-8b11-00144feabdc0.html#axzz1fHKcTLBn [Accessed December 1, 2011].

Khanna, P., 2010. A Second Tour Through the "Second World." *World Politics Review*. Available at: http://www.worldpoliticsreview.com/articles/6021/a-second-tour-through-the-second-world [Accessed August 19, 2010].

Khatami, S.M., 2010. Globalization and Dialogue among Cultures and Civilizations. In K. Schwab et al., eds. *Faith and the Global Agenda: Values for the Post-Crisis Economy*. Geneva: World Economic Forum, pp. 25–27.

Kim, H., 2010. Comparing Measures of National Power. *International Political Science Review*, 31(4), pp. 405–427.

Kirill, I., 2010. Statement on the Global Financial and Economic Crisis. In K. Schwab et al., eds. *Faith and the Global Agenda: Values for the Post-Crisis Economy*. Geneva: World Economic Forum, pp. 29–31.

Kissinger, H., 2011. Mao Might Consider Modern China to Be Too Materialistic. Available at: http://www.spiegel.de/international/world/0,1518,772292-2,00.html [Accessed July 13, 2011].

Klau, T., 2011. Two Challenges for Europe's Politicians. *European Council on Foreign Relations*. Available at: http://ecfr.eu/content/entry/commentary_two_challenges_for_europes_politicians [Accessed December 2, 2011].

Kohut, A. et al., 2011. *Twenty Years Later: Confidence in Democracy and Capitalism Wanes in Former Soviet Union*, Washington: Pew Research Center. Available at: http://www.pewglobal.org/2011/12/05/confidence-in-democracy-and-capitalism-wanes-in-former-soviet-union/ [Accessed December 13, 2011].

Kurlantzick, J., 2010. Avoiding a Tempest in the South China Sea. *Council on Foreign Relations*. Available at: http://www.cfr.org/publication/22858/avoiding_a_tempest_in_the_south_china_sea.html?utm_source=feedburner&utm_medium=feed&utm_campaign=Feed%3A+cfr_main+%28CFR.org+-+Main+Site+Feed%29&utm_content=My+Yahoo [Accessed September 2, 2010].

Lambert, R., 2011. Blueprint to Put Bosses' Pay in Order. *FT.com*. Available at: http://www.ft.com/cms/s/0/54b217b0-0625-11e1-ad0e-00144feabdc0.html#axzz1cpmYTs41 [Accessed November 5, 2011].

Lamont, J. and Bokhari, F., 2011. China and Pakistan: An Alliance is Built. *FT.com*. Available at: http://www.ft.com/cms/s/0/417a48c4-a34d-11e0-8d6d-00144feabdc0.html#axzz1QqPth8ub [Accessed July 1, 2011].

Layard, R., 2009. Now is the Time for a Less Selfish Capitalism. *FT.com*. Available at: http://www.ft.com/cms/s/0/3f6e2d5c-0e76-11de-b099-0000779fd2ac,dwp_uuid=ae1104cc-f82e-11dd-aae8-000077b07658.html [Accessed March 18, 2009].

Layne, C., 1994. Kant or Cant: The Myth of Democratic Peace. *International Security*, 19(2), pp. 5–49.

Layne, C., 2008. China's Challenge to US Hegemony. *Current History*, 107(705), pp. 13–18.
Lebow, R. and Valentino, B., 2009. Lost in Transition: A Critical Analysis of Power Transition Theory. *International Relations*, 23(3), pp. 389–410.
Lemke, D., 1997. The Conituation of History: Power Transition Theory and the End of the Cold War. *Journal of Peace Research*, 34(1), pp. 23–36.
Levy, A., 1986. Second-Order Planned Change: Definition and Conceptualisation. *Organisational Dynamics*, 15(1), pp. 4–20.
Levy, J., 1988. Domestic Politics and War. *The Journal of Interdisciplinary History*, 18(4), pp. 653–673.
Lynch, M., 2010. Veiled Truths. *Foreign Affairs*. Available at: http://www.foreignaffairs.com/articles/66468/marc-lynch/veiled-truths?page=show [Accessed December 1, 2011].
Maddison, A., 1998. Measuring the Performance of a Communist Command Economy: An Assessment of the CIA Estimates for the USSR. *Review of Revenue and Wealth*, 1–27.
Mahbubani, K., 2009. Can America Fail? *The Wlison Quarterly*. Available at: http://www.wilsoncenter.org/index.cfm?fuseaction=wq.essay&essay_id=518042 [Accessed April 14, 2009].
Mahbubani, K., 2011. The New Asian Great Game. *Financial Times*. Available at: http://blogs.ft.com/the-a-list/2011/11/23/the-new-asian-great-game/ [Accessed February 1, 2012].
Mammone, A., 2009. The Eternal Return? Faux Populism and Contemporarization od Neo-Fascism across Britain, France and Italy. *Journal of Contemporary European Studies*, 17(2), pp. 171–192.
Mammone, A., 2011. The Future of Europe's Radical Right: Why the Politics of Race Are Here to Stay. *Foreign Affairs*. Available at: http://www.foreignaffairs.com/articles/68286/andrea-mammone/the-future-of-europes-radical-right?page=show [Accessed October 6, 2011].
Marx, R., 2010. A Decisive Turning Point. In K. Schwab et al., eds. *Faith and the Global Agenda: Values for the Post-Crisis Economy*. Geneva: World Economic Forum, pp. 29–31.
Matsunaga, Y., 2010. Some Suggestions Offered from Japanese Buddhism. In K. Schwab et al., eds. *Faith and the Global Agenda: Values for the Post-Crisis Economy*. Geneva: World Economic Forum, pp. 39–41.
Mauboussin, M., 2011. Embracing Complexity. *Harvard Business Review*, (September), 89–92.
Mearsheimer, J., 2003. *The Tragedy of Great Power Politics*, New York: Norton.
Mearsheimer, J., 2010. Australians should Fear the Rise of China. *The Spectator*.
Meikie, J., 2011. English Defence League filling Vacuum left by Mainstream Politics, says Report. *The Guardian*. Available at: http://www.guardian.co.uk/world/2011/sep/22/far-right-doorstep-hearts-minds [Accessed December 2, 2011].
Micklethwait, J. and Wooldridge, A., 2001. *A Perfect Future: The Challenge and Hidden Promise of Globalisation*, London: Random House.

Mill, J., 1861. *Considerations on Representative Government*, London: Parker, Son, & Bourn. Available at: http://books.google.co.uk/books?id=grtLAAAAcAAJ&printsec=frontcover#v=onepage&q&f=false [Accessed March 22, 2012].

Mintzberg, H., 1990. The Design School; Reconsidering the Basic Premises of Strategic Management. *Strategic Management Journal*, 11, pp. 171–195.

Mintzberg, H. and Waters, J., 1985. Of Strategies, Deliberate and Emergent. *Strategic Management Journal*, 6, pp. 257–272.

Monk, P., 2009. The Rise of the Market State. *Quadrant Online*. Available at: http://www.quadrant.org.au/magazine/issue/2009/9/the-rise-of-the-market-state [Accessed July 13, 2011].

Moran, T., 2010. Is China Using its Checkbook to Lock up Natural Resources Around the World? *Peterson Institute: Real Time Economic Issues Watch*. Available at: http://www.piie.com/realtime/?p=1148&utm_source=feedburner&utm_medium=%24%7Bfeed%7D&utm_campaign=Feed%3A+%24%7BRealTime%7D+%28%24%7BRealTime%7D%29&utm_content=My+Yahoo [Accessed January 22, 2010].

Moubayed, S., 2011. Will there be another Arab Spring in 2061? *Asia Times Online*. Available at: http://www.atimes.com/atimes/Middle_East/MK29Ak02.html [Accessed December 2, 2011].

Nasr, V., 2009. *The Rise of Islamic Capitalism: Why the New Muslim Middle Class Is the Key to Defeating Extremism*, New York: Free Press.

Nelson, D., 2010. India to Overtake China as World's Biggest Country by 2026, says Report. *Telegraph.co.uk*. Available at: http://www.telegraph.co.uk/news/worldnews/asia/india/7885896/India-to-overtake-China-as-worlds-biggest-country-by-2026-says-report.html [Accessed March 14, 2011].

Neslon, D., 2011. Afghanistan is a Proxy War Between India and Pakistan. *Telegraph.co.uk*. Available at: http://www.telegraph.co.uk/news/worldnews/asia/afghanistan/8863073/Afghanistan-is-a-proxy-war-between-India-and-Pakistan.html [Accessed March 14, 2012].

Nesvetailova, A. and Palan, R., 2010. The End of Liberal Finance? The Changing Paradigm of Global Financial Governance. *Millennium: Journal of International Studies*, 38(3), pp. 797–825.

Noland, M. and Pack, H., 2004. *Islam, Globalization and Economic Performance in the Middle East*, Washington: Peterson Institute.

Nossel, S., 2004. Smart Power. *Foreign Affairs*, 83(2), pp. 131–142.

Nye, J., 2011a. Power in the 21st Century. *World Politics Review*. Available at: http://www.worldpoliticsreview.com/articles/8260/power-in-the-21st-century [Accessed April 4, 2011].

Nye, J., 2011b. The Future of Power. Available at: http://www.chathamhouse.org.uk/events/view/-/id/1946/.

Nye, J., 2011c. *The Future of Power*, New York: Public Affairs.

Obama, B., 2012. Remarks by the President on Fair Trade. *The White House*. Available at: http://www.whitehouse.gov/the-press-office/2012/03/13/remarks-president-fair-trade [Accessed March 25, 2012].

O'Hagan, J., 2000. A "Clash of Civilizations"?. In G. Fry & J. O'Hagan, eds. *Contending Images of World Politics*. Houndmills: MacMillan, pp. 135–149.

Ohmae, K., 1990. *The Borderless World: Power and Strategy in the Global Marketplace*, New York: HarperBusiness.

Ohmae, K., 1995. *The End of the Nation State: The Rise of the Regional Economies*, London: HarperCollins.

O'Neill, J., 2001. *Building Better Global Economic BRICs*, New York: Goldman Sachs. Available at: http://www2.goldmansachs.com/ideas/brics/building-better-doc.pdf [Accessed November 24, 2010].

Packer, G., 2011. The Broken Contract. *Foreign Affairs*. Available at: http://www.foreignaffairs.com/articles/136402/george-packer/the-broken-contract [Accessed October 16, 2011].

Payne, A., 2003. Globalization and Modes of Regionalist Governance. In D. Held, and A. McGrew, eds. *The Globalization Transformations Reader*. Cambridge: Polity, pp. 213–222.

Pearson, S., 2012. Brazil declares New "Currency War." *Financial Times*. Available at: http://www.ft.com/cms/s/0/76d1d4d0-63d0-11e1-8762-00144feabdc0.html#axzz1ns7flkgj [Accessed March 2, 2012].

Pearson, S. and Pfeifer, S., 2011. BP in $680m Brazilian Bioethanol Deal. *FT.com*. Available at: http://www.ft.com/cms/s/0/63fc17aa-4be7-11e0-9705-00144feab49a.html#axzz1qPNXpUg2 [Accessed February 12, 2012].

Pettigrew, A. and Whipp, R., 1991. *Managing Change for Competitive Success*, Oxford: Blackwell.

Pettis, M., 2011. The Contentious Debate Over China's Economic Transition. *Carnegie Endowment*. Available at: http://www.carnegieendowment.org/2004/09/09/putin-s-burden/8zda [Accessed January 12, 2012].

Popescu, N., 2011. How the Eurozone Crisis Undermines EU power. *Euobserver*. Available at: http://blogs.euobserver.com/popescu/2011/11/25/eurozone/ [Accessed January 21, 2012].

Porter, M. and Kramer, M., 2011. Creating Shared Value: How to Reinvent Capitalism – and Unleash a Wave of Innovation and Growth. *Harvard Business Review* (January/February), 62–77.

Posen, A., 2009. What Has Been the Lasting Damage? *Peterson Institute*. Available at: http://www.piie.com/publications/opeds/oped.cfm?ResearchID=1305 [Accessed October 11, 2009].

Prince, R., 2011. The Amilcar Notes (Part 4): Tunisia – Profoundly Islamic. *Foreign Policy In Focus*. Available at: http://www.fpif.org/blog/the_amilcar_notes_part_4_tunisia_-_profoundly_islamic?utm_source=feedburner&utm_medium=feed&utm_campaign=Feed%3A+FPIF+%28Foreign+Policy+In+Focus+%28All+News%29%29 [Accessed December 16, 2011].

Ramo, J., 2004. *The Beijing Consensus*, London: The Foreign Policy Centre. Available at: http://fpc.org.uk/fsblob/244.pdf [Accessed January 10, 2012].

Ranson, S., Hinings, C. and Greenwood, R., 1980. The Structuring of Organisational Structures. *Administrative Science Quarterly*, 25(2), pp. 1–17.
Rapley, J., 2006. The New Middle Ages. *Foreign Affairs*. Available at: http://www.foreignaffairs.com/articles/61708/john-rapley/the-new-middle-ages?page=show [Accessed November 16, 2011].
Rashid, A., 2011. Al-Qa'eda's New War. *The Spectator*. Available at: http://www.spectator.co.uk/essays/all/7460188/alqaedas-new-war.thtml [Accessed December 18, 2011].
Reinhardt, A., 2011. Must Democracy Be Sacrificed to Save Europe? *Business Week*. Available at: http://www.businessweek.com/global/euro-crisis/archives/2011/11/must_democracy_be_sacrificed_to_save_europe.html [Accessed November 19, 2011].
Reuters, 2010. Timeline: Flashpoints and Flare-ups in India-Pakistan Ties. *Reuters*. Available at: http://www.reuters.com/article/2010/02/25/us-pakistan-india-timeline-idUSTRE61O0B620100225 [Accessed March 28, 2012].
Richardson, M., 2010. China's Navy Changing the Game. *The Japan Times Online*. Available at: http://search.japantimes.co.jp/cgi-bin/eo20100513mr.html [Accessed May 17, 2010].
Richardson, M., 2012. Eventually not a Drop of Groundwater to Drink? *The Japan Times Online*. Available at: http://www.japantimes.co.jp/text/eo20120202mr.html [Accessed February 3, 2012].
Rodrik, D., 2011. *The Globalization Paradox: Why Global Markets, States and Democracy Can't Coexist*, Oxford: Oxford University Press.
Rogoff, K., 2011. Is Modern Capitalism Sustainable? *Project Syndicate*. Available at: http://www.project-syndicate.org/commentary/rogoff87/English [Accessed December 30, 2011].
Rojas, M. and Zahidi, S., 2010. Global Public Opinion on Values and Ethics. In K. Schwab et al., eds. *Faith and the Global Agenda: Values for the Post-Crisis Economy*. Geneva: World Economic Forum, pp. 3–15.
Roosevelt, F., 1941. The Four Freedoms. Available at: http://www.americanrhetoric.com/speeches/fdrthefourfreedoms.htm [Accessed March 21, 2012].
Rothberg, M., 2011. Neo-Nazi Terror and Germany's Racism Problem. *Open Democracy*. Available at: http://www.opendemocracy.net/michael-rothberg/neo-nazi-terror-and-germany%E2%80%99s-racism-problem [Accessed December 16, 2011].
Roubini, N., 2011. The Instability of Inequality. *Project Syndicate*. Available at: http://www.project-syndicate.org/commentary/roubini43/English [Accessed October 16, 2011].
Roubini, N. and Mihm, S., 2011. *Crisis Economics: A Crash Course in the Finance of the Future*, London: Penguin.
Roughneen, S., 2011. Japan Muddies Water in South China Sea Debate. *The Irrawaddy*. Available at: http://www.irrawaddy.org/article.php?art_id=22155 [Accessed March 28, 2012].

Rubin, T., 2010. We are too Vulnerable. *The Miami Herald*. Available at: http://www.miamiherald.com/2010/12/16/1975612/we-are-too-vulnerable.html [Accessed December 16, 2010].
Ruggie, J., 1993. Territoriality and Beyond: Problematizing Postmodernity in International Relations. *International Organization*, 47, pp. 139–174.
Sabra, H., 2011. Which Islamists? *Foriegn Policy – The Call*. Available at: http://eurasia.foreignpolicy.com/posts/2011/12/06/which_islamists [Accessed December 16, 2011].
Sachs, G., 2010. America's Deepening Moral Crisis – Project Syndicate. *Project Syndicate*. Available at: http://www.project-syndicate.org/commentary/sachs170/English [Accessed October 29, 2010].
Sachs, D., 2011. Understanding Populist Extremists. *European Council on Foreign Relations*. Available at: http://ecfr.eu/blog/entry/understanding_populist_extremists [Accessed December 17, 2011].
Sassen, S., 2009. A Global Financial Detox. *Open Democracy*. Available at: http://www.opendemocracy.net/article/a-global-financial-detox [Accessed September 4, 2009].
Sayigh, Y., 2012. One Year On: The Challenges of Democratic Transition in the Wake of the Arab Uprisings. Available at: http://www.chathamhouse.org/sites/default/files/public/Meetings/Meeting%20Transcripts/250112sayighQ&A.pdf [Accessed February 17, 2012].
Schwab, K. et al., 2010. *Faith and the Global Agenda: Values for the Post-Crisis Economy*, Geneva: World Economic Forum. Available at: http://www.weforum.org/issues/faith-and-religion [Accessed March 22, 2012].
Scissors, D., 2011. The China Models. *The Foundry*. Available at: http://blog.heritage.org/2011/09/06/the-china-models/ [Accessed January 10, 2012].
Shamoo, A., 2011. Arab Islamists Are Here to Stay. *Foreign Policy In Focus*. Available at: http://www.fpif.org/articles/arab_islamists_are_here_to_stay?utm_source=feedburner&utm_medium=feed&utm_campaign=Feed%3A+FPIF+%28Foreign+Policy+In+Focus+%28All+News%29%29 [Accessed December 16, 2011].
Shani, G., 2002. "A Revolt Against the West": Politized Religion and the International Order – A Comparison of the Islamic Umma and the Sikh Qaum. *Ritsumeikan Annual Review of International Studies*, 1, pp. 15–31.
Shankar, S.R., 2010. Values: Elusive Reality. In K. Schwab et al., eds. *Faith and the Global Agenda: Values for the Post-Crisis Economy*. Geneva: World Economic Forum, pp. 47–48.
Shell International, 2005. *The Shell Global Scenarios to 2025 – the Future Business Environment: Trends, Trade-Offs and Choices*, London: Shell.
Sheridan, M., 2012. Meet China's Secret Bosses. *The Sunday Times*, pp. 1, 8.
Silvestri, S., 2007. Does Islam Challenge European Identity?. In L. Faltin & M. Wright, eds. *The Religious Roots of Contemporary European Identity*. London: Continuum.
Skelton, D., 2011. Government of the Technocrats, by the Technocrats, for the Technocrats. *New Statesman*. Available at: http://www.newstatesman.

com/blogs/the-staggers/2011/11/european-greece-technocrats [Accessed November 19, 2011].
Smith, J., 2009. The China-India Border Brawl. *The Wall Street Journal*. Available at: http://online.wsj.com/article/SB124578881101543463.html [Accessed March 1, 2012].
Soros, G., 2011. A New World Architecture. *Project Syndicate*. Available at: http://www.project-syndicate.org/commentary/soros52/English [Accessed December 1, 2011].
Souaiaia, A., 2012. Egypt and the Islamists. *FPIF*. Available at: http://www.fpif.org/articles/egypt_and_the_islamists [Accessed February 15, 2012].
Stiglitz, J., 2002. *Globalization and Its Discontents*, London: Penguin.
Stockholm International Peace Research Institute, 2012. The SIPRI Military Expenditure Database. *Stockholm International Peace Research Institute*. Available at: http://milexdata.sipri.org/ [Accessed March 28, 2012].
Strange, S., 1988. *States and Markets*, London: Pinter.
Strange, S., 1996. *The Retreat of the State: The Diffusion of Power in the World*, Cambridge: Cambridge University Press.
Strategic Foresight Group, 2011. *The Himalayan Challenge – Water Security in Emerging Asia*, Strategic Foresight Group. Available at: http://www.strategicforesight.com/Himalayan%20Challenge%20ES.pdf [Accessed March 28, 2012].
Subramanian, A., 2011. The Inevitable Superpower. *Foreign Affairs*, (September/October 2011). Available at: http://www.foreignaffairs.com/articles/68205/arvind-subramanian/the-inevitable-superpower?page=show [Accessed January 11, 2012].
Sull, D., 2005. Steering Through Uncertainty. *European Business Forum*, 21(Spring), 25–27.
Taleb, N., 2008. *The Black Swan: The Impact of the Highly Improbable*, London: Penguin.
Tharoor, S., 2011. India's Nuclear Path. *Project Syndicate*. Available at: http://www.project-syndicate.org/commentary/tharoor37/English [Accessed October 15, 2011].
The Economist, 2006. The Myth of Chindia. *The Economist*. Available at: http://www.economist.com/node/8311987?story_id=8311987 [Accessed March 24, 2012].
The Economist, 2011. Alternative Investments in Brazil: The Buys from Brazil. *The Economist*. Available at: http://www.economist.com/node/18178275 [Accessed March 27, 2012].
The Heritage Foundation, 2012. 2012 Index of Economic Freedom. *2012 Index of Economic Freedom*. Available at: http://www.heritage.org/index/ [Accessed March 25, 2012].
The Resource Wars of Tomorrow, 2010. The Resource Wars of Tomorrow. *Geopolitical Monitor*. Available at: http://www.geopoliticalmonitor.com/the-resource-wars-of-tomorrow-4243/ [Accessed December 10, 2010].
The World Bank, 2012. GDP Growth (annual %). *The World Bank*. Available at: http://data.worldbank.org/indicator/NY.GDP.MKTP.KD.ZG/countries/BR-RU-IN-CN?display=graph [Accessed March 28, 2012].

Thomas, S., 2000. Taking Religious and Cultural Pluralism Seriously: The Global Resurgence of Religion and the Transformation of International Society. *Millennium: Journal of International Studies*, 29(3), pp. 815–841.
Thomas, S., 2005. *The Global Resurgence of Religion and the Transformation of International Relations*, New York: Palgrave MacMillan.
Topol, S., 2012. Egypt's Salafi Surge. *Foreign Policy*. Available at: http://www.foreignpolicy.com/articles/2012/01/04/egypt_s_salafi_surge?page=0,0 [Accessed January 5, 2012].
University of Maryland, 2012. Global Terrorism Database. *Global Terrorism Database*. Available at: http://www.start.umd.edu/gtd/ [Accessed March 28, 2012].
Usmani, M., 2010. Post-Crisis Reforms: Some Points to Ponder. In K. Schwab et al., eds. *Faith and the Global Agenda: Values for the Post-Crisis Economy*. Geneva: World Economic Forum, pp. 51–54.
Walt, S., 2009. Alliances in a Unipolar World. *World Politics*, 61(1), pp. 86–120.
Walt, S., 2012. Do I believe in international law? *Foreign Policy Blogs*. Available at: http://walt.foreignpolicy.com/posts/2012/02/09/a_response_to_david_bosco [Accessed February 23, 2012].
Waltz, K., 1959. *Man, the State and War a Theoretical Analysis*, New York: Columbia University Press.
Weber, T., 2005. Is the Global Economy Set for Trouble? *BBC News*. Available at: http://news.bbc.co.uk/1/hi/business/4209709.stm [Accessed November 24, 2010].
Wei, S., 2008. *In the Mood for Multilateralism? China's Evolving Global View*, Centre Asie IFRI.
Wei, Z., 2011. Anatomy of a Miracle: China Model and its Significance. *www.qstheory.cn*. Available at: http://www.qstheory.cn/hqwg/2011/201106/201103/t20110325_74156.htm [Accessed January 11, 2012].
Weick, K., 1995. *Sensemaking in Organisations*, Thousand Oaks: Sage.
Weitz, R., 2011. Are China and US Destined to Clash? *The Diplomat*. Available at: http://the-diplomat.com/2011/08/01/are-china-and-us-destined-to-clash/ [Accessed August 3, 2011].
Wike, R., 2011. From Hyperpower to Declining Power. *Pew Research Center*. Available at: http://www.pewglobal.org/2011/09/07/from-hyperpower-to-declining-power/ [Accessed December 13, 2011].
Williams, R., 2010. Human Well-Being and Economic Decision-Making. In K. Schwab et al., eds. *Faith and the Global Agenda: Values for the Post-Crisis Economy*. Geneva: World Economic Forum, pp. 57–60.
Williamson, J., 2004. *A Short History of the Washington Consensus. in From the Washington Consensus Towards a New Global Governance*, Barcelona: Institute for International Economics.
Williamson, J., 2012. Is the "Beijing Concensus" Now Dominant?. *Asia Policy*, 13, pp. 1–16.
Wilson, E., 2008. Hard Power, Soft Power, Smart Power. *The Annals of the American Academy of Political and Social Science*, 616(March), 110–124.

Wohlforth, W., 2009. Unipolarity, Status Competitionand Great Power War. *World Politics*, 61(1), pp. 28–57.
Wohlforth, W., 2011. Gilpian Realism and International Relations. *International Relations*, 25(4), pp. 499–511.
Wolf, M., 2005. The Pull of a Free and Prosperous Europe. *FT.com*. Available at: http://www.ft.com/cms/s/1/3f90b804-7483-11d9-a769-00000e2511c8.html#axzz1QqPth8ub [Accessed July 1, 2011].
Wolf, M., 2010. India's Elephant Charges on through the Crisis. *FT.com*. Available at: http://www.ft.com/cms/s/0/750747e0-262c-11df-aff3-00144feabdc0.html#axzz1q1vrC3Oh [Accessed March 22, 2012].
Wolfers, A., 1962. *Discord and Collaboration: Essays on International Politics*, Baltimore: John Hopkins University Press.
Wong, E., 2012. China's President Lashes Out at Western Culture. *The New York Times*. Available at: http://www.nytimes.com/2012/01/04/world/asia/chinas-president-pushes-back-against-western-culture.html?_r=1&ref=world [Accessed January 4, 2012].
Wright, R., 2011. The Islamists Are Coming. *Foreign Policy*. Available at: http://www.foreignpolicy.com/articles/2011/11/07/the_islamists_are_coming?page=0,1 [Accessed December 16, 2011].
Yao, Y., 2010. The End of the Beijing Consensus. *Foreign Affairs*. Available at: http://www.foreignaffairs.com/articles/65947/the-end-of-the-beijing-consensus?page=show [Accessed January 10, 2012].
Youngs, R., 2009. Dicing with Democracy. *The World Today*, 65(7), pp. 7–9.
Zizek, S., 2007. The Dreams of Others. *In These Times*. Available at: http://www.inthesetimes.com/article/3183/ [Accessed November 21, 2011].
Zizek, S., 2009. *First as Tragedy then as Farce*, Verso.

Index

Acemoglu, Daron, 114
Afghanistan, 49, 148, 152
Africa, 141
Aitken, Carolyn, 17
Algeria, 99
Aljazeera, 148
Al Qaeda, 39, 54
Altman, Roger, 49
Angola, 49
ANI, *see* Asian News International (ANI)
Applegate, Lynda, 11
Arab Spring, 39, 44, 46, 124–5
Arrata, Philippe, 17
Asia, 86, 141–2, 163, 165
Asia, East, 113
Asian News International (ANI), 148
Aslund, Anders, 143
Astill, James, 147
Atsmon, Yuval, 102
Augustine, Norman, 15
Australia, 149
autocracy, 63, 164, 186
Ayoob, Mohammed, 124, 127

Babones, Salvatore, 134
Baden-Fuller, Charles, 25
Badkar, Mamta, 143
Bajoria, Jayshree, 54, 113, 148
balance of power, *see* power, balance of
Balogan, Julia, 25
Bangladesh, 151
Bardham, Pranab, 153
Barnett, A., 130
Barton, Dominic, 105
Barysch, Katinka, 143
BBC, 62, 144–5, 151
Becker, Gary, 105
Beer, Michael, 12

Beijing Consensus, 70, 113, 117, 121, 128–3, 144, 160, 164
  Great Leap, 137
  phase, China Reforms, 130, 134
  phase, China Reverts, 130–2, 134
  See also China; Washington Consensus
Belgium, 53
Bequelin, Nicholas, 131
Bergsten, Fred, 53
Berlin Wall, 3, 5, 29, 74
Bernard, Michael, 70
Berthelsen, John, 102
Berti, Benedetta, 59
Betto, Frie, 106
bipolar systems, 82, 84
  See also unipolar systems; multipolar systems
Bivens, Josh, 105
Black swan, 119
Bobbitt, Philip, 36–9, 44, 54, 62, 71
Bogle, John, 105
Bokhari, Farhan, 147
Boland, Vincent, 115
Bone, James, 40
Bower, Joseph, 105
Bowley, Graham, 53
Bradsher, Keith, 152
Braithwaite, Tom, 91, 160
Brazil, 32, 33, 100, 142, 150
Bremmer, Ian, 4, 99, 113, 135, 142
Breslin, Shaun, 114, 129–34
Bretton Woods, 76, 78, 104
BRICs (Brazil, Russia, India, China), 4, 89, 140–6
Brooks, David, 108
Bruno, Greg, 54
Buckley, Neil, 53, 143, 149
Bull, Hedley, 50–5, 57, 103
Bunderson, J. Stuart, 17

business planning, *see* strategy, planned
Buzan, Barry, 75

Cagrici, Mustafa, 106, 107
Callinicos, Alex, 5, 45
Canada, 32
capabilities, organisational, 20–4
capitalism, 31, 38, 39, 45, 55, 76, 99, 105–7
  long test of, 106, 138, 159–61, 165–78, 183
  See also Beijing Consensus; communism; cultural capitalism; free market capitalism; Islamic capitalism; Planned economies; social capitalism; state capitalism; Washington Consensus
Cardenas, Mauricio, 142
Cerny, Philip, 49, 50, 54, 68, 70
Chakravorti, Bhaskar, 11
change, organisational, *see* organisational change
Chellany, Brahama, 151, 179
Chidambaram, P., 147
China, 29, 32, 42, 58, 85, 86, 93, 99, 102, 108, 111, 113, 114, 115, 128–3, 161, 163, 177
  Assets Supervision and Administration Commission, 132
  Communist Party, 132, 146
  and conflict, 142, 145–52, 167, 169, 174
  democratisation of, 174
  Great Leap, 137
  See also People's Liberation Army Navy; South China Sea
China Model, *see* Beijing Consensus
Chindia, 144–6
Chovanec, Patrick, 137
Chu, Yun-han, 113–14
CINC, *see* Composite Index of National Capabilities (CINC)

Clark, Ian, 36, 74
Clinton, Bill, 4, 31
Cohen, Stephen, 42
Cold War, 3–4, 28
communication, 18–19
communism, 56, 120, 179
competitive advantage, 156
competitive strategy, *see* strategy, competitive
Composite Index of National Capabilities (CINC), 27
conflict, 73, 89–91, 93–4, 95, 162–4, 168, 170, 179
  See also dissonance, status and order; security community; status competition; transition, conflict pathway
Consumerism, 102, 103, 123, 162, 164
Cooper, Robert, 36–7
Corrales, Javier, 115
Crandell, Russell, 38
Crooks, Ed, 163
cultural CAPITALISM, 67
cultural CLOUDS, 66, 67
cultural empires, 65, 66
culture and values, 66, 69, 97–102, 107–9, 117, 120–8, 161–2, 164
custodians of security, 66
cyber warfare, 54, 91

Davidson, Jason, 84, 90
Davies, Robert, 18, 25
Day, George, 119
Deep assumptions, 19–24, 45, 97, 154–65, 183–4
Delong, J. Bradford, 42
democracy, 29, 31, 38, 45, 59, 76, 85, 86–7, 97–8, 100, 110–115, 117, 160–1, 182
  backsliding of, 86–7, 110–114, 161–2, 164
  See also legitimacy, democracy
democratic peace theory, 85–7, 162–4
democratic recession, 115

Dennison, Susi, 114
Denoeux, Guilain, 124–5
DePetris, Daniel, 124
Desai, Seema, 147, 150
Dewan, Sabina, 105, 160
dissonance, status and order, 92–4
  matrix, 91–4, 155, 165, 168–74
  See also conflict
diversity
  functional, 18
  intrapersonal functional, 17–18
Doucouliagos, Hristos, 114
Doyle, Michael, 86
Dyer, Geoff, 91, 160

East Asian free trade area, 53
Eckstein, Alexander, 137
economic freedom, 142–3
economic growth trajectory, 28
Economic warfare, 91, 160, 164, 179
economist, The, 142, 144, 145
Egypt, 99
EIA, *see* U.S. Energy Information Administration (EIA)
Eisenstadt, Shmuel, 99, 100
Elias, Juanita, 96
Emmerson, Charles, 150
Emmott, Bill, 146, 152–3
Engdahl, F. William, 143
Eurasia, 143
Eurasian Zone, 53, 143
Euro crisis, 41, 42, 48–9
Europe, 48, 85, 106, 110, 115, 116, 133, 162
European Union, 41–2, 46, 151
Evans, Michael, 54
experimentation, 14, 15–16
exploration, framework for, 14
extremism, 115–17

failure, 15–16
Falk, Richard, 44
Featherstone, Mike, 99, 102
Ferguson, Niall, 163
First World War, 83, 89
Foley, Stephen, 151–2

Follath, Eric, 145
Førland, Tor, 91
Fortune, 11
Fortune Global, 132, 500
France, 100
free market capitalism, 63, 66, 67, 104
Friedman, George, 174
Friedman, Thomas, 4, 40
Friedrichs, Jorg, 52, 55–7, 62–3
Fry, Greg, 38, 45
Fukuyama, Francis, 4, 29, 85, 102–3

Gapper, John, 160
GDP, *see* Gross Domestic Product
Georgetown University, 100, 118
Germany, 116
Ghannouchi, Rachid, 126
Gillis, Charlie, 152
Gilpin, Robert, 27, 43, 57, 60, 83–4, 87–8, 90
Gini coefficient, 131
  See also inequality
Glauber, Robert, 107
globalisation, 6, 7, 21–2, 37, 38, 39, 44, 48–9, 60–1, 68, 97–9, 180–6
  challenges of, 37–38, 98–110, 116, 155–165, 180–186
  definitions of, 6–7, 108–110, 180–181
Godemont, Francois, 143, 146
Gokhale, Nitin, 146
Golden Arches Theory, 40
Goldman Sachs, 4, 62, 140
Goodwin, Matthew, 115–16
Gray, John, 6, 55, 99
great depression, 64, 77
great recession, 3, 32, 37, 45, 57, 59, 62, 64, 67, 68, 70, 78, 85, 89, 95, 105, 106, 114, 115–16, 120, 138, 140, 158, 161, 168
Greenwood, Royston, 13, 79–80
gross domestic product, 27, 29, 105, 134

groupthink, 18
Guzansky, Yoel, 59

Hadar, Leon, 45
Hailin, Ye, 146
Hamid, Shadi, 124
Hanson, Stephanies, 142
Harding, Luke, 142
Harreld, Bruce, 11
Harvey, David, 5, 57, 58
Hearst, David, 142
Helliwell, John, 114
Heritage Foundation, The, 142–4
Hille, Kathrin, 144, 167
Hinings, Bob, 13, 79–80
Hobbes, Thomas, 112–13, 115
Hobson, Christopher, 100
Hong Kong, 113
Hope Hailey, Veronica, 25
Hoyos, Carola, 167
Huang, Yanzhong, 134
human rights, 37, 38, 56, 76–7, 179
Huntington, Samuel, 6, 45, 68, 118
Husain, Ben, 127
Hu, Zuliu, 130

Ibarra, Herminia, 17
idealists, 85–6
Ikenberry, G. John, 75–7
IMF, *see* International Monetary Fund (IMF)
India, 29, 31, 32, 99, 143–8, 150–1, 179
Indonesia, 141, 149
inequality, 104–5, 113, 131, 160, 164
  See also Gini coefficient
innovation, 11, 163, 165
International Monetary Fund (IMF), 35, 54, 135
international order, *see* world order
internet, 7, 37, 39, 54–5, 159, 186
interpretive schemes, 13, 17, 19–20, 79, 156
Iranian revolution, 121–2

Islam, 123–8
  See also Islamic capitalism; religion
Islamic capitalism, 121–8, 138
Italy, 48–9

Jacobs, Elizabeth, 160
James, Howard, 3, 88
Janis, Irving, 18
Japan, 29, 39, 85, 87, 113, 144, 151, 162
J-curve, 113, 135
Jervis, Robert, 85–7, 145
Johne, F. Axel, 18
Johnson, Simon, 140
Jones, Bruce, 159
Judah, Ben, 49

Kabraji, R., 147
Kaplan, Robert, 68, 110, 149, 150
Kaufmann, Eric, 122–3
Keidel, Albert, 113
Keller, Scott, 17
Khalaf, Roula, 123
Khan, Mohsin, 130
Khanna, Parag, 125
Khatami, Seyed Mohammad, 59, 108, 109, 181
Kim, Hyung, 27
Kirill, I, 59, 108, 110
Kissinger, Henry, 41
Klau, Thomas, 116
Kohut, Andrew, 105, 107, 113
Kramer, Mark, 183
Kurki, Milja, 100
Kurlantzick, Joshua, 149
Kuusito, Maria, 147, 150

Lambert, Richard, 5
Lamont, James, 147
Layard, Richard, 105
Layne, Christopher, 86
leadership team
  alignment of, 16–17, 156
  diversity of, 17–18
Lebow, Richard, 27
Legislation, 37

legitimacy
  capitalism, 104, 138
  communism, 131, 137, 138
  democracy, 104, 110–113, 123–124, 135–136, 161
  sources of, 55–56
Lemke, Douglas, 27
Levy, Amir, 74
Levy, Jack, 85
liberal order, 5, 63, 70, 75–8, 82, 86, 89, 91, 92, 103, 104, 105–6, 108, 113, 129, 141, 145, 160, 162, 168
Lithuania, 105, 107, 113
long test, *see* capitalism, long test of
Lynch, Marc, 124

Mackinder, Halford, 143
Magni, Max, 102
Mahbubani, Kishore, 125
Malaysia, 149
Mammone, Andrea, 115–16
management, *see* leadership team
market elites, 58, 59, 60, 65, 67, 68–9, 92, 95, 120–1, 157–9, 173, 179, 181
market states, 36, 38–9, 41, 42, 44, 46, 66
Marx, Reinhard, 109, 110
Maryland, University of, 147
Matsunaga, Yukci, 109
Mauboussin, Michael, 18
Mearsheimer, John, 26, 83, 86, 95, 141–2
Medievalism, 68
  21st century, 51–70
  new, 52–70
Meikie, James, 116
Mexico, 100, 141
Micklethwait, John, 4, 109, 181
Middle Ages, 46, 51–2, 54, 62, 110
Middle East, 40, 120–8, 141
Mihm, Stephen, 119
military expenditure, 27, 29, 31, 149, 157, 167, 176, 177
military prowess, 27, 28

Mill, John Stuart, 110–113, 114, 115, 135–6
Mintzberg, Henry, 12, 13, 14
MNCs, *see* Multi-national corporations (MNCs)
money markets, 48–9
Mongolia, 113
Monk, Paul, 37
Moran, Theodore, 145
Motorola, 11
Moubayed, Sami, 124
multi-national corporations (MNCs), 40, 88
multipolar systems, 82–3, 84, 141
  See also bipolar systems; unipolar systems
Murphy, Kevin, 105

Nasr, Vali, 126–8
nationalism, 84, 85, 116, 132, 133, 149, 158–9, 162–3, 177
NATO, *see* North Atlantic Treaty Organization (NATO)
natural resources, *see* rare earths; resources; water
Nelson, Dean, 144
neo-liberalism, 62, 78, 160, 173
Nepal, 151
Nesvetailova, Anastasia, 78
New Security Dilemma, 50
NGOs, *see* non-governmental organisations (NGOs)
Nohria, Nitin, 12
Noland, Marcus, 126
non-governmental organisations (NGOs), 54
non-state actors, 35, 37, 40, 44, 46, 48, 49
  See also market elites; social movements; post-state elites
North Atlantic Treaty Organization (NATO), 152
North Korea, 58
Nossel, Suzanna, 42
nuclear weapons, 147–8
Nye, Joseph, 39, 40, 43, 91, 144, 145–6

Obama, Barack, 152
O'Hagan, Jacinta, 45
Ohmae, Kenichi, 4, 36–7
O'Neill, Jim, 4, 140
order-chaos model, 112–13
organisational capabilities, *see* capabilities, organisational
organisational change, 11, 12, 73–4, 79
organisational focal points, 15
organisation, exploring, 15
organisation, stable, 15, 183
organisations, transnational, 54, 61, 76

Packer, George, 5
Pack, Howard, 126
Pakistan, 147–8, 150
Palan, Ronen, 78
Payne, Anthony, 55
peace, 73
Pearl Harbor, 39
Pearson, Samantha, 142, 160
People's Liberation Army Navy, 149
Pettigrew, Andrew, 17
Pettis, Michael, 137
Pfeifer, Sylvia, 142
Phillipines, 113
Pinker, Steven, 96
planning, *see* strategy, planned
Popescu, Nicu, 41
population, 27
Porter, Michael, 183
Posen, Adam, 140
post-modern state, 36
post-state elites, 59–61, 65, 157–8, 168, 179
power
  actors and, 34–40
  balance of, 150
  definitions and types, 26–36, 40–46
  gap, 90
  maps of, 28–34, 165–168, 175
  measurement of, 27–9, 43–4

  ownership of, 44–45
  proliferation of, 88, 89
  relational, 34, 40, 42, 43, 49, 54, 74, 77, 87, 89, 90, 168, 170, 177
  smart, 42–3, 46, 90, 92, 164, 168–9
  soft, 40–4, 46, 90, 135–6, 164, 168, 170
  structural, 34–36, 40, 42, 43, 77, 87, 89, 90, 141, 168, 177
  transition theory, 26
power transition theory, *see* power, transition theory
Prince, Rob, 108, 125
Private international violence, 54
protectionism, 75–6, 135, 142, 160, 183, 191
Putin, Vladimir, 53, 143

quadrilemma
  rules of, 62–3
  settling points, 63
  twenty-first century, 60–70, 72, 73, 77–78, 98, 119–120, 155, 158–159, 161, 165

Ramo, Joshua, 129–30
Ranson, Stewart, 13
Rapley, John, 48
rare earths, 511–12
  See also resources
Rashwan, Diaa, 124, 127
realists, 82–5
Reinhardt, Andy, 49
religion, 48, 56, 59, 64, 68, 69, 88, 97, 100–2, 103–4, 117, 120–8, 161
Resource Wars of Tomorrow, 163
resources, 90, 150–2, 163
  See also rare earths; Water
Reuters, 147
Revlon, 11
Richardson, Michael, 149, 150
Rodrik, Dani, 56
Rogoff, Kenneth, 106
Rojas, Milagros, 100–2

Roosevelt, Franklin, 76–7
Rothberg, Michael, 116
Roubini, Nouriel, 5, 104, 119
Roughneen, Simon, 149
Rubin, Trudy, 54
Ruggie, John, 50, 69
rules of the game, 75, 77–8, 79, 83–4, 87, 90, 94, 168
Russia, 29, 85, 93, 99, 107, 113, 115, 142–3, 173–4

Sabra, Hani, 127
Sachs, Jeffrey, 107, 116
Saleh, Heba, 123
Sassen, Saskia, 140
Saudi Arabia, 99
Sayigh, Yezid, 127
Schoemaker, Paul, 119
Schwab, Klaus, 118
Scissors, Derek, 130, 134
Second World War, 34, 64, 77, 89, 99, 116, 147
secularism, 22, 98, 102–10, 122
security binding, 76
security community, 162–3
Shamoo, Adil, 125–6
Shani, Giorgio, 103
Shankar, Sri Ravi, 59, 110
Shell International, 56–7
Sheridan, Michael, 132
Silvestri, Sara, 123–4
Singapore, 149
Sinister interests, 111, 113
Skelton, David, 49
Smith, Jeff, 146
social actors, 56
    See also social movements
social bargain, 76, 104
social capitalism, 67
social identity theory, 88–91
social movements, 58–9, 60, 62, 65, 70, 87, 92, 95, 117, 122, 157–9, 168, 172, 179, 181
Soros, George, 70, 115
Souaiaia, Ahmed, 125, 128

South Africa, 99–100
South China Sea, 148–50
South Korea, 113
Soviet Union, 5, 29, 31, 49, 58, 61, 74, 89–90, 105
Spain, 53
Splintered states, 179
stability-Change model, 19–24, 182, 185
state capitalism, 63, 179
    empires of, 66
    See also custodians of security
state elites, 58, 60, 61, 69, 83, 84, 87, 90, 92, 95, 157, 168, 173, 179
states, 33, 36–40, 42, 43, 55, 57, 65, 83, 87, 89, 157–9
    allegiance to, 103
    authority of, 50–51
    definition, 50
    erosion of power, 48–55, 157–158
    fragmentation of, 53–4
    legitimacy of, 74, 86
    regionalisation of, 53
    revisionist, 84
    See also legitimacy, sources of; market elites; market states; post-modern state; post-state elites; splintered states; state elites; states of terror
states of terror, 39, 44, 54
status competition, 90, 168–9
    See also conflict
Stiglitz, Joseph, 6, 7, 108–9, 180
Stockholm International Peace Research Institute, 144
Stopford, John, 25
Strange, Susan, 34–6, 40, 43
Strategic Foresight Group, 151
strategy, competitive, 7, 12, 156, 182–6
    See also competitive advantage; strategy, emergent; strategy, planned

strategy, emergent, 12, 14–15
strategy, planned, 12–15
Subramanian, Arvind, 27, 136
Sull, Donald, 15, 18
Sutch, Peter, 96
systems of rule, 50, 57

Taiwan, 113, 149
Taleb, Nassim, 119
Taliban, 148
technology, 36, 38–9, 44, 55, 68
Thailand, 113
Tharoor, Sashi, 147–8
Theocracy, 65
Thomas, Scott, 58, 59, 102, 104, 121–3
Tibet, 146, 149
Topol, Sarah, 127
transition
  conflict pathway, 80, 82, 93–4, 170
  definition, 72–73
  first order, 74, 75, 77, 79, 91–2
  incremental change pathway, 80–81, 93, 170–173
  paths and routes, 72, 79–82, 91–94, 170–173
  process of, 6, 9, 46, 79–82
  scenarios, 92–94
  second order, 74, 75, 77, 81, 82
  splintering pathway, 80–81, 93, 170
  stasis pathway, 80–1, 93, 170–2
  transformation pathway, 80–81, 93, 170
  types of, 72–74
  unsuccessful assaults pathway, 80, 82, 94, 170–171
  See also conflict; peace
transnational organisations, *see* organisations, transnational
transnational threats, 37
Treaty of Westphalia, *see* Westphalia, Treaty of
trilemma, 56–7
Turkey, 141, 179

twenty-first century quadrilemma, *see* quadrilemma, twenty-first century
Twin Towers, 46, 49

Ukraine, 99, 107, 113
Ulabasoglu, Mehmet, 114
United Arab Emirates, 99
United Kingdom, 53, 140, 144
United Nations (UN), 54, 61
  Security Council, 142
United States, 5, 29, 30–1, 32, 35, 42, 64, 68, 74–7, 81, 83, 85, 86, 87, 89–90, 91, 92–4, 106, 115, 131, 133, 136, 141, 143–5, 148–9, 151, 157, 159–60, 162, 167, 170, 173–7
UN, *see* United Nations (UN)
unipolar systems, 82, 84, 89, 159
  See also bipolar systems; multipolar systems
U.S. Energy Information Administration (EIA), 148
Usmani, Muhammad, 110, 125–6

Valentino, Benjamin, 27
Values, *see* culture and values
Vietnam, 149

Walt, Stephen, 61, 87
Waltz, Kenneth, 27, 43, 82–3
Washington Consensus, 129, 133, 135, 137–8, 164, 174
  See also Beijing Consensus; capitalism; democracy
water, 150–1, 179
  See also resources
Waters, James, 12, 14
Weapons of mass destruction (WMDs), 37
Weber, Tim, 5
Weick, Karl, 13
Weitz, Richard, 86
Wei, Zhang, 133
Westphalian system, 69, 87, 103, 122, 168
Westphalia, Treaty of, 36

Whipp, Richard, 17
Whittell, Giles, 54
Wike, Richard, 5
Williamson, John, 129, 131
Williams, Rowan, 109
Wilson, Ernest, 42–3
WMDs, *see* Weapons of mass destruction (WMDs)
Wohlforth, William, 83, 88–91
Wolfers, Arnold, 51
Wolf, Martin, 41, 143
Wong, Edward, 108
Wooldridge, Adrian, 4, 109, 181

World Bank, 35, 54, 140
World Economic Forum, 100, 118
world order, 75
World Trade Organization (WTO), 151
Wright, Robin, 124, 127
WTO, *see* World Trade Organization (WTO)

Yao, Yang, 137
Youngs, Richard, 115

Zahidi, Saadia, 100–2
Zizek, Slavoj, 56, 120

If you have any concerns about our products,
you can contact us on
ProductSafety@springernature.com

In case Publisher is established outside the EU,
the EU authorized representative is:
**Springer Nature Customer Service Center GmbH
Europaplatz 3, 69115 Heidelberg, Germany**

Printed by Libri Plureos GmbH
in Hamburg, Germany